Civil Procedure in Slovenia

Civil Procedure in Slovenia

Aleš Galič

This book was originally published as a monograph in the International Encyclopaedia of Laws/Civil Procedure.

Founding Editor: Roger Blanpain
General Editor: Frank Hendrickx
Volume Editor: Piet Taelman

Wolters Kluwer

Published by:
Kluwer Law International B.V.
PO Box 316
2400 AH Alphen aan den Rijn
The Netherlands
E-mail: international-sales@wolterskluwer.com
Website: lrus.wolterskluwer.com

Sold and distributed in North, Central and South America by:
Wolters Kluwer Legal & Regulatory U.S.
7201 McKinney Circle
Frederick, MD 21704
United States of America
Email: customer.service@wolterskluwer.com

Sold and distributed in all other countries by:
Air Business Subscriptions
Rockwood House
Haywards Heath
West Sussex
RH16 3DH
United Kingdom
Email: international-customerservice@wolterskluwer.com

ISBN 978-94-035-1865-7

e-Book: ISBN 978-94-035-1891-6
web-PDF: ISBN 978-94-035-1903-6

The Author

Prof. Aleš Galič was born in 1968. He graduated in Law (LL.B.) in 1991 and accomplished the LLM programme of civil and commercial law in 1994. He earned a PhD Degree in 1998 with his thesis 'Constitutional Procedural Guarantees in Civil Procedure: A Research Emphasized at the Case Law of the Constitutional Courts of Slovenia and Germany and the European Court of Human Rights'; all at the University of Ljubljana, Faculty of Law. After the traineeship at the Ljubljana Court of Appeals, he passed the bar exam (the state law exam) in 1995. He is professor at the Faculty of Law in Ljubljana, with major interests in teaching and research being Civil Procedure, International Private Law, International and European Civil Procedure, Arbitration and Alternative Dispute Resolution. He has published numerous books (as a sole or co-author) and articles in these fields of law. Besides full-time employment at the University of Ljubljana, Faculty of Law, Professor Galič worked part-time as legal advisor to the Constitutional Court of Slovenia from 1996 to 2018. He is a vice-president of the Ljubljana Arbitration Chamber (attached to the Slovenian Chamber of Commerce and Industry). He has participated in expert groups for drafting Civil procedure Act – 1999 and its amendments of 2002 and 2008, the Labour and Social Courts Act, the Amendment of Enforcement of Judgments and Protective Measures Act, Protection of Competition Act – 1999, Arbitration Act and Collective Claims Act. Besides Slovenian, he speaks English, German, Croatian and Serbian languages.

The Author

Table of Contents

Table of Contents

List of Abbreviations

AA	Arbitration Act
ADR	Alternative Dispute Resolution
CPA	Civil Procedure Act (*Zakon o pravdnem postopku*)
ECHR	European Convention of Human Rights
ECJ	European Court of Justice
ECourHR	European Court of Human Rights
EU	European Union
EJPMA	Enforcement of Judgments and Protective Measures Act (*Zakon o izvršbi in zavarovanju*)
JSA	Judicial Service Act (*Zakon o sodniški službi*)
MFRA	Marriage and Family Relations Act (*Zakon o zakonski zvezi in družinskih razmerjih*)
NCPA	Non-Contentious Procedures Act
NGO	Non-governmental organization
PILPA	Act on Private International Law and Procedure (*Zakon o mednarodnem zasebnem pravu in postopku*)
UNCITRAL	United Nations Commission on International Trade Law
VAT	Value Added Tax

List of Abbreviations

General Introduction

§1. General Background

1. Slovenia is a small central European and Mediterranean country – it covers an area of approximately 20,000 km^2. Its population is about 2 million (thus, about 100 inhabitants/km^2). Due to a low birth-rate, population is stagnating. The immigration to Slovenia is low, but such is – in contrast to several other ex-socialist states – also the emigration from Slovenia. The capital of Slovenia is Ljubljana. Slovenia borders Italy to the west, Austria to the north, Hungary to the northeast and Croatia to the southeast, with a 47 km Adriatic Sea coastline. Official language is Slovenian, which belongs to a Slavic linguistic group. Slovenes also form the largest ethnic group (approximately 90% of the whole population). In nationally mixed areas, the languages of ethnic groups, whose existence is recognized already by the Constitution, Italian and Hungarian language respectively are an official language besides Slovenian.

2. Slovenia was a part of the Austrian part of the Austro-Hungarian Empire till the end of World War I. Then it was incorporated to the newly formed Kingdom of Yugoslavia. After the World War II, Yugoslavia became a socialist and federal state, consisting of six republics, which Slovenia was one of. Although the introduction of socialism brought many far reaching changes to the legislation (and to the functioning of the justice system), it must however be stressed that these changes were much less radical in comparison to the other communist states. Yugoslavia was not a part of the Soviet dominated economic and military block. At least after the late fifties, Yugoslavia opted for what could most easily be described as a 'milder version of socialism' which distinguished it from the states of the so-called Soviet block. For example, companies, although officially 'social property', retained a considerable degree of independence at the making of commercial decisions (the system of 'self-management') – the system of 'central planning' did not apply in Yugoslavia.[1] Thus, real commercial disputes, decided in regular course of litigation (based on the use of the Civil Procedure Act (*Zakon o pravdnem postopku,* CPA)) were common, unlike in other socialist countries where tools of a more administrative nature were used for deciding disputes (as much as genuine disputes could at

1. About features of the socialist system in former Yugoslavia before democratic changes *see,* e.g., M. Cerar, *From Elite Consensus to Democratic Consolidation*, in *Democratic Consolidation in Eastern Europe* 378–406 (Zielonka ed., Oxford U. Press 2001); L. Ude, *Entwicklung der demokratischen Institutionen und Geltendmachung von Menschenrechten und Grundfreiheiten*, in *Zehn Jahre Danach* 195–214 (D. Pfaff, ed.,Suedosteuropa-Gesellschaft 2000).

all occur in a system of centrally planned economy).[2] Besides, the degree of allowed private businesses was considerably higher than in any other socialist state. A concept of real commercial arbitration was also retained – also for disputes between domestic companies. Bankruptcies (a concept, unthinkable of in other socialist states) could occur. Also in the field of respect (or violations) of human rights, the Yugoslav version of socialism was more bearable than in the countries of the soviet block. For example, travelling to western countries was unrestricted and visa-free.

3. Following a growing economic crisis in the 1980s, a major political crisis took place in Yugoslavia and pro-reform and pro-independence movement constantly gained ground in Slovenia. In 1991, Slovenia became an independent state (a full international recognition followed in 1992) and at the same time, this meant a shift to a parliamentary democratic system and a market economy. Slovenia's independence was, unlike what happened in other parts of former Yugoslavia, implemented relatively peacefully, also as a result of a fact that the population of Slovenia was ethnically compact and not so mixed as in other parts of former Yugoslavia. Slovenia's transition from a socialist economy to a capitalist free market was gradual and cautious but steady, clearly rejecting ideas and often hard-lobbied proposals for 'shock therapy'. Today the country enjoys substantial economic and political stability. As the first one among former Yugoslav Republics, it joined the European Union (EU) in May 2004 and (as the first one among the 'new Member States') it fulfilled 'the Maastricht criteria' for adoption of the Euro (EUR), which became a national currency in January 2007. In 2017, the gross domestic product per capita was USD 25,700 (USD32,000, adjusted by Purchasing Power Parity).

4. The Republic of Slovenia is a parliamentary democracy. The Constitution, adopted in December 1991, proclaims that supreme power is vested in the people and that its legal system is based on respect for human rights and fundamental freedoms, on the principle of rule of law, a principle of social state and the principle of separation of state powers into legislative, executive and judicial. The Constitution (Article 7) is also based on the principle of separation of church and state (whereby the freedom of religion is guaranteed). The highest legislative authority is the National Assembly (*Državni zbor*) consisting of ninety representatives elected for a term of four years by secret ballot in proportional electoral system. The second house of the Parliament – The National Council (*Državni svet*) – is a mainly advisory body composed of representatives of social, economic, professional and local interests. The head of state is the President of the Republic (elected for a maximum of two consecutive five-year terms). According to the constitution, he or she represents the Republic of Slovenia and is the commander-in-chief of its defence forces, but in fact, his or her role is mostly formal, without any substantial powers (and it is therefore unusual that although with such a limited role in the parliamentary system, he or she is elected in general public elections). Executive authority is vested in the Prime Minister and the cabinet. For the policies it adopts, the Government is responsible to the National Assembly.

2. Cf. R. Stuerner, *The Principles of Transnational Civil Procedure*, 69 RabelsZ222(2005).

5. In Slovenia, international law becomes a part of domestic law after its incorporation into the Slovenian legal system. Ratified and proclaimed international treaties, to which Slovenia adheres, take an immediate effect (Article 8 of the Constitution). The Constitutional Court can supervise the conformity of laws and other regulations with ratified treaties and with the general principles of international law. In the process of ratifying a treaty, the Constitutional Court, on the proposal of the President of the Republic, the Government or a third of the deputies of the National Assembly, have to issue an opinion on the conformity of such treaty with the Constitution. The National Assembly is bound by the opinion of the Constitutional Court (Article 160 of the Constitution). With regard to EU legislation, an amended Article 3a of the Constitution provides that legal acts and decisions adopted within international organizations to which Slovenia has transferred the exercise of part of its sovereign rights are applied in Slovenia in accordance with the legal regulation of these organizations.

6. According to the Constitution (Article 127), the Supreme Court is the highest court in the state. Independence of judges is guaranteed by the Constitution. There is no explicit provision that would guarantee an independence of a judiciary as an institution, but this stems already from the proclaimed principle of the separation of powers (Article 3 of the Constitution). In one of its most influential decisions, the Constitutional Court confirmed that the guarantee of independence applies not only to individual judges but to the judiciary as a whole as well.[3] According to the Constitution, judges exercise their duties independently in accordance with the Constitution and with the law (Article 125 of the Constitution). The Constitution lays out the basic principles on the organization and jurisdiction of the courts, the participation of citizens in the performance of judicial functions, the permanence of office of judges, the election of judges, the Judicial Council, the termination and dismissal from office of a judge, the incompatibility of judicial office and judicial immunity (Articles 129–133).

7. Courts, including the Supreme Court, are not empowered to decide upon the conformity of the law with the Constitution. This is reserved for the Constitutional Court (*Ustavno sodišče*).[4] If, in course of proceedings, a judge of an 'ordinary court' suspects that the law they should apply is unconstitutional, they must stay the proceedings and refer the matter to the Constitutional Court (Article 156 of the Constitution). According to Article 160.6 of the Constitution, one of the powers of the Constitutional Court is also to decide on constitutional complaints in case of alleged violation of human rights and fundamental freedoms by the judgments of (*inter alia*) courts in civil litigation. Despite this competence, the Constitutional Court cannot be regarded as a further Court of Appeals for civil cases. When deciding upon constitutional complaints, the Constitutional Court is not empowered to control the correctness of the application of procedural and substantive law and finding of facts, but only whether an ordinary court has interpreted laws in such a manner

3. Decision of the Const. Court, U-I-60/06, 7 Dec. 2006.
4. A. Mavčič, *The Slovenian Constitutional Court and its Activities During the Period of Transition*, 2 *Revue de justice constitutionnelle Est-Européenne*229–251(2001).

that contravenes a certain constitutional right.[5] The power of the Constitutional Court to decide on constitutional complaints is a consequence of the Constitutional Court's fundamental jurisdiction, which is to review the conformity of statutes with the Constitution: the system of constitutional protection is not complete if a law itself is in conformity with a Constitution, but is then interpreted in an unconstitutional manner in a particular case.

8. Retrospective legislation is prohibited by the Constitution: no statute, regulation or other legislative measure shall, in general, be interpreted as having retrospective effect (Article 155/1). In exceptional circumstances, a statute can be given a retrospective effect, if that is in public interest and provided that no accrued rights are infringed thereby (Article 155/2). The Constitution also stresses out the importance of the principle of finality of judgments (Article 158).

9. Other independent authorities, already mentioned in the Constitution, are: the State Prosecutor (responsible for prosecuting cases brought against those suspected of committing criminal offences), the local self-government, the Court of Audit (the highest body for supervising state accounts, the state budget and all public spending; however with no real judicial functions), the Bank of Slovenia, the Ombudsman for Human Rights and Fundamental Freedoms (elected by the National Assembly for a period of six years, responsible for factual supervising and safeguarding protection of human rights through informal channels).

§2. Delimitation of the Subject Matter

I. Definition of the Term 'Civil Procedure'

10. According to Article 1 of the CPA, courts hear and decide on disputes arising out of personal and family relations, and on disputes arising out of property and other civil relations of natural and legal persons, unless a specialized court or a different body is vested with the jurisdiction over some of the said disputes by a special statute.

11. In broader sense, the term 'civil procedure' refers to all proceedings that belong within the jurisdiction of courts (thus not within the jurisdiction of administrative authorities) of general jurisdiction (thus, not to specialized labour courts and administrative courts), except for criminal matters. In the narrower sense, the term '(contentious) civil procedure' excludes civil matters that are decided upon in non-contentious proceedings (including, *inter alia*, procedures referring to entry into land and company register, matters of inheritance, commitment of psychiatric

5. *See,* e.g., Decision of the Const. Court, Up 408/00, 20 Nov. 2001 and A. Mavčič, *The Specialities of Slovenian Constitutional Review as Compared with the Current Systems of Souch Review in the New Democracies*, in *Giustizia constituzionale e sviluppo democratico nei paesi dell'Europa centro-orientale*161–188(De Vergottini ed., Giappichelli 2001).

patients, certain family law matters etc.), proceedings for enforcement of judgments and bankruptcy proceedings. Thus, although enforcement of judgment falls into competence of courts, it is not considered to be a 'continuation' of civil procedure.[6] Unlike in certain other continental European jurisdictions, it is regulated in a separate piece of legislation (Enforcement of Judgments and Protective Measures Act (*Zakon o izvršbi in zavarovanju*, EJPMA)).

12. The doctrine also differentiates between 'organizational civil procedure' and 'functional civil procedure'.[7] The former covers issues like organization of the court system and the regulation of professions, including election, rights and duties of judges, attorneys at law and bailiffs. The law of evidence is not considered to be a separate discipline. It is regulated by CPA (like for criminal cases, in Criminal Procedure Act) and in law schools, it is taught as a part of general course on Civil procedure (just like evidence in criminal matters is taught as a part of course on Criminal procedure).

II. Distinction with Other Types of Procedure (Administrative, Criminal)

13. The doctrine tried to rely on the above-mentioned provision of Article 1, CPA, in order to determine the substantive criteria for a differentiation between administrative and civil matters.[8] However, these criteria are only of an auxiliary value. In any case, the delimitation between civil and administrative matters is not of a paramount importance. According to the case law of the Constitutional Court, the right of access to court is not violated if a dispute, although of a civil law nature, falls within jurisdiction of administrative authority, provided that the parties have a right to challenge the administrative decision in court (if this judicial review meets certain standards; the most important of which is that the court must have the power to control both the correctness of the application of law by the administrative authority as well as the correctness of the finding of facts).[9] Thus, there is no constitutional guarantee that an (independent and impartial) court will have 'the first word' in settling of a dispute, but only a guarantee that such a court shall have 'the last word'.

14. However, although that might be constitutionally permissible, there are no cases in Slovenian legislation, that 'classical' or 'traditional' civil and commercial matters would fall within administrative jurisdiction. In fact, the legislator is obviously favouring the competence of courts by referring ever more matters within

6. D. Wedam Lukić, *Civilno izvršilno parvo* [Enforcement of Civil Judgments Law] 20(ČZ Uradni List 1992).
7. J. Juhart, *Civilno procesno parvo* [Civil Procedure] 4(Univerzitetna založba 1961).
8. L. Ude, *Posebni sodni in upravni postopki v novi zakonodaji*[*Special Judicial and Administrative Procedures in New Legislation*], 26 *Podjetje in delo*, 1378 et seq.(2000)
9. Decision of the Const. Court, Up 280/00, 18 Sep. 2001.

the competence of (civil) courts. This, however, is often criticized as it puts additional burden onto courts, which are already overburdened and can hardly cope with huge backlogs. It is often pleaded that the legislator should be more reserved at imposing new competences to courts.

15. Furthermore, the legislator is free to decide in which kind of proceedings (contentious, non-contentious ...) a certain matter shall be decided on.[10] The only constitutional limitation is that there may be no arbitrary division that the law would refer a certain matter to one type of procedure, but in another case, a substantially equal matter would be referred to another kind of procedure.[11]

16. It is possible (but not obligatory) for a victim (an aggrieved person) to file a civil claim against the accused for damages or restitution which is based on an act giving rise to criminal proceedings, in the court seized with criminal proceedings. If the accused is acquitted, the criminal court may never decide on the civil claim, but must refer the party to file a new claim in a civil procedure. But even if the accused is convicted, the criminal court is not obliged to decide upon the civil claim. It is a matter of discretion; if the criminal court finds it too complicated or time-consuming to adjudicate upon a civil claim, it may refer a party to file a new claim in a civil court.

17. In a case when the same cause of action resulted in previous conviction of the wrongdoer in criminal procedure, it is easier for the aggrieved party to pursue its civil claim. The CPA (Article 14) determines that when the claim is based on the same state of facts that has already been adjudicated in criminal proceedings, the court shall be bound by the final condemnatory sentence issued in criminal proceedings, but only in respect of the existence of criminal offence and criminal liability of the offender. For instance, in such a claim, the defendant will be precluded from raising an objection that his act was not illegal or objection that there was no causal link or that no damage occurred. In fact, this is the only case of the so-called collateral estoppel in Slovenian civil procedure (there is no such effect between two civil procedures, just between a criminal and a subsequent civil procedure).[12] In the opposite situation, if the accused was acquitted in criminal proceedings, the outcome of these proceedings has no effect on subsequent civil litigation. As civil liability is in many aspects stricter than criminal liability (also with regard to the standard and the burden of proof), the fact that the wrongdoer was acquitted in criminal case (e.g., for lack of guilt), does not mean that the same occurrence does not give grounds for civil liability (e.g., if strict liability applies).[13]

10. Decision of the Const. Court, Up 42/96, 30 May 2000.
11. The Constitutional Court found it contrary to the Constitution that according to the Family Act, the decision on custody rights over children of divorced parents was in the competence of a court, but the decision on custody rights over children of parents, who were never married, was in the competence of an administrative authority (subject, of course, to a subsequent judicial review in administrative court). Decision of the Const. Court, U-I-273/98, 1 Jul. 1999.
12. 1L. Ude et al., *Pravdni postopek – zakon s komentarjem*[*Civil Procedure – Act with the Commentary*]140 et seq. (GV Založba in ČZ UL 2005).
13. *Ibid.*

18. If a question of administrative law is a preliminary question in civil litigation, necessary to be solved in order to decide on a civil claim, a court is bound by the final decision of the administrative authority (or, following the decision of the administrative body, a decision of the administrative court) if such a decision already exists (Article 13, CPA; the same rule applies with regard to preliminary questions from any field of law). If, however, such a question has not yet been solved in administrative procedure, a civil court has two options: it may either suspend proceedings and wait for the outcome of administrative procedure or it may decide on such a question as on a preliminary question (with effect only applying to the particular case).

19. Concerning the interaction between criminal and civil law, there are extremely few cases in Slovenian legislation where the existence of a criminal offence is a precondition for the application of a certain consequence in the field of civil law. The only such a case in the field of Law of Obligations concerns the length of the prescription period for obligations in torts; if the event that caused the damage was a criminal offence, the prescription period may be longer (Article 353, Code of Obligations). In such a case, a civil court is bound by both the conviction and the acquittal of the wrongdoer in criminal procedure (thus, if the wrongdoer was acquitted, the civil court may not in a later action for damages use a longer prescription period based on a finding that the wrongful act was a criminal offence). If, however, a criminal procedure has not taken place yet and the civil court is faced with a preliminary question of whether a criminal offence was committed (because this is decisive for the determination of the length of the prescription period), the civil court may not, in principle, decide on this preliminary question by itself. According to the position of the Supreme Court, if a civil court would find, even if just as a preliminary question, that the wrongful act was a criminal offence although a criminal procedure has not been accomplished yet, it would violate the constitutional presumption of innocence (Article 27 of the Constitution).[14]

III. Are There Separate Court Systems and Rules of Procedure?

20. According to the Constitution, judicial power is implemented by courts of general jurisdiction and by specialized courts. However, there are only two kinds of specialized courts in Slovenia: labour and social courts and administrative courts. The former courts deal with individual and collective labour disputes and disputes arising out of decisions of bodies responsible for social security. The latter deal with requests for judicial review of administrative acts.

21. There are no special commercial courts and no special family courts. However, commercial and family divisions within district courts exist (and the CPA contains certain, though limited, rules, applicable only in commercial and family cases, respectively). Also non-contentious matters and enforcement procedures are dealt

14. Judgment of the Supreme Court, II Ips 548/2002, 18 Sep. 2003; in line with the position of the European Court of Human Rights (*Ringvold v. Norway*, No. 34964/97; 11 Feb. 2003).

with by regular courts (whereby bigger courts have specialized divisions for non-contentious matters). The same rule applies to the matters of enforcement of judgments.

22. Extraordinary courts are prohibited by the Constitution (Article 126). Furthermore, courts martial cannot be established in peacetime.

23. The Constitution (Article 23) explicitly guarantees a right of access to court. The notion of 'court' is interpreted in a strict sense – meaning that it must be a proper (state) court, and the judicial power must be exercised by a judge in the sense of Judicial Service Act (*Zakon o sodniški službi,* JSA) (unlike Article 6 of the European Convention of Human Rights (ECHR) which provides for a broader notion of a 'tribunal'). Thus, in Slovenian system, for the right of access to court to be respected, it is not possible to vest a judicial power into certain non-state tribunals, even if these would comply with conditions of (relative) permanency, independence and impartiality of the tribunal and of the position of its members.

§3. Sources of Civil Procedure Law

24. The CPA of Slovenia is closely related to the Austrian Code of Civil Procedure (ZPO). This is not surprising as until 1918 the territory of what is nowadays Slovenia was a part of Austria. It is, however, interesting that this development was not interrupted when Slovenia became a part of the newly formed Yugoslavia after the First World War (1918). Yugoslavia, when adopting a new unified legislation in the fields of private law and civil procedural law (in some areas, such as the law of obligations, unified laws were not enacted at all) decided to transplant Austrian laws because they were considered to be more modern and advanced than, for example, laws of the former Kingdom of Serbia, which was also integrated into the newly formed Yugoslavia. Thus, the first Yugoslav CPA, adopted in 1929, was nearly a complete translation of the Austrian ZPO.[15] As it has already been explained, the introduction of socialism to Yugoslavia after the Second World War did not bring such drastic changes as it did in other communist states (*see* above paragraph 2). It is logical that the mentioned characteristics of the Yugoslav version of socialism also influenced the development of the law of civil procedure. The aforementioned is namely a field of law that very clearly shows what concept – authoritarian or liberal – of relations between the state and the individual prevails in a certain political system and which also very clearly shows whether a state is willing to respect the autonomy as an expression of a broader notion of freedom of an individual. In this regard, it can be established that the civil procedural law did not suffer such degradation and distortion in Yugoslavia as it did in the countries of the Soviet block (e.g., East Germany).

25. The above-mentioned findings that Yugoslav CPA remained closely linked to its Austrian predecessor could implicit that this statute was not unsuitable for the

15. J. Juhart, *Civilno procesno parvo* [Civil Procedure]21(Univerzitetna založba 1961).

new social and economic order in independent Slovenia after 1991. There was nevertheless a general consent that a reform was needed. The main reason was (and still is) a great public dissatisfaction with the functioning of civil justice – predominantly caused by the excessive length of proceedings. The reasons for this condition are numerous, but the old CPA was perceived as one of the factors that contributed to the inability of civil justice in Slovenia to respect the right to trial within a reasonable time. There were heated debates on whether a more radical reform was needed but in the end the new Slovenian CPA,[16] which came into force in 1999 (i.e., eight years after the proclamation of independence) did not radically depart from the Yugoslav CPA-1976. For example, the principle of substantive material guidance (*materielle Prozessleitung*) was retained. However, some important novelties were introduced. One of the most important changes is that a restriction is now imposed with regard to until when a party is allowed to assert new facts and evidence (preclusions) – *see* below. Also – and this is one of the results of the heated proposals for a more passive role of a judge – the power of a court to take evidence not proposed by parties was abolished.

26. Since its coming into force in 1999, the CPA has been amended several times. The amendment of 2002 (the CPA-A) brought certain changes, predominantly in the field of promoting settlement. The amendment in 2004 (the CPA-B) broadened the courts jurisdiction in family law matters. The amendment in 2007 (the CPA-C) founded a basis for an 'e-service' and use of modern technology in civil litigation (but implementary measures have not been achieved yet). The amendment of 2008 (CPP-E) emphasized on the strengthening of judges' powers in order to achieve a concentration of procedure and at the same time strengthen the system of procedural sanctions against parties. It also implemented a groundbreaking reform of access to the Supreme Court and, by empowering this court to accept cases by discretion, emphasized the importance of the role of the Supreme Court in creating precedence. This reform was further strengthened with the 2017 reform (the CPP-E). With this amendment, important changes concerning the disclosure of evidence, the preparatory stage of proceedings as well as proceedings in appellate courts were implemented.

27. Besides the CPA, there are other important formal sources of civil procedural law in Slovenia. It has already been mentioned that several norms, important also for civil procedure, are contained in the Constitution. These refer to the position of courts (e.g., independence), to the position of judges (e.g., permanence, election, immunity, termination of office) and to fundamental procedural guarantees (e.g., right of access to court, right to an impartial and independent court, right to have a case decided by a natural judge, pre-determined by a statute, right to trial within reasonable time, right to be heard and of equality of arms, right to public trial, right to appeal, guarantee of unchangeability of final of judgments; *res iudicata*). There are also several statutes, which contain norms, relevant for civil procedure. Rules on international jurisdiction (and on recognition and enforcement of foreign judgments) are found in the Private International Law and Procedure Act

16. Official Gazette RS, No. 36/04 – consolidated version.

(PILPA) (*Zakon o mednarodnem zasebnem pravu in postopku*).[17] For matters which are decided in a non-contentious procedure (e.g., certain family law matters and certain patrimonial matters such as the division of joint property, regulation of relations between co-owners, land border disputes, tenants relations rules of Non-Contentious Procedure Act (*Zakon o nepravdnem postopku*)[18] apply. The enforcement of judgments as well as provisional (protective) measures is not regulated by the CPA but by a separate statute (EJPMA).[19] The composition, status and subject matters, the jurisdiction of courts as well as the position of employees of the courts (such as administrative staff, judges' assistants, legal advisors, court clerks), except for judges, a system of assigning cases to judges within the same court, the position of the Judicial Council and so on are regulated in the Courts Act (*Zakon o sodiščih*).[20] The JSA[21] determines the status of a judge, in particular concerning access to office, elections, rights, responsibilities, dismissal from office and disciplinary procedures. Legal aid is regulated in the Free Legal Aid Act (*Zakon o brezplačni pravni pomoči*).[22] The profession, election, status, rights and obligations of attorneys are regulated by the Attorneys Act (*Zakon o odvetništvu*).[23] The Labour and Social Courts Act (*Zakon o delovnih in socialnih sodiščih*)[24] establishes five specialized courts and determines some particularities in their procedure, while the Administrative Disputes Act (*Zakon o upravnem sporu*)[25] establishes the Administrative Court. The Court Order (*Sodni red*)[26] contains detailed provisions concerning administrative, technical and organizational matters of the courts, the case flow management, detailed rules on the assignment of cases, the court recess (from 15 July to 15 August), during which all cases, except the determined urgent cases, are suspended, and the functioning of the court administration. Remedies against the violation of the right to trial within reasonable time are regulated by the Act on Protection of the Right to Trial without Undue Delay (*Zakon o varstvu pravice do sojenja brez nepotrebnega odlašanja*).[27] In 2008, the Arbitration Act (*Zakon o arbitraži*)[28] was enacted (until then, the chapter on Arbitration was included in the CPA) as well as, the Act on Mediation in Civil and Commercial Matters (*Zakon o mediaciji v. civilnih in gospodarskih zadevah).*[29] This is in line with the legislator's goal of promoting Alternative Dispute Resolution (ADR). Mediation was further recognized by the Alternative Legal Dispute Resolution Act (*Zakon o alternativnem reševanju sodnih sporov*), which promotes court-annexed (or court-connected)

17. Official Gazette RS, No. 56/99.
18. Official Gazette SRS, No. 30/86.
19. Official Gazette RS, No. 40/04 – consolidated version.
20. Official Gazette RS, No. 23/05 – consolidated version.
21. Official Gazette RS, Nos 19/94 ... 57/2007.
22. Official Gazette RS, Nos 48/01 and 50/04.
23. Official Gazette RS, No. 18/93 ... 48/01, 54/08 (latest substantial amendment adopted on 20 May 2008).
24. Official Gazette RS, No. 2/04.
25. Official Gazette RS, No. 105/06.
26. Official Gazette RS, Nos 17/95 ... 138/2004.
27. Official Gazette RS, No. 49/2006.
28. Official Gazette RS, No. 45/2008.
29. Adopted in the Parliament on 23 May 2008.

ADR.[30]With the coming into force of the Collective Claims Act in 2018, a collective recovery of mass monetary claims is available in Slovenia (although not universally available for all sectors).Until then, only injunctive and not compensatory relief was available.

28. Since Slovenia is a member of the EU, all EU regulations in the field of European civil procedure are directly applicable in Slovenia and should be considered a part of a Slovenian legal order. Of particular importance are both Brussels Regulations concerning jurisdiction in civil and commercial matters (Regulation Number 44/2001) and in family law matters (Regulation Number 2201/2003), respectively, as well as regulations in the field of cross-border aspects of taking of evidence (Regulation Number 1206/2001) and service of documents (Regulation Number 1348/2000, now repealed by the Regulation Number 1393/2007), furthermore the Regulation creating a European enforcement order (Regulation Number 805/2004). The Regulation Number 1896/2006 creating a European order for payment procedure and the Regulation Number 861/2007 establishing a European Small Claims Procedure.

29. Case law is not formally recognized as a source of law. But in practice, an established case law is an important authority, and lower courts tend to follow the position of the appellate courts and of the Supreme Court. One of the functions of the Supreme Court of Slovenia is also to safeguard the uniformity of the case law (Article 110, Courts Act). Already in the late nineties, the Slovenian Constitutional Court established a doctrine linking the uniformity and consistency of case law on the one hand with the constitutional guarantees of the fair trial on the other. Through case law of the Constitutional Court the argument of precedent won direct constitutional significance in Slovenia to the extent that the violation of an arbitrary departure from settled (established, uniform) case law can amount to a violation of constitutional procedural guarantees and be remedied through a constitutional complaint. It is one of the elements of fair trial that a judge may not arbitrarily (without providing extensive reasoning) depart from a settled and uniform case law.[31] If such a departure occurs, the Constitutional Court may, upon a constitutional complaint, quash a judgment and order a retrial. That being said, the requirement that 'like cases should be decided alike' must not be framed in absolute terms. Otherwise, as the Constitutional Court explains, the independence of judges (Article 125 of the Constitution) would be jeopardized and, concurrently, the development of case law frustrated.[32] Therefore, even if the relevant case law is uniform and settled, the Constitutional Court does not ascribe to it the significance of an absolutely binding legal source. According to the established doctrine of the Constitutional Court, the Constitution does not prevent any departure from case law, but only arbitrary departure.[33] In order for a violation of the mentioned constitutional right to be found, the complainant must thus demonstrate the following: (1) there must exist settled and

30. Official Gazette RS, No. 97/2009.
31. For example, Decision of the Const. Court, Up 188/02, 11 Dec. 2003.
32. Decision of the Const. Court, Up-342/96, 8 Jun. 1998.
33. Decision of the Const. Court, Up-297/96, 15 Jun. 2000, Up-452/02, 9 Sep. 2004.

uniform case law; (2) the court's decision in the case at issue, which concerns an essentially similar legal and factual situation, departs from this settled and uniform case law; and (3) such departure is arbitrary.[34] The Constitutional Court comprehensively, and by reference to the positions taken in the legal literature, defined the criteria of the applicable test: '*[T]he Constitution does not prevent all departure from the case law, but only arbitrary departure. This concerns the requirement that when the court decides to depart from settled case law it must specifically explain its reasons (which presupposes that it knows the previous case law in the first place). Thus, the constitutional aspect of the inadmissibility of the departure from the case law does not entail that the Constitutional Court reviews the substantive correctness of the challenged judgment, but only whether the departure from the case law was appropriately reasoned (in the procedural sense).*'[35]

30. Courts are not authorized to determine procedural rules for themselves. It is only formally determined that the Supreme Court may give prior opinion on the draft of the Court order –*Sodni red* (*see* above), which is then adopted by the Ministry of Justice. It is however a well established practice that judges are members of expert groups for drafting legislation in the field of procedural law, and that the opinion of judiciary is sought with regard to draft-laws in that field.

§4. General Features of the Administration of Justice in Civil Matters

I. Basic Principles of Civil Procedure

A. *Principle of Free Disposition and Adversarial Principle*

31. The principle of free disposition is recognized in Slovenian civil procedural law and its importance is underlined already in the introductory part of the CPA (Articles 2 and 3). Without an action, there can be no judgment and when deciding on a dispute (except in some cases in family matters), the court is bound by the claim as determined by the claimant (a court may not decide neither extra nor ultra petitum). The action must contain a specified relief or remedy claimed in respect of the cause of action, the lateral claims, the statement of facts constituting the cause of action and the statement of evidence proving these facts (Article 180, CPA). Thus, it is obligatory for the claimant to state a concise and concrete claim already in the initial statement of the claim. When, for example, demanding damages, the claimants must always state a concrete amount of money which they are requesting from the defendant.[36] The court is not authorized to impose on the defendant to pay a higher amount, even if it finds that the plaintiff would be entitled to it according to substantive law. The same strict rules apply in the case when the court finds that

34. Decision of the Const. Court, Up-188/02, 11 Dec. 2003.
35. *Ibid.*
36. 2 L. Ude et al., *Pravdnį postopek – zakon s komentarjem*[*Civil Procedure – Act with the Commentary*], (GV Založba in ČZ UL 2005) 122–125(2005).

the plaintiff is not entitled to the sanction which they have stated in their claim (e.g., the damages in amount of money), but they are entitled to another sanction (e.g., a specific performance *–restitutio in integrum).* The court must, in such case (if the claim is not amended, *see* below), simply dismiss the action for the amount of money and the court is not authorized to impose another sanction, although such would be proper according to substantive law applied to the facts which the court has established.[37]

32. Parties are also free to dispose of their claim and defences during the trial. The voluntary dismissal of the claim, the acknowledgement (admission) of the claim and the in-court settlement result in a termination of litigation and produce a *res iudicata* effect thereby preventing a relitigation regarding the same claim. The court is not authorized to prevent parties from the mentioned acts of disposition with the claim – except if it finds out that they are conducted in a field where the principle of free disposition is revoked also in substantive law or if it finds out that the parties use these procedural acts of free disposition in an abusive way with a goal to fraudulently avoid (*in fraudem legis agere*) certain compulsory norms of substantive law (Article 3/3, CPA).[38] The above-stated in no way means that, for example, a court would not allow a defendant to admit a claim which has no foundation in substantive law or that a court would not allow a claimant to voluntarily dismiss a claim although it is founded in substantive law. It just means that the court can prevent parties from abuse of proceedings.[39]

33. Besides the voluntary dismissal of a claim (which results in effect of finality), there is also a possibility of a withdrawal of a claim (Article 188, CPA). This however does not have an effect of *ne bis in idem*. In order to protect the legitimate interests of the defendant, their consent is necessary for the latter.

34. Admission of a claim refers to the claim as a whole. It needs to be differentiated from the admission of facts. The admission of facts also has binding effects and the court is obliged to consider the facts which were admitted to be true which makes the evidence superfluous (Article 214, CPA). However, even if a defendant admits all facts, the court still has the duty to check whether the claim is founded in substantive law.

---

37. *See ibid.*, Vol. 1, p. 41.
38. If, for example, there is a compulsory norm in substantive law, that a person who does not have a status of a farmer, may not purchase real estate in a certain protected area, the parties are not able to avoid this prohibition in such a way, that a buyer would sue a farmer for a transfer of the land while the latter would then admit the claim. The purpose of the whole operation in this case is clearly to avoid the prohibition, imposed by substantive law. Only in such a case a court may refuse to accept the admission of a claim because the aim of the parties was to abuse the process. *See*, e.g., Judgment of the Supreme Court, II Ips 217/87, 15 Oct. 1987.
39. *See* 1L. Ude et al., *Pravdni postopek – zakon s komentarjem*[*Civil Procedure – Act with the Commentary*]45(GV Založba in ČZ Uradni list 2005).

35. The initiative of the parties prevails also in the field of assertions of facts and evidence. It is a responsibility of the parties to assert facts and present means of evidence (Article 7). The court is not permitted to introduce new facts and take evidence not previously advanced by the parties. The same applies with regard to evidence. Thus, the court may not take evidence which was not proposed by the parties, but can refuse to take evidence although it was proposed by the parties if it finds that evidence irrelevant (i.e., that it is meant to prove facts, which are not relevant for the case). On the other hand, it is the responsibility of the court to determine the issues of law (which covers not only domestic law but also foreign law).[40] The iura novit curia rule applies (Article 180, CPA). The court may not require the parties to make any legal assessment of the claim. Parties may, of course, present their contentions of law but they are not obliged to. If they do, the court is not bound by them and is responsible to find and apply the norms of substantive law which correspond to the factual situation. As stated above, the court is bound to the factual frame given by the parties when considering the legal basis of the dispute.

B. Active Case Management

36. Strict rules regarding the respect of the initiative of the parties are significantly softened by the rules on active case management.[41] Following the well-known patterns of Austrian and German law, the Slovenian CPA provides for the so-called substantive procedural guidance (*materialno procesno vodstvo*; in German: *materielle Prozessleitung und Aufklärungspflicht*) of a judge (Article 285, CPA).

37. The judge must ask questions, and shall in other appropriate manner see that all ultimate facts be stated during the hearing, that incomplete statements concerning important facts be supplemented, that means of evidence relating to the parties' statements be adduced or supplemented, and that all necessary explanations be given in order to establish the facts and legal relation in dispute.
The judge, as explained above, is bound by factual assertions and evidence, offered by the parties, but has a right and a duty to stimulate the parties (with questions, hints and observations) to amend and clarify their assertions of facts. The judge also needs to warn the parties if they considered the evidence, which the parties offered, as insufficient and warn them on the distribution of the burden of proof. The judge also needs to openly consult with the parties the legal viewpoints which the parties

40. J. Juhart, *Zbiranje procesnega gradiva[Production of Facts, Evidence and Legal Basis]*, 12 Pravnik, 227(1957).
41. *See*, e.g., D. Wedam Lukić, *Vloga strank in sodišča pri zbiranju procesnega gradiva[The Role of the Parties and the Judge at the Collection of Procedural Material]*, 24 Podjetje in delo, 984–990(1998); J. Juhart, *Zbiranje procesnega gradiva[Production of Facts, Evidence and Legal Basis]*, 12 Pravnik,223(1957); 2L. Ude et al., *Pravdni postopek – zakon s komentarjem[Civil Procedure – Act with the Commentary]*, 582 et seq.; M. Dolenc, *Materialno procesno vodstvo v luči odločb Ustavnega sodišča[Material Procedural Guidance in the Light of Jurisprudence of the Constitutional Court]*, 1 Pravosodni bilten, 70(2007).

have neglected.[42] With all of these measures, the judge can influence the proper factual basis and evidence to be determined, which is relevant from the point of view of applicable substantive law. It is beneficial for the ensuring of the effective right to be heard that the judge discloses to the parties his or her legal positions (which are also decisive according to the rule of iura novit curia) and thereby encourages them to state the facts that are legally relevant from a legal perspective that they would have otherwise overlooked.[43] If a judge carries out his or her powers of case management in a proper way, this can largely contribute to the rationalization of the proceedings also from the view of encouraging in-court settlements. Moreover, by enabling the judge and the parties to define as soon as possible which issues are disputed, and particularly which are relevant for adjudication, if properly performed, such trial and conduct of proceedings do not delay the proceedings but make possible for faster, more rational and economical proceedings and thus for a better access to justice.[44] It enables the proceedings to quickly concentrate to the points really relevant for the case which is extremely important for the rationalization of the taking of evidence. The material procedural guidance is practised mainly during the trial, but since the Amendment of the CPA in 2008, additional tools were implemented, which enable a judge to pose written questions and demand written clarifications already in the preparatory stage of litigation (Article 286a, CPA).

38. The duty of material procedural guidance covers just one part of a broader notion of case management. It concerns the substantive part of adjudication. Of course, also in this regard, a judge's activity can contribute to the concentration of proceedings – it can assure that factual assertions and proposed evidence will be narrowed to the extent that is really relevant for the case and that the activity of the court and the parties shall concentrate on relevant points. But, however, a judge in Slovenia lacks certain other powers of case management, those which would make it possible for the judge to assure a timely presentation of facts and evidence and a thorough preparation of a case for trial.[45]

39. In early 1990, when a reform of civil procedural law was discussed and a need to guarantee a more effective civil justice was more than evident, it was perceived by many that the goal of acceleration of proceedings should be achieved

42. This requirement follows also from the case law of the Constitutional Court; decisions Nos Up 130/04 (24 Nov. 2005) and Up 133/04 (1 Dec. 2005).
43. *See* J. Juhart, *Zbiranje procesnega gradiva*[*Production of Facts, Evidence and Law*], 12 Pravnik, 223–245(1957); S. Triva, *Esej o otvorenom pravosudjenju*[*An Essay on Open Adjudication*], Godišnjak PF u Sarajevu, 343–364(1973); Z. Trampuš, *Metode racionalnega vodenja postopka*[*Methods of Rational Case-management*], 2 Pravosodni bilten, 39–57(1999); 2 L. Ude et al., *Pravdni postopek – zakon s komentarjem*[*Civil Procedure – the Act with a Commentary*]585(GV Založba in ČZ UL 2006); *see also* the Decision of the Const. Court Up 130/04, 24 Nov. 2005.
44. *Ibid.*
45. *See* N. Betetto, *Pospešeni pravdni postopek*[*An Accelerated Civil Litigation*], 24 Pravna praksa, 37, 5(2004).

through a more passive position of a judge.[46] The heated discussion – often burdened by excessive amount of ideology – regarding the passive or active role of a judge developed. There were numerous proposals (many given by judges) that the court should remain absolutely passive in the litigation, that the rules regarding case management ('substantive procedural guidance', *materielle Prozessleitung*) should be abolished and that a strict and rigid system of time limits should be introduced.[47] These proposals were often based on a lack of knowledge of comparative procedural law. Many of those who advocated the idea of a passive judge have perceived the concept of an active judge as an expression of the soviet law, characteristic only for socialist states and introduced after the socialist revolution, and thus unsuitable for the new political and legal order. Simplifications in the sense that a judge has an active role in the 'east' (i.e., in the soviet system), but remains passive in the 'west', were common.[48] It is superfluous to say that these were serious misconceptions, since the concept of an active judge in the Yugoslav CPA in fact derived from the Austrian (*Klein's*) ZPO and was not a result of legislative changes after the introduction of socialism. The advocates of a concept of a passive judge also totally neglected the modern trends and developments in comparative procedural law, which undoubtedly speak in favour of a more active role of a judge in the field of preparation of a trial and in case management. However, the same reproach of ignorance of comparative civil procedure can also be addressed to at least some of the proponents of retaining an active role of a judge. These were obviously not familiar with the recent trends, for example in German and Austrian law, where the obligation of parties to contribute to the concentration and acceleration of procedure is emphasized and the system of procedural sanctions strengthened.[49]

40. Nevertheless, the warnings of the legal science (which also drove attention to the developments in foreign civil procedural laws), that – it goes without saying, within the limits of respect of the autonomy of the parties and free disposition – an active case management by the judge can contribute not only to the substantive quality of civil justice, but also to the concentration and acceleration of litigations, finally prevailed.

---

46. *See* P. Oberhammer, *Richterbild im Zivilprozess, Zwischenbilanz eines Jahrzents der Reformen in Mitteleuropa*in *Richterbild und Rechtsreform in Mitteleuropa*132 ff. (P. Oberhammer et al., ed. Wien, Manz2001).
47. M. Šipec, *Med liberalnim in socialnim civilnim procesom*[*Between Liberal and Social Civil Procedure*], 25 Podjetje in delo, 1201 ff(1999).
48. Typically *ibid.*, p. 1201 et seq.; *see also* L. Koman-Perenič, *Izpeljava ustavnih določil v civilnih procesnih zakonih*[*Application of Constitutional Norms in Civil Procedural Laws*], 23 Podjetje in delo, 801(1997).
49. *See,* e.g., P. Oberhammer, *Die Aufgabenverteilung zwischen Gericht und Parteien,* in *Commentaren op fundamentele herbezinning*, No. 1, p. 88 et seq.(Ingelse, Goslings eds., Prinsengrachttreeks 2004).

C. Principle of Obligation of Parties to Contribute to Acceleration of Procedure

41. To the rights of the parties in litigation corresponds their responsibility to contribute to the fulfilment of these rights and also to contribute to the quality, concentration and acceleration of litigation (*see* Article 11 CPA).[50] The Slovenian system of civil procedure does not only aim to establish a proper balance between a claimant and a defendant but also a proper balance and distribution of procedural burdens between the parties and the court.[51] Parties, of course, cannot be forced to actively participate in litigation; however, their passivity can cause them negative consequences. A default judgment can be entered in case of total passivity. Furthermore, the facts that were not explicitly denied or were denied in an unsubstantiated manner will be presumed to be admitted. As explained, a certain degree of active case management by the court contributes not only to substantive quality of adjudication but also to the concentration and acceleration of litigation. These positive effects can, however, be achieved only if the parties are also active and diligent at the participating in litigation. Thus, it should be a responsibility and obligation of both the parties and the court, to assure the concentration and acceleration of litigation. To make this obligation effective, a certain system of imposing sanctions against parties who do not fulfil this obligation may and should be imposed. This is not a question of diminishing or even abolishing the principle of autonomy of the parties in civil procedure or a question of ideologically burdened discussions about inquisitorial or adversarial or even 'eastern' or 'western' civil procedure. Parties do remain *dominus litis* ('the master') of litigation. This refers to the respect of their autonomy with regard to framing the issue of litigation (claim and facts upon which the claim is based), the respect for the acts of claim disposition (settlement, withdrawal, admission of claim) and the full respect for the parties' constitutional right to be heard. But, there is no plausible reason to consider the parties as of a litigation regarding the question whether it should be left to the parties to decide when (if whenever at all) the litigation would be allowed to proceed from one stage to another and whether a hearing of a court would be carried out or adjourned. Especially the amendment of the CPA in 2008 emphasized the importance of the obligation of the parties to contribute to the acceleration and efficiency of procedure by strengthening the procedural obligations, combined with the system of sanctions. This is not to be seen as a formalization of the procedure but as a measure, aimed at stimulating parties diligently to participate in procedure in order to assure a timely gathering of procedural material. In consequence, this contributes also to the substantive quality of adjudication.[52]

---

50. Decision of the Const. Court Up-2089/06, U-I-106/07, 18 Oct. 2007.

51. *See,* e.g., J. Zobec, *Predlagane novosti glede zamudne sodbe in posledic izostanka ter glede vmesne sodbe[The Proposed Reform Concerning Default Judgment, Sanctions for Inactivity and Interim Judgment]*, 33 Podjetje in delo, 1060(2007); L. Ude et al., 2 *Pravdni postopek – zakon s komentarjem[Civil Procedure – Act with the Commentary]* 596(GV Založba in ČZ UL, 2006).

52. *See* J. Zobec, *Predlagane novosti glede zamudne sodbe in posledic izostanka ter glede vmesne sodbe[The Proposed Reform Concerning Default Judgment, Sanctions for Inactivity and Interim Judgment]*, 33 Podjetje in delo, 1060(2007).

42. The Slovenian Constitutional Court very positively evaluated the extended system of procedural sanctions of disregarding new facts and evidence as it was introduced by the 2008 CPA amendment. It clearly emphasized the principle that the responsibility or burden to contribute to efficient and expeditious proceeding, as well as to the substantive quality of judicial protection, also falls on the parties. Thereby, it should be noted that the very same Constitutional Court otherwise has little or no understanding for procedural novelties which amount to an excessive formalization of procedure. The 2008 CPA amendment indeed included such novelties, many of which have already been declared unconstitutional by the Constitutional Court. The rule that a claim filed by an attorney is immediately stricken out, without the possibility of rectification, if it does not fulfil all formal criteria (Article 108/2 CPA)[53] or if a correct power of attorney is not submitted (Article 98/5 CPA) has been declared unconstitutional by the Constitutional Court.[54] The Constitutional Court also annulled strict procedural sanctions of automatic striking out of a claim in cases where the claimant did not attend the main hearing[55] and the sanction of an automatic judgment by default, if it was the defendant who did not attend the main hearing (regardless of whether he had previously duly filed a defence plea).[56] The rule that the service of a claim to a physical person can always be validly effected on the address, entered in the official administrative register, regardless of whether the addressee actually (still) lives at that address and regardless of whether the addressee could, upon reasonable effort actually be found at certain other address (Article 143 CPA), has also been declared unconstitutional since it disproportionally restricts the constitutional right to be heard.[57]

43. All the aforementioned issues prove that a real danger of abuse of procedural instruments leading to a pure formalization of proceedings without any real benefits of legitimate aims of civil justice truly exist, and that they can put the fairness of the trial in jeopardy. It must, therefore, be constantly and critically assessed whether both the legislature and the judge in every individual case, have managed to find a proper balance between the goals of concentration, speed and procedural economy on the one hand, and the goal of achieving justice on merits on the other. Furthermore, the quest for a proper balance must also include the aspect of adequately protecting procedural guarantees such as the right to be heard. Review of the case law of the Slovenian Constitutional Court, however, shows that an individual assessment must be made in each specific case, since it is not possible to attach the label of a mere formalization of procedure to every accentuated procedural requirement or every procedural sanction. The system of the judge's powers to disregard late facts and evidence proves that such requirements and sanctions attached to cases of non-compliance can, if applied properly, benefit all of the aforementioned aims of civil justice.

53. Decision of the Slovenian Constitutional Court No. U-I-200/09-14 of 20 May 2010.
54. Decision of the Slovenian Constitutional Court No. U-I-74/12-6 od 13 Sep. 2012.
55. Decision of the Slovenian Constitutional Court No. U-I-164/09-13 of 4 Feb. 2010.
56. Decision of the Slovenian Constitutional Court No. U-I-161/10-12 of 9 Dec. 2010.
57. Decision of the Slovenian Constitutional Court No. U-I-279/08 of 9 Jul. 2009.

D. Principles of Orality, Immediacy and Free Evaluation of Evidence

44. According to Article 4 of the CPA, the court shall decide upon the claim on the basis of an oral, immediate and public consideration of the case. Only in cases specified by the present act, claims may also be determined on the basis of procedural acts made in writing, and on the basis of circumstantial evidence. An oral hearing is an obligatory phase of every civil procedure. Only in exceptional cases can a court decide the case on merits without a hearing. Besides the obvious cases of default judgment (which can be rendered already if the defendant fails to file an answer to the claim) and acknowledgement or voluntary dismissal of the claim (which can occur even before the hearing and in such a case makes a hearing obsolete) the only real exception is that a court may waive a hearing in commercial dispute and in small claims procedure if it finds, on the basis of claim and answer to the claim that only the law is in dispute and not the facts.

45. Although the principle, envisaged in Article 4, CPA, speaks in favour of orality, in fact, civil procedure in Slovenia is a mixture between written and oral proceedings.[58] Often, practice even tends to a greater importance of written procedural acts. On the other hand, the importance of the main hearing is diminished because it is often conducted in a 'piece-meal' manner; with a number of short consecutive short hearings. True, Article 298.2 of the Slovenian CPA provides that litigation, whenever possible, should be terminated in one single main hearing (trial). In this provision, a principle of concentration is envisaged. But in reality, litigations which are terminated after one hearing are rare. However, during the time period between consecutive hearings parties often file preparatory submissions and in practice, these are very important. Although according to the wording of the act (Article 286/3, CPA) in these written submissions parties should only announce facts, which they will later assert during a hearing. Besides, according to the wording of the Act, preparatory submissions should not contain legal views, but only facts. However, the practice has long ago abandoned such a restrictive approach. In practice, it is never demanded that facts and legal observations, asserted in preparatory submissions, are then pleaded orally.[59]

46. Another instrument that gives importance to written form is the obligatory answer to the claim. If a defendant fails to answer a claim, a judgment by default can already be entered against him. Besides, it also speaks in favour of the finding that in reality, the character of civil procedure in Slovenia gravitates more towards written proceedings, that the procedure before the Supreme Court is always and before appellate courts almost always purely written, as these courts decide in camera, without parties and their attorneys having a chance to be present and to plead orally.

---

58. L. Ude, *Civilno procesno parvo* [*Civil Procedure*] 122(ČZ UL 2002).
59. 2 L. Ude et al., *Pravdni postopek – zakon s komentarjem*[*Civil Procedure – Act with the Commentary*]607(GV Založba in ČZ UL 2006).

47. The principle of free evaluation of evidence means that the judge is not bound by any formal rules as to the weight of particular evidence. According to Article 8, CPA: 'the decision on facts which will be deemed to have been proven shall be based upon the opinion which the court shall take after a careful and thorough evaluation of every piece of evidence in itself, and of the evidence as a whole, and considering the outcome of the entire proceedings'. In broader sense, the principle of free evaluation of evidence also means that the court is not limited in deciding which evidence (offered by the parties) it can use in order to establish the existence of disputed facts. There are very few exceptions – one is that a prorogation agreement may be proved only by submitting a document, containing such an agreement (this is not just a question of written form as a matter of substantive law, but a procedural rule on evidence).

48. The principle of free evaluation of evidence is logically connected to the principle of immediacy. This principle means that only judges, who conducted the trial and were thus personally present at the time of taking of evidence, may render the judgment. The only exception is that witnesses and parties may be examined by a requested judge if they live in the area of another court and are prevented from appearing in court by insurmountable obstacles (usually concerning health conditions), or unreasonable costs would be incurred by their appearance (Article 259, CPA). From the same principle, it also follows that appellate courts cannot overturn the judgment based on a different evaluation of witness evidence just from their statements, as contained in the protocols of the file. It is only possible for appellate courts to either fix a public hearing and take such evidence again or quash a judgment and order a retrial.

49. If a judge changes during the trial, all oral evidence needs to be, as a principle, taken again. But with the consent of parties (which is usually given) a new judge may rely on protocols taken during the examination of witnesses and experts (Article 302, CPA).

E. Principle of Prevention from Abuse of Procedural Rights

50. Article 9 of the CPA proclaims that in court, the parties, their statutory representatives and attorneys shall speak the truth and exercise the rights stipulated by the present act in a fair manner. However, the obligation to speak the truth is a mere programmatic principle, without any real sanctions (except for when a party is cross-examined as evidence). Besides, Article 10 of CPA determines that in the event that the parties, interveners, their statutory representatives or attorneys, with intention of harming another person or achieving goals contrary to the custom and usage or good faith and fairness, abuse the rights stipulated by the act, the court may impose on them a fine or other measures provided hereinafter. In the case of abuse the fine imposed may not exceed EUR 1,300. Previously, the CPA also provided for a possibility of this pecuniary fine to be transformed into a prison term (up to one month) if the fine was not paid. But the Constitutional Court found that this possibility violated the Constitution. At the same time, the Constitutional Court determined that it is permissible to impose such fines (in casu: against defamatory written submissions, which damage the reputation and impede the authority of the court and of the judiciary) in the course of civil procedure. These sanctions are more of disciplinary nature and a tool of case management, aimed to achieve a proper administration of justice and not a real penal sanction.[60] However, in order to maintain that this is their real character, these sanctions may not be too severe (such as a prison sanction obviously is).[61]

51. An abuse of procedural rights can also result in the court's decision not to accept a procedural act or not to decide on merits on a motion of a party which constitutes an abuse of rights.[62]

II. Fundamental Guarantees

A. Introduction

52. The Slovenian Constitution contains an extensive chapter on human rights and fundamental liberties (Part II; Articles 14–65). Many of these concern guarantees in civil procedure: right of access to court, right to independent and impartial judge, pre-determined by law, right to trial within reasonable time (all of Article 23); right to due process (Article 22); right to appeal (Article 25); right to public trial (Article 24). International treaties in the field of human rights, such as the ECHR are directly binding and are applied by Slovenian courts. However, as all of the rights and freedoms, contained in ECHR, are guaranteed also by the Slovenian Constitution, the Constitutional Court examines allegations regarding violations of the ECHR in the framework of examining the violation of corresponding rights under the Constitution.[63] For example, a party's allegation of a violation of a right of access to court, guaranteed by Article 6 ECHR, would be considered (and reasoned) from the viewpoint of the right to judicial protection, guaranteed by Article 23 of the Constitution. In any case, influence of the jurisprudence of the European Court

---

60. Decision of the Const. Court, U-I-145/03, 23 Jun. 2005.
61. *Ibid.*
62. In a particular case, the Supreme Court stroke out as inadmissible a motion for disqualification of a Supreme Court judge for an alleged reason of lack of impartiality on grounds that this motion constituted an abuse of procedural rights. The Supreme Court explained that the same attorney at law has already on numerous occasions filed a motion for disqualification of that judge with exactly the same reasoning and the Supreme Court has on all of these occasions gave a reasoned decisions in which it dismissed the motion. The attorney thus already had to know the position of the Supreme Court and the repeated filing of identical motions constituted an abuse of rights. *See,* e.g., Decision of the Supreme Court, II Ips 306/99, 13 Jan. 2002 and the Decision of the President of the Supreme Court, Su 29/2004, 14 Jan. 2005.
63. *See,* e.g., Decision of the Const. Court, Up 262/99, 25 Apr. 2002.

of Human Rights (ECourHR) on Slovenian courts is evident.[64] Especially the Constitutional Court often relies on the case law of the ECHR and its positions concerning particular procedural guarantees (such as right to be heard and right to equality of arms). Judgments of the ECourHR are often cited in the decisions of the Constitutional Court.

53. It has already been mentioned that the Slovenian legal system provides for a constitutional complaint. A party, who alleges that a certain human right was violated by a court judgment, can, after exhaustion of all available remedies, file a constitutional complaint with the Constitutional Court.[65] However, this does not mean that it is only the Constitutional Court that has to apply provisions of the Constitution (and the ECHR); both the provisions of the Constitution and the ECHR concerning procedural guarantees are directly applicable also in proceedings before regular courts. Thus, also the motivations (reasons) of the regular courts' judgments should and often do contain aspects of constitutional guarantees.[66] Also the parties to litigations are expected to include arguments about constitutional rights into their pleadings. If they fail to do so, they might be precluded from submitting such arguments in the subsequent constitutional complaint (for the lack of exhaustion of remedies on substance).[67] One of the conditions for admissibility of the constitutional complaint is also the exhaustion of all other remedies; this condition is construed in such a manner, that it does not suffice to exhaust remedies just formally, but the party needs to exhaust them in substance. Thus, if it is possible to seek redress against a certain violation already by remedies, available in civil procedure (appeal, revizija – the further appeal on points of law), a party, who fails to do so, will later be precluded from referring to such violations in a constitutional complaint.[68] This condition seeks to achieve, *inter alia*, a goal that the parties would, in fact, plead human rights arguments already in 'ordinary' court proceedings and not 'reserve' such arguments only for the procedure in the Constitutional Court.

B. Right of Access to Court

54. The 'right to judicial protection' (right of access to court), determined in Article 23 of the Constitution, guarantees everyone the right to have any decision regarding his rights, duties and any charges brought against him or her made without undue delay by an independent, impartial court constituted by law. This right guarantees that a person can submit his or her civil dispute to a court and obtain the

64. A. Mavčič, *The Influence of the European Court on Human Rights Case-Law on Slovenian Constitutional Case-Law: The Right to Fair Trial, Revue de justice constitutionnelle Est-Européenne*, numéro spécial, str. 103–123 (2003).
65. Article 50 of the Constitutional Court Act (Zakon o Ustavnem sodišču); Official Gazette RS, No. 15/94 and 108/07.
66. *See* D. Wedam Lukić, *Vloga in odgovornost sodnika v civilnem pravdnem postopku*[*The Role and Responsibilities of the Judge in Litigation*], 29 Podjetje in delo, 1675(2003).
67. For example, Decision of the Const. Court, Up 39/95, 16 Jan. 1997.
68. Decision of the Const. Court, Up 39/95, 16 Jan. 1997.

court's judgment on the merits.[69] The right of access to court is effectively fulfilled only if a court decides on a submitted dispute on merits. Thus, rejecting the claim as inadmissible for procedural reasons is not an effective fulfilment of the right of access to court. This, of course, does not mean that the law cannot impose procedural conditions for admissibility of actions and formal requirements that a claim should comply with. However, as such conditions restrict the right of access to the court; they must be based on reasonable and constitutionally acceptable grounds.[70] Concerning the time limits, for example, the Constitutional Court stated that they must always be predictable and that both their length and preclusive nature must clearly follow from the wording of the law; besides, they must not be so short as to make an effective accomplishment of certain procedural act practically impossible.[71] Also the standpoint that any kind of action is inadmissible if the claimant does not have legal interest or standing for achieving a court judgment is constitutionally acceptable.[72] In the opinion of the Constitutional Court, it is no violation of the right to access to court protection in case of a lack of international jurisdiction in a dispute on damages against a foreign state due to immunity. The Constitutional Court found that such immunity does restrict the right of access to court, but it is constitutionally acceptable as an expression of international law standards; besides the right of access to court is not entirely frustrated as the claimant can file an action in a foreign state.[73] However, the right of access to court was found to be violated in a case, in which the court had dismissed the action for reason of a lack of subject matter jurisdiction, instead of transferring the case to the court with jurisdiction.[74]

55. The right of access to court can also be violated if the court dismisses a motion to order an interim measure if it turns out that this entails ineffective subsequent judicial protection. With this reasoning, the Constitutional Court enabled for the issuing of regulatory interim measures in favour of the creditor in cases when unrecoverable damage would be sustained without such a measure.[75]

56. A part of an effective right of access to court is also the guarantee that a final judgment shall be binding; principle of *res iudicata* is an expression of the right of access to court.[76] Besides, a part of the broader notion of 'access to court' is also that a party can rely on an effective enforcement proceedings if the debtor does not voluntarily fulfil the obligation imposed by a final judgment.[77]

57. The Slovenian Constitutional Court has also dealt with the problem of the relationship between financial burdens of the litigation and the right of access to court. The Constitutional Court confirmed that it is a constitutional demand that an

69. Decision of the Const. Court, Up 107/99, 23 May 2002.
70. *Ibid.*
71. Decision of the Const. Court, Up 268/00, 21 May 2002.
72. Decision of the Const. Court, Up 334/98, 10 Feb. 2000.
73. Decision of the Const. Court, Up 13/99, 8 Mar. 2001.
74. Decision of the Const. Court, Up 54/704, 3 May 2005.
75. Decision of the Const. Court, Up 275/97, 16 Jul. 1998.
76. Decision of the Const. Court, Up 206/02, 16 Apr. 2002.
77. Decision of the Const. Court, U-I-339/98, 21 Jan. 1999.

effective access to court is guaranteed and thus it is not sufficient if the right of access is recognized only theoretically. From this demand, it also follows that financial burden of litigation must not form an insurmountable obstacle for the access to court for a poor party. This is a consequence of not only the right of access to court but also of the right of equality before the law and the prohibition of discrimination with regard to financial status (Article 14 of the Constitution).[78] Regulations on court and attorney fees and legal aid are therefore important from this point of view. The Constitutional Court has also stated that this right by its nature calls for a statutory regulation, and it is not unreasonable if the law imposes the obligation that the applicant for legal aid must provide certain certificates to prove his financial status.

C. *Right to Be Heard*

58. Article 22 of the Constitution (the right to equal protection of rights in court) imposes a constitutional demand for 'equality of arms' in any court proceedings – including in civil litigation. As the general demand of this provision, the constitutional court defines that every party of the litigation should be given equal opportunity to present his case, including the evidence under circumstances that do not put the party in substantial disadvantage against the opponent.[79] The most important consequence (however, not the only one) of this constitutional guarantee is the right of each party to be heard (also sometimes referred to as the right to a contradictory procedure). This is one of the most fundamental procedural guarantees, contained not only in the Constitution but also in the CPA (Article 5). Both the Supreme Court as well as the Constitutional Court have on many occasions reaffirmed the importance of this procedural guarantee and many aspects that it includes. The importance of the right to be heard is not merely to assure an equal treatment of the parties (after all, both parties are treated equally in a case when none of the parties are assured the right to be heard) but to assure that a person shall have full opportunity to 'come to word' (to have 'a day in court'), that is to have an opportunity to influence the decision of the court in proceedings concerning his or her rights and legal interests.[80] The Constitutional Court stresses out that the right to be heard is based on the respect for human dignity.[81] This is a necessary precondition for a democratic state, devoted to the respect for human rights and rule of law. A party must be ensured the possibility to state the arguments in favour of his or her position, make statements in any dispute regarding both factual and legal questions, make statements concerning the assertions of the opposing party and the results of the evidence taken, to be present in the taking of evidence and to cross-examine witnesses and experts.[82] In the broadest terms, a party must be able to get knowledge of and to comment on the whole procedural material on the file, thus all evidence

78. Decision of the Const. Court, Up 103/97, 26 Feb. 1998.
79. Decision of the Const. Court, Up 39/95, 16 Jan. 1997.
80. 1L. Ude et al. *Pravdni postopek – zakon s komentarjem*[*Civil Procedure – Act with the Commentary*]54 et seq. (GV Založba in ČZ UL 2005).
81. Decision of the Const. Court, Up 39/95, 16 Jan. 1997.
82. *Ibid.*

adduced or observations filed, even if they were provided by a third neutral body (such as a judge of a lower court in his report for the Court of Appeals), but with the purpose of influencing the decision of the court.[83] In any case, when a law foresees that a certain person – although a neutral public body – shall have powers to present its comments to a litigation between two (other) litigants, such comments have to be served to parties and their right to answer must be guaranteed.[84]

59. If a party defaults a certain procedural act and this default results in a preclusion of a particular right, it is a constitutional demand that a party must have an opportunity to achieve a reinstatement (*restitution in integrum*) if the default was due to justified reasons.[85] However, it is a burden for the party to prove that the default was due to justified reasons.

60. A system of preclusions with regard to the question till when can a party submit new facts and evidence, has to be considered as a restriction of the right to be heard. However, such a restriction can be constitutionally acceptable if it is a necessary precondition to achieve conformity with the right to trial within reasonable time and if, despite these preclusions, a party still has a reasonable opportunity to present its case.[86]

61. Another consequence of the right to be heard is that the court must drive the attention of the parties to legal grounds which it intends to use when solving the dispute and which the parties did not rely on. The rule of *iura novit curia* applies in Slovenian law and thus, a court may use a legal norm, which none of the parties has relied on. However, if a court decides to do so, it is a constitutional demand that a court should drive the parties' attention to the possibility of relying on such a norm and thereby enable the parties to comment on it and to adjust their factual assertion to facts, relevant from the viewpoint of such a norm.[87] This obligation of a court should, however, not mean that parties are totally free from obligation to diligently prepare their case, also with studying relevant legislation and case law in order to determine what is the proper legal basis of the dispute.[88]

62. Concerning the evidence, the fact that a party can propose evidence is not the only consequence of the right to be heard, but there is also a corresponding obligation of the court to, as a principle, take all evidence offered by the parties, under a condition that such evidence is relevant for the case.[89] Thus, for the court to be

83. Decision of the Const. Court, Up 108/00, 20 Feb. 2003.
84. *Ibid.*
85. Decision of the Const. Court, Up 487/01, 21 May 2002.
86. Decision of the Const. Court, Up 184/98, 2 Feb. 1999.
87. Decision of the Const. Court, Up 130/04, 24 Nov. 2005.
88. *See*, e.g., M. Dolenc, *Materialno procesno vodstvo v luči odločb Ustavnega sodišča*[*Material Procedural Guidance in the Light of Jurisprudence of the Constitutional Court*], Pravosodni bilten, 1, 70 (2007); 1L. Ude et al., *Pravdni postopek – zakon s komentarjem*[*Civil Procedure – Act with the Commentary*]59(GV Založba in ČZ UL 2005).
89. Decision of the Const. Court, Up 121/00, 18 Sep. 2001. It must be stressed out that this procedural guarantee is not violated if the court rejects evidence on the grounds that facts, which it aims to

able to reject the offered evidence there must be a constitutionally acceptable ground for such a rejection. As a principle, the constitutional court confirmed that also the fact that evidence was illegally obtained might be an acceptable ground for rejecting such evidence in civil (and not just in criminal) procedure. However, the test of proportionality must be applied to solve the conflict of rights, for example the right to privacy (which would be impeded if such evidence was taken by the court) and the right to effective judicial protection and the right to evidence as one of the expressions of the right to be heard (which is impeded if evidence is rejected by the court).[90] Besides, an evidence may be rejected if it is obvious that it is totally inappropriate for establishing the asserted facts or if it is not properly substantiated (i.e., a party who offers evidence has a burden to explain exactly which fact is to be proved, why is that fact relevant for the case and how the offered evidence could contribute to establishing such a fact).[91] However, it is not constitutionally acceptable (as a principle) to reject offered evidence with reasoning that it is unlikely that the evidence will succeed.[92]

63. Although the Constitutional Court admits that there may be some justified exceptions, the general principle (as a consequence of the constitutional right to be heard) is that a judgment may bind only the parties of the litigation (procedural privity). A result of litigation may not harm a person who was not a party in that litigation – neither by the *res iudicata* effect of the judgment nor by the fact that in a certain later litigation a court would apply evidence, produced in a prior litigation.[93]

64. The right to be heard must already be guaranteed in the Court of First Instance. It would not suffice that the opponent would obtain this right only with a possibility to file an appeal. In exceptional circumstances, for example in case of an interim measure of freezing of bank accounts when an effect of surprise is essential, it is permissible that the right to be heard is assured ex post facto – with the debtor's right to file an objection against the interim measure. But also in such case, it is essential that this objection is then decided by the Court of First Instance, who must again, in the light of debtor's submissions in objection, reconsider the interim measure.[94]

---

establish, are not relevant for the case; however, it later (in the course of appeal or revision) appears that the application of substantive law by the First Instance Court was erroneous. True, the erroneous application of substantive law resulted in an erroneous decision on which facts are relevant for the case, but the basis for this error is in the field of substantive law, not in the field of procedural law and procedural constitutional guarantees.

90. Decision of the Const. Court, Up 472/02, 7 Oct. 2004.
91. Decision of the Const. Court, Up 266/01, 25 Apr. 2002.
92. Decision of the Const. Court, Up 121/00, 18 Sep. 2001, N. Betetto, *Ustavna jamstva v dokaznem postopku*[*Constitutional Guarantees Concerning Taking of Evidence*], 22 Pravna praksa, 8 (2003).
93. Decision of the Const. Court, Up 39/95, 16 Jan. 1997. In case, it was unacceptable that an expertise and a statement of an expert witness in a litigation between parties A and B was later used by the court in the litigation between parties A and C (in order to prove the illegality of C's conduct). The party C namely had no opportunity to participate in litigation between A and B, had no chance to cross examine the expert witness and had no chance to challenge his expertise. His right to be heard was thus violated.
94. Decision of the Const. Court, Up 321/96, 15 Jan. 1997.

65. A violation of the right to be heard is an absolute ground for appeal (Article 339/1, point 8, CPA) and revizija (the further appeal on points of law; Article 370, CPA). It is also a ground for a constitutional complaint.

D. Obligation to Give a Reasoned Judgment

66. A duty corresponding to the party's right to be heard is the duty of the court to take into consideration all of the statements of a party, weigh their relevancy, and take positions concerning the relevant statements. An obligation of the court to give a reasoned decision is a necessary consequence of the party's right to be heard; only in such a way is the party's right to be heard effective and only in such a way is also the party's right to appeal effective.[95] The extent to which this duty to give reasons applies may vary according to the nature of the decision and must be determined in the light of the circumstances of the case. It is not necessary to answer every single argument of the parties, however at least the crucial arguments of the parties have to be dealt with specifically. Besides, it is also not always necessary to specifically answer a certain point, if already other parts of the reasons can be construed as an implied rejection of the party's position.[96] The standards as to the question how extensive reasons in a judgment should be lower for appellate courts, especially for courts, against whose decisions there are no further appeals. If a court of a lower instance already gave extensive reasons concerning a rejection of a party's position and if that party's appeal does not bring any new standpoints, but merely repeats the positions that it already presented during the procedure in the first instance, then it is admissible for the appellate court, simply to endorse reasons of the judgment of the First Instance Court.[97]

E. Equality before the Law

67. The right to equal protection before the court expands beyond the demand of equality of the parties of one litigation – it also implies that equal cases should be decided alike.[98] In the opinion of the Constitutional Court, this constitutional right would, therefore, be violated in a case when a court in a civil litigation arbitrarily decides on the case differently as courts regularly decide similar cases. Thus, the constitutional complaint will have success if the appellant can prove that the judgment in his case contravenes the well-established case law and that the court's decision not to follow the established case law lacks sufficient reasons – in procedural sense, the constitutional court will not determine whether the previous or the new case law is (more) appropriate or correct in substance.[99] From the reasons

95. Decision of the Const. Court, Up 77/01, 4 Mar. 2004.
96. Decision of the Const. Court, Up 286/001, 5 Mar. 2001.
97. Decision of the Const. Court, Up 429/01, 18 Oct. 2001.
98. M. Pavčnik, '*Argument sodnega (pravnega) precedensa*[*Argument of Judicial (legal) Precedent*], 30 Podjetje in delo, 1032 et seq, (2004).
99. Decision of the Const. Court, Up 188/02, 11 Dec. 2003.

(grounds), contained in the judgment it should be evident that the departure from the established case law was intentional (and not just a result of a judge's lack of knowledge of case law) and that there were, according to the opinion of that judge, good grounds for a change in the case law. It is expected from the judge to specifically explain the reasons that substantiate the departure: this means that they must know the case law, explain why they do not agree with such, and provide reasons for a different decision and thereby an attempt to change the case law for the future.[100]

68. It is however not within a jurisdiction of the Constitutional Court to adjudicate which interpretation of law is correct if both such interpretations are acceptable from the viewpoint of conformity with the Constitution. In such a case, the final word in interpreting statutory law is reserved for ordinary courts (especially the Supreme Court) and the Constitutional Court would exceed limits of its jurisdiction if it interfered with the interpretation of statutory law, given by the ordinary courts. Furthermore, the prohibition of the arbitrary departure from case law does not mean that case law (precedents) cannot be changed. The Constitutional Court has already taken the position that it cannot and should not prevent changes and thereby the development of case law.[101]

69. However, the constitutional court rejected the plea that it is a consequence of the equality before the law that a new procedural legislation ought not to be used in cases already pending. The Constitutional Court reaffirmed the traditional position in procedural law that the new procedural legislation may be applied also to cases which are already pending.[102] There is just a guarantee that an immediate application of new legislation should not result in a deprivation of the position of the party, who relied on the old (then valid) legislation. It was therefore permissible that a new law substantially raised a limit concerning the value of claim, which determines whether a revizija (a further appeal on points of law to the Supreme Court) is permissible, and that such new law was applicable also to cases, in which an action to the Court of First Instance was filed already before the new law came into force.[103]

F. Right to Appeal

70. Article 25 of the Slovenian Constitution guarantees a right to appeal against decisions of courts (no such right is laid down in the ECHR with regard to decisions concerning civil rights and obligations, a right to appeal is guaranteed by the Seventh Protocol to the ECHR, however only in criminal procedure). The right to appeal as a constitutional right of course does not mean that the Constitutional Court is empowered to review the correctness of the appellate court's decision concerning

100. *Ibid.*
101. Decision of the Const. Court, Up 22/94, 7 Mar. 1997.
102. Decision of the Const. Court, U-I-21/02, 12 Sep. 2002.
103. *Ibid.*

the application of law and assessment of facts. The right to appeal as a constitutional right is a procedural guarantee, imposing an obligation upon appellate court to take the appeal into consideration and to answer all of the appellant's relevant arguments. Therefore, it is a consequence of the constitutional right to appeal that the decision of the appellate court must be reasoned; however, standards as to the question how detailed a motivation of the judgment should be, are lower for appellate courts than for the Courts of First Instance.[104] A precondition for the right to appeal is that a judgment of a Court of First Instance must always be reasoned because only in such way can a party effectively fulfil his or her right to appeal against that decision. In the opinion of the Constitutional Court, the right under Article 25 of the Constitution is also not violated if due to a different legal evaluation the appellate court overturns the judgment of the Court of First Instance. The Constitutional Court, however, found a violation of this right in a case in which the party missed the time limit to file an appeal due to erroneous legal instructions,[105] and in a case in which the court issued a default judgment, but from the reasoning it did not follow which legal norm was the basis for finding that the claim was substantiated.[106]

71. The Constitutional Court has also stated that the right to appeal as a constitutional right only guarantees a right of access to appellate courts, but not an appeal to the Supreme Court (revizija) against appellate courts' judgments.[107] However, if a statute does provide for access to the Supreme Court, then the procedure before the Supreme Court must conform with all constitutional procedural guarantees – such as right to be heard and equality of arms.[108]

72. The Constitution (unlike, for example, in case of a right to public trial) does not foresee that a statute could restrict the right to appeal. Therefore, it is not possible for a legislator in Slovenia to exclude an appeal in toto, for example, for small-value claims. It is however considered to be acceptable to restrict grounds for appeal – in Slovenian civil procedure, for example, an appeal against a decision in small claims procedure may only be based on an erroneous application of substantive law and on a grave ('absolute') procedural error (Article 458, CPA).

G. Right to a Trial without Undue Delay

73. The Constitution of Slovenia (like the Article 6/1, ECHR) explicitly provides for a guarantee of a trial within reasonable time ('without undue delay'– Article 23 of the Constitution). The principle of speedy trial is envisaged also by

104. Decision of the Const. Court, Up 458/02, 13 Oct. 2003.
105. Decision of the Const. Court, Up 148/01, 29 Oct. 2001.
106. Decision of the Const. Court, Up 201/01, 6 Oct. 2003. Pursuant to Art. 318.1 of the CPA, the default of a defendant results in a conclusion that he or she admits the facts, stated in the claim, however the court must still prove whether, based on such facts, the claim is well-founded in substantive law.
107. Decision of the Const. Court, Up 188/01, 25 Mar. 2002.
108. Decision of the Const. Court, Up 373/97, 22 Feb. 2001.

Article 11 of the CPA. However, it can be critically assessed that the CPA, although proclaiming a principle of a trial within reasonable time, does not contain sufficient procedural tools that would enable the achievement of this goal. Although the new CPA from 1999 brought some improvements, it can be realistically assessed that the crisis of the civil justice in Slovenia continues. Slovenia is still hampered by excessive duration of civil litigations and by huge backlogs in courts. This seriously undermines the reputation of the courts in public opinion as well as the legal certainty. Both The ECourHR[109] and the Constitutional Court of Slovenia[110] delivered influential judgments stating that there is a structural defect in the functioning of Slovenian civil justice and that the right to trial within a reasonable time is too often violated. There certainly are fields where improvements are possible and desirable. One of these is the organization of a preparatory stage of civil litigation. It is not an exaggeration to assess that the current CPA does not provide sufficient tools for an effective preparation of a trial. Besides, the law still does not provide for sufficient tools (or sometimes it is just that courts do not apply the already existing tools often enough), which would effectively prevent parties and their attorneys from dilatory tactics and from non-diligent preparation of their cases, which often results in undue delays in litigations.[111]

74. Regarding the criteria to review the violations of the right to trial without undue delay, the Constitutional Court of Slovenia relied on the standards, established by the case law of the ECourHR. These are in particular the complexity of the case, the conduct of the applicant and of the relevant authorities, and the importance of what is at stake for the applicant in the litigation. But recently, foremost the question whether there are any effective procedural remedies against an excessive duration of procedure, gained on importance. The ECourHR has namely started to examine the length of proceedings cases from the viewpoint of two conventional rights: right to trial within reasonable time (Article 6/1 ECHR) and the right to effective legal remedy against the violation of conventional rights (Article 13 ECHR). The European Court found in the *Lukenda* case that also the Slovenian legal system does not provide for adequate and effective legal remedies against the violation of a right to trial within reasonable time.[112] It found that a party could neither invoke such remedies when the proceedings in question were still pending, nor can he or she effectively claim a compensation foremost for non-pecuniary damages after the termination of proceedings, in which the right to trial within reasonable time was violated. With regard to the damages it should be noted that the Slovenian Code of Obligations provided for a state's responsibility for damages caused by state authorities, but the Code contains an exclusive list of legally recognized non-pecuniary damages and the suffering, caused by an excessive duration of proceedings is not included in that list.

109. ECHR Judgment, *Lukenda v. Slovenia* (no. 23032/02), 4 Oct. 2005.
110. Decision of the Const. Court, No. U-I-65/05, 5 Oct. 2005.
111. *See*, e.g., J. Zobec, *Predlagane novosti glede zamudne sodbe in posledic izostanka ter glede vmesne sodbe*[*Proposed Reform of Default Judgment, Sanctions for Inactivity and Interlocutory Judgment*], 33 Podjetje in delo, 1060(2007); A. Butala, *Pravdni postopek brez nepotrebnega odlašanja*[*Litigation without Unnecessary Delay*], 25 Podjetje in delo, 1156(1999).
112. *Lukenda v. Slovenia*, No. of the application 23032/02; Judgment dated 6 Oct. 2005.

75. Shortly after the decision of the European Court in the *Lukenda* case, the Slovenian Constitutional Court also rendered a judgment in which it declared that the Slovenian legal system does not provide for adequate remedies against the violation of the right to trial without undue delay.[113]

76. Following the decisions of the European court and the Constitutional Court, the legislator adopted a new law – the Act on Protection of the Right to Trial without Unnecessary Delay.[114] The Act provides that in the event of a delay in the proceedings any party may lodge a request for supervision (*nadzorstvena pritožba*) with the president of the court. The president of the court may request the presiding judge to report on progress in the proceedings and is required to indicate in writing to the presiding judge any irregularities he finds. He or she may put the case on the priority list or set deadlines for procedural measures, but it must be stressed that no supervision of substantive or procedural decisions is possible and the principle of independence of the judge is maintained. If the delay has been caused by a heavy caseload, the president of the court may order the case concerned or other cases to be transferred to another judge. If this remedy proves unsatisfactory a further remedy is available: a motion for setting of deadlines with the president of a superior court.

77. Furthermore, the Act provides for a civil action for compensation after the proceedings had terminated. It specifically defines a non-pecuniary damage, caused by an excessive duration of court proceedings as a legally recognized damage. The Act limits the amount of non-pecuniary damages to EUR 300–EUR 5,000, whereby a court can, when appropriate, taking in the account foremost the behaviour of the applicant in the previous procedure, reject the claim for monetary damages if it finds that a mere declaration of violation (and a possible publication of a judgment) presents a sufficient remedy. The Act also imposes a procedural prerequisite that prior to an action the claimant must seek a consensual dispute resolution with a state attorney. An action may be filed only if a settlement is not reached.

78. It would be unrealistic to expect that the presented new law would substantively contribute to the acceleration of court proceedings in Slovenia (it will just contribute to lessening of a burden to the ECourHR as an appeal to this court will only be admissible after the exhaustion of these remedies.[115] This is probably what

---

113. Decision of the Const. Court, No. U-I-65/05, 22 May 2005. The Constitutional Court thereby overturned its previous case law, according to which there were two remedies available to a party, who believed that this right was violated: first, such a party could file an action in administrative court and after that remedy was exhausted a constitutional appeal against the violation of trial without unnecessary delay could also be filed. However, the European court found that these two remedies are not effective and the Constitutional Court later also changed its case law and stated that a comprehensive legislative reform is necessary in order to rectify the situation.

114. *Zakon o varstvu pravice do sojenja brez nepotrebnega odlašanja* (ZVPSBNO); Official Gazette, No. 49/06.

115. *See* Judgment of the ECourtHR, *Grzinčičv. Slovenia*, No. 26867/02, 3 May 2007, and P. Pavlin, *Prva pozitivna sodna presoja Zakona o varstvu pravice do sojenja brez nepotrebnega odlašanja[The First Positive Judicial Examination of the Law on Protection of the Right to Trial without Unnecessary Delay*], 26 Pravna praksa, 25(2007).

the European Court foremost had in mind when it started imposing obligations to the Member States to establish domestic remedies). Remedies such as a motion for setting of deadlines and a request for supervision can be very effective in a system which in general functions well with the exception of individual cases of violation. However, Slovenian judiciary suffers from huge backlogs in courts and overburdening of judges, therefore violations of the right to trial within reasonable time are not that often a result of inadequate measures of a judge in particular case but rather of the mere fact that the case did not yet get on the agenda due to backlogs. In such conditions, the mentioned remedies cannot really be effective – unless they result in taking the cases 'over the queue', which however jeopardizes the right to equality before the law. It still remains an unfulfilled obligation for Slovenia that it should organize its judicial system in such a way that its courts can meet each of its requirements, including the obligation to hear cases within a reasonable time.

H. Right to Public Trial

79. Save where expressly provided by law, all court proceedings are conducted in public, and all judgments are delivered in open court (Article 24 of the Constitution). The CPA defines circumstances which entail an exclusion of the public. The public may be excluded from all or part of the main hearing, where so required by the interest of state, business or personal secrets, or for moral considerations. Furthermore, public may be excluded from the main hearing also when by application of measures for maintenance of order if it cannot otherwise secure an undisturbed progress of the proceedings (Article 294, CPA). Exclusion of the public does not apply to the parties, their statutory representatives, attorneys and interveners. The panel may give permission that the main hearing from which the public is excluded be attended by certain designated officials, court personnel, scholars or public representatives, if this is necessary for performance of official tasks, scientific activity, or public service. On request of a party, the panel may allow that the hearing be attended by not more than two persons designated by the party (Article 295, CPA). In certain type of disputes, public is always excluded – family disputes (Article 407, CPA) and non-contentious matters concerning family matters and personal status (Article 38, Article 72, Non-Contentious Procedures Act (NCPA)).

80. Even if public is excluded from a hearing, a judgment must always be pronounced in public. The public may only be excluded from the part when the judge is giving oral explanation of the judgment. However, as judgments are in most cases not proclaimed on the hearing (not just the reasons, but also the verdict), but are only sent to parties later in a written form, the guarantee of public pronouncement of a judgment is practically diminished. What remains possible is an insight into a judgment in the case file, which must be allowed to anyone (just the judgment, except for certain parts of its reasons, if the public was excluded, other parts of the case file can be accessed only by persons who prove their legal interest).

81. As the right to public trial is established in public interest, it is not left to the parties' free disposition to agree that their case will be decided on in a non-public trial. The court must disregard such an agreement.[116] An unlawful exclusion of public is a grave procedural error and an absolute ground for appeal (Article 339/2, point 13, CPA).

82. The importance of the right to public trial is diminished in appellate courts and in the Supreme Court. Appellate courts almost always and the Supreme Court always decides in camera. Neither parties nor their attorneys may be present in the sessions of these courts (unless, which in practice happens just exceptionally, the appellate court decides to have an appeals hearing). However, the judgments of these courts are accessible to public, just as the judgments of the Courts of First Instance.

83. The constitutional guarantee of public trial does not include the right of direct transmission of court proceedings by media, such as TV or radio.[117] A president of a court may merely allow short parts of a trial (in the trial room) to be photographed or filmed; however just a visual, without sound (Article 19 of the Court Order).

116. 2 L. Ude et al. *Pravdni postopęk – zakon s komentarjem*[*Civil Procedure – Act with the Commentary*]293(GV Založba in ČZ UL 2006).
117. *Ibid.*, p. 626.

Part I. Judicial Organization

Chapter 1. The Courts and Their Members

§1. COURTS

I. Structure of the Court System

84. Judicial power is implemented by courts of general jurisdiction (which cover civil, commercial, family law and criminal cases) and by specialized courts. There are forty-four county courts (*okrajno sodišče*), eleven district courts (*okrožno sodišče*), four higher courts (*višje sodišče*) as Courts of Appeal and the Supreme Court of the Republic of Slovenia (*Vrhovno sodišče*). There is also the Constitutional Court, but it is not a part of the regular court system (although a party to civil litigation can, after the exhaustion of all legal remedies within civil procedure, file a constitutional complaint if he or she believes that a judgment, rendered in civil litigation violated certain human right or liberty). There are only two kinds of specialized courts (labour and social courts and administrative courts), but neither of these deal with civil litigation.

85. County courts are not subordinated to district courts. Both are Courts of First Instance (about subject matter jurisdiction, *see* below paragraph 137) and appeals from both courts are decided by the higher courts. The Supreme Court predominantly decides upon the so-called extraordinary appeals (revizija, request for protection of legality) and only in certain exceptional cases with regular appeals (such as if the Court of Appeals (as a Court of a First Instance) punishes a party for abuse of procedural rights or for defamatory submission). Since the CPA amendment of 2017, the Supreme Court is also vested with the power to issue, upon request of first instance courts, non-binding advisory opinions as to the interpretation of a question of law in case of conflicting case law of appellate courts regarding such question of law (Article 206 CPA). The procedure is a kind of preliminary ruling. Serious doubts as to its compatibility with the role of courts – which is deciding disputes, not rendering advisory opinions in abstract manner – however exist.

86. The Supreme Court is the highest appellate court, and it functions primarily as a court of third instance (court of cassation). Besides its appellate functions, it also determines certain cases of jurisdiction between lower courts, grants the transfer of jurisdiction to another court in cases, provided by law, and keeps record of the case law. The Supreme Court also exercises certain inspection of the lower courts' activities. It can demand an insight into a work of a lower court by examining cases, which are already closed, chosen at random. It must be stressed that this only refers to cases, already closed, and is done mostly for research and educational purposes, and therefore it cannot be regarded as an infringement of judicial independence of lower courts' judges.

II. Administration of the Court

87. The system of the administration of courts is mixed. The management and supervision of the courts' operation is divided between the Ministry of Justice, the Judicial Council, the personnel boards, presidents of the courts and the Supreme Court.

88. Each court has a president, who autonomously administers it concerning day-to-day operations (thus, it is not the Supreme Court who administers the whole court system). Presidents of the courts are nominated by the Minister of Justice upon a recommendation of the Judicial Council (*Sodni svet*).[118] Only the president of the Supreme Court is nominated by the Parliament (following a proposal by the Minister of justice and subject to the opinion of the Judicial Council and opinion of the plenary session of the Supreme Court). According to Article 7 of the Courts Act, the president of the court manages the operations of the court, including internal organization, financial operations, public relations, personnel policy, etc. Only a judge can be nominated to be a president of a court. In practice, this condition often results in lack of proper managerial skills. Management training for (prospective) presidents of courts has unfortunately not been a priority. A president is assisted by one or (at bigger courts) more vice-presidents. Each court also has a General Secretary, which is a professional position, but still reserved to a lawyer, usually a person, who had previously been engaged as a judge's assistant.

89. The Ministry of Justice and presidents of superior courts are also granted the power to supervise court presidents' administrative activities, except of the president of the Supreme Court. Presidents of courts are often required to submit reports on various issues. But in any case, this cannot interfere with the individual judge's independence at deciding particular cases (Article 60 of the Courts Act). The Ministry of Justice is responsible for the overall administration of the judiciary (Article 10, Courts Act). The minister prescribes 'the Court Order', which determines the internal organization and operation of the courts, and supervises its implementation. The administration of courts includes, in particular, the preparation of laws and other regulations in the field of organization and operation of the courts, care for

---

118. Even if a judicial council recommends only one person, the minister of justice is not bound by that proposal and may still refuse to nominate the candidate. However, reasons for such rejection must be given. Decision of the Const. Court, Up–679/06 and U–I–20/07, 10 Oct. 2007, critique of that decision: A. Zalar, *Mednarodni pravni standardi imenovanja predsednikov sodišč*[*International Legal Standards on Appointment of Presidents of Courts*], 26 Pravna praksa, 2, 2 (suppl.)(2007).

the education and in-service training of personnel, the provision of personnel, material, professional and physical conditions, the provision of international legal aid, statistics and other research into the operation of the courts (Article 74 of the Courts Act). The ministry adopts statistical data on a half-yearly basis, concerning the number of incoming and pending cases, their structure, the duration of proceedings, the number of appeals and of their success etc.

90. The personnel boards decide on the assignment of judges to different divisions within a court and on the determination of judges' specializations. They also give opinions on candidates for judges of Courts of First Instance, and the personnel boards of appellate courts assess the performance of judges of the Courts of First Instance. The personnel boards exist at every district court, at higher courts and at the Supreme Court and consist of judges of that court (except for district court personnel boards, which also include a certain number of county court judges).

91. The performance of matters of court management in Courts of First Instance is monitored by the president of the court of higher instance, and in courts of all instances by the president of the Supreme Court (Article 67 of the Courts Act). However, this supervisory competence is limited to the right to demand written reports about administrative activities of the subordinate court's president.

92. The president of the court and the immediately superior court may conduct official supervision of the work of a judge (Article 79a, JSA). Official supervision is conducted ex officio or upon a motion of the Human rights Ombudsman, the president of the immediately superior court, the president of the Supreme Court, the minister of justice, the personnel board of the court or the Judicial Council. Besides, whenever a party believes that a court is unreasonably delaying the resolving of the case, he may address a supervisory appeal to the president of the court, in which the case is pending.

93. The proposal for a budget for courts is formulated by the Supreme Court, in coordination with the Ministry of Justice (whereby the Judicial Council also gives its opinion). In the process of budget preparation, each court has to set targets, and the achieving thereof must be reported yearly to the Ministry of Finance. The final yearly budget for the courts is proposed by the Government and confirmed by the Parliament. Within the approved budget, the judiciary autonomously disposes of the allocated sources, whereby salary of judges is pre-determined by the law.

94. The Constitutional Court had an opportunity to examine the question of judges' remuneration from the viewpoint of the principle of separation of powers and from the viewpoint of the constitutional guarantee of independence of judiciary. It imposed a requirement that only an act, adopted by the Parliament, and not a governmental decree, may determine the questions of the judges' salaries. Besides, it imposed a restriction that a judge's salary may not, except in highly exceptional circumstances, be diminished from what it was at the moment when the judge was nominated to the post. Furthermore, it declared that it might be permissible to make a judge's salary dependent also on his work-performance, but this may not be evaluated solely on quantitative criteria (the number of solved cases).[119]

III. The Bench

95. In Courts of First Instance, a single professional judge constitutes the bench (Articles 31 and 33 of the CPA. Although the Constitution includes a provision that a direct participation of citizens in the exercising of judicial power is regulated by statute (Article 128), this has been extremely rare and was finally totally abolished with the CPA amendment in 2008 for civil cases. Lay judges only still sit as members of a panel of three, presided by a professional judge in labour disputes, pursuant to the Labour and Social Courts Act. This, however, is not a jury system and, furthermore, not a system where the decision-making on legal and factual issues would be split between a judge and a jury.

96. Higher courts decide on appeals in panels of three professional judges (Article 36, CPA). Since the CPA amendment in 2008, certain less important matters (like small claims cases and appeals against certain decisions on procedural issues) can be decided by a single judge in the appeals level as well. The Supreme Court decides in proceedings on revizija (further appeal on points of law) and other extraordinary legal remedies in panels of five professional judges (Article 38, CPA). Otherwise, the Supreme Court also decides in panels of three judges (e.g., concerning appeals against a decision of the higher court, which imposed a fine for contempt of court). The procedure of constitutional complaint in the Constitutional Court is split into two steps – first, a panel of three judges decide upon the admissibility of the complaint. If the constitutional complaint is declared admissible and accepted for consideration, it is then decided by the plenary session of the Constitutional Court (of nine judges).

97. A public prosecutor or a similar body cannot sit as amicus curiae or in any other role in any court. A public prosecutor may bring an action in certain family law cases and he or she may file an extraordinary remedy (request for a protection of legality), but in such case, he or she holds a position of a party or a complainant and not a position of a member of the bench.

IV. Appointment of Judges

98. Judges are elected by the Parliament (*Državni zbor*) after a proposal by the Judicial Council (which has eleven members: six judges and five other lawyers – usually members of the Bar or academics). According to Constitution, judges are independent in carrying out their functions, but are bound by the Constitution and the Law. The conditions of election, as well as the age of retirement of a judge, are determined by statute (JSA).

119. Decision of the Const. Court, U–I–60/06, 7 Dec. 2006.

99. To be appointed a judge, a candidate must have a degree in law (bachelor of law) and must have passed the state legal examination (bar exam). Before taking the state legal examination, one must have worked as a trainee for a minimum of two years, of which at least one must be in a court. After the examination, a candidate must have further three years of work experience in the field of law (usually as a legal assistant at a court). A further condition is that a candidate must be at least 30 years old (Article 8, JSA).

100. When a vacant judge post is announced, the Ministry of Justice first determines which of the candidates fulfil the formal criteria for the post (Article 15, JSA). The list of such candidates, including their evaluation during the traineeship at court, is then submitted to a court personnel board, which participates in the system of selection and promotion of judges. The personnel board evaluates the candidates who apply for positions in judiciary. Finally, the proposal, together with the opinion of the Ministry of Justice and of the personnel board is submitted to the Judicial Council for a final proposal. The candidate must then be confirmed by the Parliament.[120]

101. Once elected, a judge is subject to regular monitoring and assessment, based on quantitative and qualitative criteria by a court personnel board. This evaluation is a basis for promotion. Judges are promoted to higher salary brackets and to higher grades by a decision of the Judicial Council. A promotion to a rank of a supreme judge is subject to a confirmation by Parliament upon a proposal of the Judicial Council. In any case, promotions are not automatic; they depend on evaluation by personal councils, established by district and higher courts and the Supreme Court.

102. A judge of the Constitutional Court is elected for a term of nine years and is not eligible for re-election. The conditions of election as well as the status of the Constitutional Court judges are regulated by the Constitutional Court Act.

103. Judges may, with their consent, be transferred to overburdened courts. Only in exceptional cases (temporary disciplinary measure, abolition of a court, a reorganization of court system, a significant decrease in the volume of work), they can also be transferred without the judge's consent (Article 66, JSA). These rigid norms on immovability of judges, whereas positive from the viewpoint of the protection of independence of judges, had negative consequences for the goal of assuring the rights to trial within reasonable time and to equal protection before the law (huge differences in backlogs in different courts are causing entirely incomparable positions of litigants in different courts with regard to when they can expect to obtain a decision in their cases). Certain programmes for reduction of court backlogs envisaged a transfer of higher court judges to lower overburdened courts – but this is subject to their consent. An important novelty in this regard was introduced by the

120. So far, only on a couple of occasions has the Parliament rejected the proposal of the Judicial Council. In all of these occasions, the Judicial Council then repeated the same proposal, with additional reasoning, and the Parliament then, insofar always, confirmed the proposed candidates.

amendment of the Courts Act in 2005. The amendment instituted an 'inter-county judge' with the aim of securing a greater mobility of judges within the area of jurisdiction of a single higher court (Article 38/5 of the Courts Act). Such judge can be transferred to a court with high backlogs or with other exceptional circumstances (such as a maternity or longer sick leave of a judge at that court) even without consent. However, the inter-county judges are already elected as such; therefore, the candidates, when filing an application for a vacant post of an inter-county judge, already know that they are applying for a post, where they can be moved from court to court (within the same appellate jurisdiction), subject to demand.[121]

§2. Members of the Judiciary

I. Incompatibilities

104. The Constitution (Article 133) provides for the incompatibility of a judicial office with an office in any other state body, local government body, or any organ of a political party.

105. A judge may not accept any other employment that would obstruct his performance as a judge, harm the reputation of the judicial service, or create the impression that he is not impartial at administering justice (Article 41, JSA). A judge is explicitly prohibited to work as an attorney at law, as a notary public, or to be engaged in any profit-making activity. A judge may only teach, publish and conduct research activity, provided that this does not infringe on his judicial performance (Article 42, JSA).

106. Judges are allowed to be members of political parties. According to the standpoint of the Judicial Council, it is an element of judicial ethics that a judge should remain reserved and should, for example, refrain from openly supporting candidates in parliamentary or local elections (the latter recently occurred on one occasion).[122]

II. End of Functions

107. The office of a judge is permanent (Article 129 of the Constitution). The compulsory age for retirement is determined by the Courts Act at age 70. Extensions are not allowed.

121. Another proposal, however not yet enacted, is the introduction of so-called movable court cases which allows for courts of the same instance within the same appellate jurisdiction to share cases among themselves. This enables the president of an appellate court to transfer cases from a court with backlogs to a less burdened court in the appellate court's area of jurisdiction, pending that the backlogged court submits a proposal to that effect.

122. *See*: B. Koritnik, *Dogodki – izjave*[*Events – Statements*], 25 Pravna praksa, 40, 42 (2006); Opposite view: J. Zobec, *Politična vzdržnost sodnikov*[*Political Abstinence of Judges*], 25 Pravna praksa, 38, 12 (2006).

108. The Constitution (Article 132) determines that when a judge infringes upon the Constitution or commits a major breach of law in the discharge of the duties and functions of his or her office, the Parliament may, upon the recommendation of the Judicial Council, dismiss such judge. Where a judge is found by a court to have intentionally committed a criminal offence in the discharge of the duties and functions of his office, and thereby to have abused that office, he or she can be dismissed from such office by the Parliament.

109. A judge is assessed every three years by the personnel board (Article 31, JSA). Before that time, the assessment is made only upon a request of the Judicial Council, the president of the court, the president of the directly higher court or of the judge himself. In the first three years of judicial function, a judge is assessed every year. The assessment of performance of a respective judge is made considering the judge's professional knowledge, working abilities, ability of dealing with judicial matters, safeguarding of the judge's and court's reputation, oral and written communication, relations with co-workers and ability of dealing with managerial tasks (Article 118, JSA). However, the most important criterion is the number of completed cases. The Judicial Council applies these norms in a strict sense: it sets a minimum number of cases completed by each judge, according to type of cases and field of law. The number of cases completed by each judge is monitored on a monthly and yearly basis for statistical and assessment reasons. The assessment is decisive to whether or not a judge will be promoted, or he will be promoted to a more senior post or he will be eliminated from judicial function.

III. Discipline

110. The Constitution guarantees judicial immunity; a judge cannot be called to account for any opinion he or she expressed in court in the course of reaching that decision. Where a judge is suspected of criminal activity in the discharge of his judicial duties and functions, he may not be detained, nor may any proceedings be instituted against him, save with permission of the Parliament (Article 134 of the Constitution).

111. When a judge infringes upon the Constitution or commits a major breach of law in the discharge of the judicial office, the Parliament may, upon the recommendation of the Judicial Council, dismiss such judge. Besides, if a judge is found, by a court in criminal procedure, to be guilty of committing a premeditated criminal offence in the discharge of judicial office and to have thereby abused that office, the Parliament shall dismiss such judge (Article 132 of the Constitution). If a criminal procedure is pending against a judge for an offence involving an abuse of judicial service, the President of the Supreme Court must order a temporary removal of such judge from service (Article 95, JSA).

112. The JSA governs disciplinary proceedings in cases of alleged irregularities and breaches of a judge's duties (whereby these standards are not defined by any act). A breach of certain ethical rules, included already in the JSA (such as an obligation to refrain from commenting pending cases, to refrain from receiving gifts and to behave impartially) can also result in disciplinary proceedings (Articles 37–39, JSA). In practice, the most common ground for initiating disciplinary proceedings is the undue delay in rendering justice. Since the Act Amending the JSA (2002), the supervision and discipline are performed exclusively by judges (the minister of justice may, however, initiate disciplinary proceedings; Articles 79a–90, JSA).

113. Disciplinary courts of first and second instance decide upon a judge's disciplinary indictments. The panel of the disciplinary Court of the First Instance consists of three judges, of which at least one member must have a status equal to the indicted judge. The disciplinary court of the second instance consists of five Supreme Court judges. The proceedings are held in camera, closed for public (unless the accused judge himself wishes a public trial). Only the final verdict is made public (for that reason it often happens in practice that a judge quits judicial service before the verdict is pronounced, which results in discontinuation of proceedings and such judge thus achieves that the disciplinary proceedings against him or her will never be known in public). The right to be heard and the right to be legally represented are safeguarded.

114. A negative assessment by the Personnel council and the Judicial council of the judge's work-performance (*see* above) may result in removal from office by Judicial Council if a judge is considered not to be suited for judicial service (Article 33, JSA).

Chapter 2. The Bar

§1. Exercise of the Legal Profession

I. Conditions for Admission

115. In the territory of Slovenia, the Bar Association exists since 1870. The current Attorneys Act (*Zakon o odvetništvu*) was adopted in 1993 and amended in 1996, 2001, and in 2008. The activity of the Slovenian Bar Association is based on Article 137 of the Constitution of the Republic of Slovenia, on the Attorneys Act, on the Code of Professional Conduct for Attorneys (1994, amended in 2001) and on the Attorney's Tariff Act (2008). Currently, there are about 1,100 attorneys at law (*odvetniki*), members of the Bar Association of Slovenia (thus, approximately 500 attorneys per 1 million inhabitants).

116. Attorneys at law perform a freelance profession. Their status is incompatible with any other employment. Thus, unlike in several other countries, a person cannot be at the same time, for example, a professor and an attorney at law, or an employee of a company and an attorney at law.

117. Conditions for an admission to the Bar Association are the following (Article 25 of the Attorneys Act): a candidate must be a national of Slovenia or the EU, must:

- hold a professional title of Bachelor of Law acquired in the Republic of Slovenia or a Bachelor's or LLM Degree in Law acquired abroad and recognized in the Republic of Slovenia;
- have passed the state legal exam, must have four years practical experience as a Bachelor of Law, thereof at least one year with an attorney at law or as a public notary, public prosecutor or a judge;
- have an active command of the Slovenian language;
- be reliable for practising the legal profession; and
- possess equipment and premises required and suitable for practising the legal profession.

A lawyer from another EU Member State can be entered into the Roll of foreign lawyers that are allowed to practice their legal profession in the Republic of Slovenia under their professional title of *odvetnik*, including all his rights and obligations associated with the practising of the legal profession, provided that such lawyer passes the examination testing the knowledge of the legal order of the Republic of Slovenia (Article 34.a of the Attorneys Act). Besides, a lawyer from another EU Member State can achieve the title of *odvetnik*, provided that he has actually and permanently performed his profession in Slovenia on the basis of the title, achieved in his own country (*see* below) for at least three years (Article 34.d, Attorneys Act).

118. A lawyer from another EU Member State can also be entered into the Roll of foreign lawyers that are allowed to practice their legal profession in the Republic of Slovenia under the professional title from his parent country, if he submits a certificate of being entered with the competent authority of his parent country. Such a foreign lawyer may give legal advice on the legislation of his parent country, on the legislation of the EU, on international law and on the legislation of the Republic of Slovenia. However, in the performance of a lawyer's services related to the representation of clients before the courts in the Republic of Slovenia, such lawyer shall act in conjunction with the lawyer who is entitled in the Republic of Slovenia to practice his legal profession under the professional title of *odvetnik* (Article 34.b of the Attorneys Act).

119. A foreign lawyer from a country, which is not a member of the EU, can apply for an entry into the Roll of foreign lawyers and practise the legal profession under the title *odvetnik* under a condition of reciprocity and if such lawyer has a good command of Slovenian language and passes the examination testing the knowledge of the Slovenian legal order (Article 34 of the, Attorneys Act). Without having accomplished an entry into the Roll of foreign lawyers, a foreign attorney at law may never represent a party in a Slovenian court.

II. Rights and Duties

120. A lawyer may practise his profession individually (which is still most common in Slovenia) or within a law firm, in compliance with the provisions of the Attorneys Act. A law firm may be established as a civil law firm (*a societas*) or as a law firm with the status of a legal entity (Article 35 of the Attorneys Act). A law firm with the status of legal entity may be established as a company with unlimited personal liability of partners or as a limited liability company. The activity of the law firm must be limited to practising the legal profession. Partners in a law firm may only be lawyers. Management of the affairs of a law firm cannot be entrusted to a person other than a lawyer. An attorney at law cannot have a subsidiary of his law office in the Republic of Slovenia.

121. As mentioned above, practising the legal profession individually is still the most usual practice in Slovenia. It is, however, common that a group of lawyers share a common office and even use a common stamp, stating names of all of them, and stating a title law office (*Pravna pisarna*). Nevertheless, such an arrangement still does not mean that there is a real law firm and that the power of attorney, given to one of them, is considered as being given to all of attorneys in such a law office.[123] A common office is just a technical cooperation. Only a suffix 'o.p.' in the official title really means that a law firm in the proper sense exists and only if such a law firm is also a legal entity (which is evident from the suffix o.p., d.n.o.) a power of attorney may be given to the firm as such – meaning that any of the partners can

123. Decision of the Supreme Court, II Ips 538/97, 15 Nov. 1998.

act on behalf of the party. However, this applies only in the case when a law firm is organized as a legal entity (d.n.o., d.o.o.) and not, if it organized as a non-incorporated *societas*.[124]

122. A client may be represented in courts against remuneration exclusively by the attorney at law. The provision of the Attorneys Act that an attorney at law may not advertise his or her activity has been declared unconstitutional by the Constitutional Court.[125] The Constitutional Court, however, added that it would be legitimate to impose strict conditions and restrictions for the advertising of attorneys at law services. Following this decision of the Constitutional Court rules concerning advertising of legal services were implemented through the 2008 amendment of the Attorneys Act. There, however, still exist substantial restrictions concerning advertising of legal services (e.g., it is forbidden to advertise number of cases won or make references to profession, which an attorney exercised before becoming an attorney at law; Article 21a of the Attorneys Act).

123. An attorney at law may freely decide whether to assume the representation of the client who has addressed himself to him. A lawyer must respect the confidentiality of all information entrusted by the client. An attorney at law is not subject to detention in criminal procedure, introduced against him for suspicion of criminal offence, committed at practising the legal profession, without preliminary consent of the Senate of three judges of a higher court, established on the territory of the Court of First Instance where the procedure is conducted. A search of the law office may be permitted only subject to a warrant of the competent court and only with reference to the records and objects explicitly stated in the search warrant. The investigation may not affect the confidentiality of other documents and objects (Article 7, Attorneys Act).

124. Governmental bodies, organizations and individuals with public powers of attorney must provide an attorney at law with the information required at his law practice relating to individual case. An attorney at law is entitled to require personal data from database administrators whenever required for procedural acts within the scope of the client's representation (Article 10, Attorneys Act).

125. The remuneration of attorneys is, in principle, regulated by the Lawyer's Fee (*Odvetniška tarifa*). Till the amendment of the Attorneys Act in 2008, the Bar Association of Slovenia was empowered autonomously to determine the Lawyers Fee. However, an agreement with the Minister of Justice had to be obtained (Article 19 of the Attorneys Act). According to the aforementioned amendment of the Attorneys Act, the powers to determine Lawyers Fee are transferred to the Parliament. Thus, the Attorneys Fee Act was adopted in July 2008 and it shall come into force on 1 January 2009. At decision-making on specification of payment and compensation of costs incurred through a lawyer's representation in procedures, courts and

124. 1L. Ude et al.*Pravdni postopek – zakon s komentarjem*[*Civil Procedure: Act with the Commentary*]376(GV Založba in ČZ UL 2005).

125. Decision of the Const. Court, U–I–212/03–14, 24 Nov. 2005.

other bodies must use the Lawyer's Fee (Article 20 of the Attorneys Act). Thus, it is possible that a party and an attorney at law agree for a higher fee than prescribed by the Lawyer's Fee. However, when a court decides upon how much expenses a winning party may reimburse from his opponent, expenses connected with an attorney's representation shall always be calculated according to the Lawyer's Fee. The amount of the lawyer's expenses in a particular case depends on the value of the claim. One of the (unfortunate) features of the Slovenian system of attorney's fees has for long, been that it also depended on the amount of procedural steps taken – every hearing at a court that an attorney attends and every preparatory submission that an attorney files entitles him to payment of a fee. Experience has shown that such a system is too often resulting in dilatory tactics of lawyers and piece-meal presentation of their cases.

126. Unlike in several other European legal orders, contingency fees (*pactum de quota litis*) are allowed, though to a limited extent, in Slovenia. In patrimonial matters, the lawyer may agree with the client on such payment that instead of the payment according to the Lawyer's Fee the attorney may claim at maximum a 15% share of the amount awarded to the client by the court. The agreement must be in writing (Article 17 of the Attorneys Act). However, when it comes to the question what costs can a winning party reimburse from his opponent; the court will again calculate this only on the basis of the applicable Lawyer's Fee.

127. The extent of power of attorney (*pooblastilo*) is determined by the party. A party may empower the attorney to perform particular procedural acts or to act generally in their behalf (Article 94, CPA). If a party has empowered an attorney at law to conduct the litigation on their behalf, without having defined the extent of the attorney's powers (which is the most common case in practice), the attorney at law is empowered to:

- perform all procedural acts and, in particular, to;
- bring an action;
- to withdraw the action;
- to acknowledge or relinquish a claim;
- to conclude a court settlement;
- to lodge any means of ordinary judicial review and to waive or withdraw the same, and to apply for interlocutory injunctions;
- to apply for execution and protection of claims and to execute any such acts as he deems fit and proper in the execution proceedings;
- to receive from the opposing party the adjudicated amount of costs of litigation; and
- to transfer the power on another attorney at law or a candidate for an attorney at law.

128. A power of attorney must be in writing (whereby it is a settled case law that a photocopy or fax is not sufficient)[126] and it must be submitted in the first procedural step taken. It is not necessary to submit a new power of attorney for an appeal procedure (and for the enforcement procedure, on the side of the creditor); but it is necessary to submit a new power of attorney for filing of an extraordinary legal remedy, including the further appeal on points of law, i.e. revizija (Article 95, CPA). The same applies to filing of a constitutional complaint.[127]

129. The power of attorney may at any time be revoked by the party or cancelled by the attorney (Article 99, CPA). This must be communicated to the court; otherwise, it does not have any effect regarding the court or another party (e.g., – which is practically important – the service effected to an attorney will be deemed valid if the court was not informed of a revocation of the power of attorney).[128] If an attorney at law cancels the representation, such attorney is obliged to continue to execute on behalf of the former client all acts required to avert the damage which that person might otherwise suffer in the said period (Article 99, CPA). The death of a party who conferred a power of attorney does not result in a termination of the power of attorney (Article 100, CPA). An attorney continues to represent a successor (who, of course, may revoke the power of attorney). However, the power of attorney granted by a legal person is terminated upon the cessation of the legal person or upon a commencement of bankruptcy proceedings against it (Article 101, CPA).

130. In Slovenia, parties may perform acts of procedure in person or through an attorney. However, in spite of being represented by an attorney, a party may be ordered to produce in court a personal statement as to the facts in dispute. Besides, a party represented by an attorney may at any time appear in court and produce statements in addition to their attorney (Article 86, CPA). Also, if a party withdraws an action, brought on her behalf by her attorney, this withdrawal will be deemed effective.[129] As a principle, a party is not obliged to be legally represented; everyone can present his or her case by himself or herself. The only exception concerns proceedings with so-called extraordinary legal remedies (such as revizija and the plea for reopening of proceedings; Article 87/3, CPA). In such case, a party is obliged to be represented by an attorney at law (except if a party or the party's legal representative personally passed the state legal exam). As explained above, even a lay party can represent himself or herself in a court (except in proceedings with extraordinary legal remedies). However, if a party chooses to be represented by another person, such party can only authorize an attorney at law or another lawyer with a state legal exam. Only in the lowest court (county court) there are no limitations as to the question, to whom a power of attorney can be conferred (Article 87/1, CPA). In any case, only a physical person can act as a representative at a court.

---

126. *See,* e.g., Decision of the Ljubljana Court of Appeals, Cpg 1586/2003.
127. Decision of the Const. Court, Up 296/02, 20 May 2002.
128. For example, Decision of the Supreme Court, II Up 8/99, 7 Feb. 2002.
129. 1 L. Ude et al., *Pravdni postopek – zakon s komentarjem*[*Civil Procedure: Act with the Commentary*]86(GV Založba in ČZ UL 2005).

The only exception is that the power of attorney can also be conferred to a law firm (which may be a legal entity; Article 87/4 of the CPA).

III. Discipline

131. A lawyer is disbarred (*inter alia*): if:

- he or she is sentenced by an effective judgment to punishment of six-month imprisonment or to a more severe punishment in case of an intentional criminal offence prosecuted under official duty;
- in case of protective or security measure of prohibition to practice the legal profession is imposed upon him or her;
- if he is engaged in activities that are incompatible with good reputation and independence of a lawyer;
- if he or she has not practised the legal profession for more than one year without justified reason;
- if he or she is discovered not to comply anymore with the legally prescribed terms and conditions for practising the legal profession; and
- in case of imposition of a disciplinary measure involving deprivation of the right to practise the legal profession (Articles 59–71, Attorneys Act).

132. In the disciplinary proceedings against attorneys at law, the following disciplinary measures may be imposed: a warning, a reprimand, a fine and a denial of the right to practise the legal profession or the practice in a law office for a limited period of up to five-year period or, in case of most grave violations, for permanently. Offences are prosecuted by a disciplinary prosecutor (himself a member of the bar). Disciplinary matters are decided upon by the disciplinary commission of the first degree. Appeals against its decisions are decided by the disciplinary commission of second degree. Two members of the disciplinary commission of the first degree are attorneys at law, nominated by the Attorneys Chamber and one member, who must have a degree in law, is nominated by the Human Rights Ombudsman. For the disciplinary commission of the second degree, it is the other way around. In case of punishment for grave violations (for offences, which may result in revoking the license) a further appeal is admissible to the disciplinary court. The disciplinary court consists of two judges of the Supreme Court of the Republic of Slovenia, of one attorney and of a representative of the Human Rights Ombudsman. The President is a judge. An appeal against the decision of the disciplinary court referred to in the preceding paragraph may be filed and shall be subject to the decision of the Supreme Court of Slovenia in the Senate of five judges. Unless otherwise provided, the procedure before the disciplinary court follows the provisions of the Criminal Procedure Act. Members of the Disciplinary Court are nominated for a three-year term. The latest amendments of the Attorneys Act substantially diminished the role of the Attorneys Chamber in nominating members of the disciplinary bodies and questions as to whether the new system is compatible with the constitutionally guaranteed independence of attorneys have already been raised.

§2. (PUBLIC) INSTITUTIONS AND (PRIVATE) ORGANIZATIONS

133. The bar is an independent service within the system of justice, and is regulated by law (Article 137 of the Constitution). Lawyers practising the legal profession in the Republic of Slovenia must be members of the Bar Association of Slovenia (*Odvetniška zbornica Slovenije*; Article 47 of the Attorneys Act). The right to law practice is acquired with the admission into the Bar Association. The Slovenian Bar Association consists of eleven regional assemblies, the membership whereof is based on territorial and functional principles. Their territories predominantly coincide with the territories of District Courts. The Bar Association autonomously adopts the Code of Professional Conduct for Attorneys at law (Article 42, Attorneys Act). The Bar Association is also responsible for the nominating of the disciplinary boards, which conduct disciplinary procedures against members of the bar (*see* above).

Chapter 3. Bailiffs and Notaries Public

§1. Bailiffs

134. The new Slovenian Enforcement of Judgments in Civil Matters and Protective measures Act was adopted in 1998. One of the most important novelties was the introduction of private enforcement officers (*izvršitelj*; bailiff).[130] The bailiff accomplishes the act of compulsory enforcement of civil judgments as his commercial activity. Bailiffs have taken over some tasks, which, under the Yugoslav law, were reserved for the court's own enforcement officers and that is direct (physical) measures of enforcement and protective measures, predominantly in the field of enforcement on movable assets. Bailiffs remain totally excluded from enforcement with attachment or garnishment of earnings and, e.g., bank accounts and practically entirely also from enforcement on immovable property. In any case, the court remains involved in the enforcement procedure, as the court has the jurisdiction for enforcement and must first render a decision allowing the enforcement. The competences of bailiffs are thus much narrower than, for example, those of French *huissier de justice*. It was expected that this partial privatization of the enforcement procedure would contribute to its greater efficiency, as it is reasonable to expect greater effort from persons, whose commercial income depends on the success of the enforcement.[131] However, it has become clear that the new system suffers from too many uncertainties and weaknesses and it, at least, insofar has not contributed to the efficiency of the enforcement procedure. Foremost, the system of communication between the court and bailiffs is not effective.[132] It is questionable whether such a 'compromise system', according to which a state court must first authorize the enforcement by means proposed by the plaintiff and then the physical enforcement only is conducted by a private bailiff, is plausible. It might nevertheless be better to either retain the system, in which all the enforcement procedure remains in the competence of state authorities on one hand, or the system, in which a bailiff is responsible for entire accomplishment of an effective enforcement and the court gets involved only in case of appeals or other remedies.

135. Bailiffs can also obtain a special license to engage in activity of service of judicial documents. So far, this remains of a low practical significance, as it is still the court that accomplishes the service of judicial documents and this is, in vast majority of cases, done through the state postal service.

136. Bailiffs are nominated by the Minister of Justice. It is not obligatory for a bailiff to have a degree in law. Only a special training and examination is a condition for obtaining a license. The bailiff can have one substitute, who must fulfil the

---

130. H. Jenull, A. Galič & M. Jan, *Zakon o izvršbi in zavarovanju – Komentar novele in uvodna pojasnila*[*Enforcement of Judgments and Protective Measures Act: Commentary of the Amendment and Introductory Notes*]35(GV Založba 2002).

131. V. Rijavec, *Civilno izvrŜilno parvo* [*Enforcement of Civil Judgments Law*]83 et seq. (GV Zalozba 2003).

132. *See* the Decision of the Const. Court, U-I-339/98, 21 Jan. 1999.

same conditions as the bailiff himself. Besides, the bailiff can employ up to five (subject to approval of the Minister of Justice, up to ten) assistants for help in performing acts of enforcement.

137. Bailiffs must obligatorily associate in the Chamber of Bailiffs of Slovenia (Article 281 of the EJPMA). The Minister of Justice performs the control over the legality of the activity of the Chamber and of the bailiffs. The presidents of courts of the territory where the bailiff has his registered office oversee the activities of the bailiff in the particular matters designated to him. This control must take place at least once a year. Every year, the bailiff must submit a report of his work to the president of the district court where he has his registered office, to the Minister of Justice and to the Bailiffs' chamber.

138. After the accomplished acts of enforcement, the bailiff must submit a report to the creditor and to the court. The bailiff is liable for all damages resulting from the acts of execution and protection, if they occur due to the breach of bailiff's duties. For their work, bailiffs are enumerated in accordance with the bailiff's fee, which is determined by the Minister of Justice. The costs incurred for the bailiff form part of the costs of the enforcement procedure (and are in the end of the day borne by the losing party).

§2. Notaries Public

139. A notary public (notar) is a public service regulated by Notaries Act (*Zakon o notariatu*). Notaries are drawing up and confirming public and private documents such as notarial records, notaries' minutes and notaries' certificates. Notaries are appointed by the Minister of Justice and the number of notary offices is limited by law. The Minister of Justice also determines the Notary Fee. The notaries must obligatory be members of the Chamber of Notaries of Slovenia. Concerning matters, related to civil procedure, the most important competence of notaries is probably that a notarized agreement or settlement can be automatically enforceable, if agreed so by the parties. In such case, it is not necessary to file an action in the event of breach of the obligation; the creditor can immediately move for enforcement against the debtor.

Part II. Jurisdiction

Chapter 1. Domestic Jurisdiction

§1. Subject Matter Jurisdiction

I. Factors to Be Taken into Account

A. County and District Courts

140. There are two types of Courts of First Instance in Slovenia: county courts (*okrajno sodišče*) and district courts (*okrožno sodišče*). There are currently forty-four county courts and eleven district courts in Slovenia. District courts deal with disputes where the value of claim is higher, and it is considered to be a step forward in a career of a judge to be promoted from a county to a district court. Nevertheless district courts have no appellate or supervisory jurisdiction over county courts; both are exclusively Courts of First Instance and appeals against their judgments are always decided by appellate courts ('higher courts', *višje sodišče*).

141. It has already been mentioned (*see* above) that there are no specialized courts in Slovenia; the only exception being labour and social courts. Thus, there are no family courts or commercial courts; family cases are dealt with (family divisions of) district courts, and commercial cases (including bankruptcy) are also dealt with by (commercial divisions of) these courts.

142. The main factor to be taken into account for a determination of a subject matter jurisdiction is the value of the claim. But for certain types of disputes there are specific rules that determine jurisdiction of either county or district courts, regardless of the value of the claim. County courts have exclusive subject matter jurisdiction to:

- decide cases concerning disturbance of possession;
- disputes concerning servitudes and real burdens;
- disputes concerning hire, lease or tenancy relations;
- cases of maintenance claims if the disputes are not adjudicated in conjunction with marriage disputes or disputes over the establishment or contestation of fatherhood;
- non-contentious procedures;
- the keeping of land registers; and

– the enforcement of judgments in civil matters.

143. However, district courts are vested with jurisdiction to decide:

– matrimonial disputes;
– disputes concerning parental responsibilities (except maintenance disputes), and disputes relating to the finding or challenge of paternity or maternity;
– commercial cases;
– copyright and intellectual property cases;
– procedures for recognition of foreign judgments;
– bankruptcy procedures (including litigations related to bankruptcy) and for keeping of the register of companies.

B. Value of the Claim and Its Calculation

144. County courts have jurisdiction in pecuniary matters where the value of the claim amount in controversy is not higher than EUR 20,000, whereas district courts have jurisdiction for disputes when the value of the claim is higher.

145. The CPA contains detailed rules concerning the determination of the value of the claim. These rules are not relevant solely for the determination of the subject matter jurisdiction but also for several other procedural questions (such as the calculation of the court taxes and the lawyers' fees, the decision whether the case should follow the rules for small claims disputes).

146. It is the claimant who determines the value of the claim. In a pecuniary dispute, this is an obligatory part of an action (Article 180, CPA); if an action does not contain a defined value of the claim, it is considered to be incomplete and is, pursuant to Article 105 of the CPA, returned to the claimant for rectification (and if the deficiency is still not rectified, the claim is rejected). A defendant may oppose the defined value of the claim if he or she considers it to be too high or too low and also the court may ex officio demand from the claimant to state a new value of the claim in such case (Article 44, CPA). Within the later stages of procedure (appellate court and the Supreme Court), the deficiency of the lack of proper determination of the value of the claim can no longer be rectified.

147. Only the value of the principal claim is relevant to determine the 'value of the claim'. Interest, costs of litigation, contractual penalty clause and other lateral claims shall be excluded from the amount in dispute, except when claimed as the principal (Article 39, CPA).

148. High practical importance is attached to the rules concerning the determination of the value of the claim in cases involving multiple claims or parties. In actions containing several claims of the same plaintiff against the same defendant which are based upon the same factual and legal ground, the amount in dispute shall be defined as the sum of values of all claims. However, if the claims are based upon a different factual and legal ground, or filed against more than one defendant, the jurisdiction shall be determined according to the value of each separate claim (Article 41, CPA).[133]

149. The examination on whether a court is vested with subject matter jurisdiction is done separately for the counter-claim (Article 183, CPA). The counter-claim may not be filed if the decision thereupon is to be rendered by a court with different subject matter jurisdiction or in a different type of procedure.

II. Delimitation Between Courts of General Jurisdiction and Specialized Labour and Social Courts

150. Concerning matters, which can be described as being of civil nature, it is important to mention individual labour disputes, which fall within jurisdiction of labour courts. Labour courts decide, *inter alia*, in disputes between:

- an employer and employees concerning the conclusion;
- existence and dissolution of employment contracts;
- disputes concerning rights and obligations arising out of employment relationships (including claims for damages against a worker and worker's claims against the employer for damages, resulting from an accident at work);[134]
- disputes arising from employment contracts, and disputes concerning intellectual property obligations, stemming out from employment relationships.

The labour court also has jurisdiction in cases when, besides an employer, an insurance company is sued as a co-defendant (Article 5 of the Labour and Social Courts Act).

§2. Venue (Territorial Jurisdiction)

I. General Jurisdiction: Jurisdiction of the Court in the Place of the Defendant's Domicile

151. The principle actor *sequitur forum rei* applies. The action must be brought into the court of the defendant's 'permanent residence', or domicile (Article 47,

133. In practice, it is often a controversial whether two claims should be considered to have the same factual and legal ground or not. According to case law, for example, a claim for pecuniary damages (such as costs of medical treatment) and a claim for immaterial damages (such as for the suffering of pain), although stemming from the same event (e.g., a traffic accident) are not considered to have 'the same legal and factual ground'. Therefore, the value of the claim is calculated separately for each of such claims and not as a sum of both. *See*, e.g., Decision of the Supreme Court, II Ips 456/2002, 5 Jun. 2003. *See* critical view in: 1L. Ude et al., *Pravdni postopek – zakon s komentarjem-* [*Civil Procedure: Act with the Commentary*], 221 et seq.

134. *See* J. Novak, in A. Cvetko, A. Galič, K. Kralj & J. Novak, *Zakon o delovnih in socialnih sodiščih s komentarjem*[*Labour and Social Courts Act with Commentary*]36(GV založba 2005).

CPA). For a residence to attain the quality of permanent residence, a clear factual base (corpus) plus an *animus manendi*, an intention to reside there indefinitely, must exist.[135] For the determination of jurisdiction, it is sufficient that a certain address of the defendant is defined as his permanent residence in The Register of Permanent Residents of Slovenia (kept by an administrative authority).[136]

152. If the defendant has a temporary residence in addition to the permanent one, and if it can be assumed from the circumstances of the case that he will stay in the place of temporary residence for a longer period of time, then the general territorial jurisdiction shall also be vested in the court on the territory of the temporary residence of the defendant.

153. In disputes against legal persons, the general territorial jurisdiction is vested in the court on the territory of which legal person has its registered office. In the event of a doubt, the registered office is deemed to be the place where the bodies of management of the legal person are located (Article 48, CPA).

II. Specific Jurisdiction

154. The CPA contains numerous provisions which provide for specific jurisdiction (in the sense of an alternative forum *–forum electivum*). A claimant may choose whether to bring an action into the court or one of the courts of specific jurisdiction or the court of general jurisdiction. For example, pursuant to Article 52 of the CPA, the territorial jurisdiction to decide upon tort liability is vested also in the court on the territory of which the tort has been committed (where a wrongdoer acted *–forum loci delicti comissi*) and in the court where the damage was suffered (*forum laesionis*). If the damages involve death or serious bodily injury, a court of the claimant's residence also has jurisdiction. These rules also apply to the disputes against insurance companies for the compensation of damages to third persons in accordance with the regulations on direct liability of insurance company.

155. The territorial jurisdiction to decide upon disputes against a legal person with a branch office outside the place of its registered office is vested also in the court on the territory of which the branch office is situated, provided that the dispute relates to a legal transaction effected by the branch office (Article 60, CPA). A similar rule applies with regard to jurisdiction over foreign persons operating business in Slovenia (Article 61, CPA). A claim against a foreign person, arising from their business operation in Slovenia may be brought into court on the territory of which the branch office is situated, or in the court on the territory of which the registered office or residence of the person entrusted with the management of the foreign person's business affairs is situated (Article 61, CPA).

135. L. Ude, *Civilno procesno parvo* [*Civil Procedure*] 152(ČZ UL 2002).
136. Decision of the Supreme Court II Ips 72/2002, 27 Jun. 2002.

156. Certain norms on territorial jurisdiction (venue) can be applied only in cases with a foreign element. For example, Article 59 of the CPA reads:

If the power of courts of the Republic of Slovenia to decide upon a dispute is based upon the fact that any object in dispute or property owned by the defendant is located in the Republic of Slovenia, the territorial jurisdiction shall be vested in the court on the territory of which the object or property concerned is located.

This provision must be read in conjunction with Article 58(2) of the PILPA, which provides for jurisdiction, based on the presence of assets – Slovenian courts are vested with international jurisdiction if any of the defendant's property is situated within Slovenia (even if not in any way connected with the dispute). Thus, if in a case with a foreign element, the Slovenian court is vested with jurisdiction on such basis, the mentioned provision of the CPA applies in order to determine territorial jurisdiction. However, in a case without any foreign element, a claimant cannot rely on the provision of the CPA concerning jurisdiction, based on the presence of assets, but must bring the claim into the court of the defendant's permanent residence.[137]

157. Also, the rule concerning the jurisdiction in the place of performance of contractual obligation applies only to cases with a foreign element (Article 51, CPA). In purely domestic disputes, the rule concerning jurisdiction in the place of performance of contractual obligation applies, on the basis of a special provision, only in commercial disputes (Article 496, CPA).

III. Jurisdiction for Ancillary Claims, Counter-Claim, Co-defendants, Multiple Claims

158. It is solely the main claim that is decisive for the determination of territorial jurisdiction. Rules of the CPA concerning jurisdiction for the counter-claim, for multiple claims and for joinder of parties (co-defendants) should also be mentioned. If the same action is brought against several persons who are in the position of so-called material co-defendants (see below, paragraphs 213–214), the court, which has territorial jurisdiction for one of them, acquires territorial jurisdiction over all of such co-defendants (*forum atractionis*). However, in case of so-called formal co-litigants, the territorial jurisdiction of the court must be determined individually for each co-defendant (Article 49, CPA). The rule of *forum atractionis* (for territorial jurisdiction, but not for subject matter jurisdiction) also applies for the counter-claim (Article 183, CPA) – even if a certain court would be vested with exclusive jurisdiction, if such claim was pursued with an independent action (e.g., a counter-claim concerning rights in rem over immovable property). The rule of *forum atractionis* also applies if an action contains multiple claims.[138] If any of the claims is subject to rules on exclusive territorial jurisdiction, the claims may be joined in the

137. M. Ilešič, A. Polajnar–Pavčnik & D. Wedam-Lukić, *Mednarodno zasebno pravo – komentar zakona*[*International Private Law: Commentary of the Act*] 81 et seq. (ČZ Uradni list 1992).

138. 2 L. Ude et al.*Pravdni postopek – zakon s komentarjem*[*Civil Procedure: Act with the Commentary*]176(GV Založba in ČZ UL 2006).

same action only if such action is filed with the court that is competent under the rules on exclusive territorial jurisdiction (Article 182).

IV. Exclusive Jurisdiction

159. The court in the place, where the property is situated, has exclusive jurisdiction in proceedings which have as their object rights in rem on immovable property or tenancies of immovable property (Article 57, CPA).[139] The court in the place, where a ship or an airplane register is kept, has exclusive jurisdiction in proceedings which have as their object rights in rem on ships or airplanes or tenancies of ships and airplanes. (Article 58, CPA). The court in the place, where a bankruptcy or civil judgment enforcement procedure is pending, has exclusive territorial jurisdiction for disputes, arising out of bankruptcy or enforcement procedure (Article 63, CPA).

V. Jurisdiction Agreement (*Prorogatio Fori*)

160. A jurisdiction agreement is only possible with regard to territorial jurisdiction, but not with regard to subject matter jurisdiction. Unless an exclusive territorial jurisdiction is vested in a certain court by the statute, the parties may conclude an agreement conferring the first instance jurisdiction upon a court without territorial jurisdiction, under the condition that this court has proper jurisdiction over the subject matter. The agreement must be in writing (strict form) and in reference to a particular dispute or future disputes that might arise from a particular legal relationship (Article 69, CPA). The party who wishes to rely on the jurisdiction agreement must attach it to the first procedural act, which such party undertakes – thus, a claimant to the claim and a defendant (who wishes to rely on the jurisdiction agreement, when the claim was brought into another court) in a written reply to the claim.

161. Since the amendment of 2017, the CPA contains protective jurisdictional norms in favour of weaker parties concerning consumers and insurance contracts (favourable jurisdictional rules for employees have already been set out in the Labour Courts Act). The weaker party may bring proceedings in the place of its domicile and if the weaker party is the defendant, it may only be sued in the place of its domicile. In addition, agreements conferring jurisdiction which are concluded before a dispute has arisen are not admissible.

139. According to Slovenian substantive law, the ownership is not transferred already with a conclusion of a contract, but with a delivery (in case of movable assets) or with an entry into a land register (in case of immovable assets). Therefore, the claim of a buyer against a seller for a transfer of land (for the enabling of an entry into the land registry), does not concern rights in rem, but merely a fulfilment of a contractual obligation. Jurisdiction to hear such an action is not vested with a court in the place, where immovable property is situated, but with a court of general jurisdiction (the place of the defendant's domicile). 1 L. Ude et al.*Pravdni postopek – zakon s komentarjem*[*Civil Procedure – Act with the Commentary*]265(GV Založba in ČZ UL 2005).

162. It has already been mentioned that the court does not examine whether it is vested with territorial jurisdiction ex officio (except in case of exclusive jurisdiction; but also in case of violation of protective jurisdictional regime for weaker parties). This can result in a tacit (conclusive) jurisdiction agreement if a claimant files an action with a court that is not vested with territorial jurisdiction, and the defendant does not object the jurisdiction in his written reply to the claim.[140] It might also need to be mentioned that, as the objection concerning the lack of jurisdiction must be made already in the written reply to the claim, the court has no possibility to warn or instruct the defendant that he or she can object the lack of jurisdiction (and about consequences of failing to do so).

VI. Delegation (Transfer) of Territorial Jurisdiction

163. If the court cannot proceed due to successful challenge of all judges at that court, the Supreme Court shall delegate the power to conduct the proceedings to another court from its territory with competent jurisdiction over the subject matter (known as 'necessary delegation'; Article 66, CPA). Besides, upon a motion by the party or by the court of competent jurisdiction, the Supreme Court may assign another court of jurisdiction over the subject matter to proceed in the case if this will evidently facilitate the completion of the proceedings or is supported by other good reasons (Article 67, CPA). Before reaching such decision, both parties must be guaranteed the right to be heard.[141] Circumstances that justify the transfer of the case must relate to the court as a whole, not individual judges (if all judges are successfully challenged, that is a ground for a 'necessary delegation', see above). In practice, however, reasons that resulted in the delegation for 'other good reasons' are often nearly identical as reasons relating to the challenge of individual judges (such as: a party is a judge or an employee of the court, where an action was filed, or a relative of a judge or other employee of a court …).[142]

164. Besides the delegation of jurisdiction (*delegatio fori*), the CPA also regulates a so-called ordination of jurisdiction (*ordinatio fori*). If, pursuant to the rules on international jurisdiction, the courts of the Republic of Slovenia have the power to hear a certain case, but the provisions of the present Act are not clear on the issue of which particular court is to assume the territorial jurisdiction, the Supreme Court shall determine, upon a motion by a party, the court of jurisdiction over the subject matter which is to assume the territorial jurisdiction (Article 68, CPA).

---

140. L. Ude, *Civilno procesno parvo* [*Civil Procedure*] 161(ČZ UL 2002).

141. Decision of the Supreme Court, I R 16/2000, 12 Apr. 2000.

142. *See* 1 L. Ude et al.*Pravdni postopek – zakon s komentarjem*[*Civil Procedure: Act with the Commentary*]292(GV Založba in ČZ UL 2005).

165. There are also two cases of so-called general delegation.[143] According to Article 103 of the Courts Act, all cases concerning intellectual property shall be heard at Ljubljana District Court, and all maritime cases shall be heard at the Koper District Court.

§3. Resolution of Jurisdiction Conflicts

I. Introduction

166. According to Article 17 of the CPA, immediately after the receipt of the action, the court must examine whether, and if so, in what composition it has the power to proceed therewith. The jurisdiction is determined on the basis of facts stated in the action, and of judicial knowledge. The examination of procedural prerequisites concerning jurisdiction is a part of a so-called preliminary examination of the claim, thus, as a principle, taking place even before the claim is served on the defendant (Article 274, CPA). If the court determines that it lacks jurisdiction it can, already in this early stage of proceedings, issue a decree on the rejection of the action or a decree on the referral of the case to the competent court (Article 274, CPA). However, the rules are quite different, depending on what kind of jurisdiction (judicial – in the sense of delimitation of powers between courts and administrative authorities, international, subject matter or territorial) is in question.

167. The rule of *perpetuatio fori* applies in Slovenian civil procedure.[144] The jurisdiction of the court is determined based on circumstances which exist at the time the action is filed. It does not affect the jurisdiction, if these circumstances change afterwards in the course of proceedings (e.g., if the jurisdiction of the court is based on the defendant's domicile and the defendant changes his or her domicile during the proceedings). This rule applies without exceptions with regard to international (Article 89, Act on Private International Law and Procedure (PILPA)) and territorial jurisdiction (Article 17, CPA). It also applies with regard to subject matter jurisdiction if the claimant reduces the amount in dispute: if the district court had jurisdiction for the original claim it will retain it, although the claimant reduces the claim to such an extent that would otherwise put the claim within the jurisdiction of county courts (Article 17, CPA). In an opposite case, the rule of *perpetuatio fori* does not apply: if the claimant before a county court amends his or her claim by increasing the value of the claim to such an extent, that a district court would have jurisdiction, the county court, where the original claim was filed, must transfer the case to a district court (Article 19, CPA).

168. If the same set of facts is relevant both from the viewpoint of the determination of jurisdiction as well as for the merits of the case (so-called double relevant facts), it is, for the jurisdiction to exist, sufficient that a claimant asserts such facts. For example, if an action is brought into a court in Ljubljana as a court in the place

143. *See ibid.*, p. 161.
144. L. Ude, *Civilno procesno parvo* [*Civil Procedure*] 164(ČZ UL 2002).

'where the damage occurred' (Article 52, CPA), a court in Ljubljana is vested with territorial jurisdiction (venue), regardless of the objection of the defendant (who resides in Maribor) that there was no harmful event and no damage occurred (anywhere). Such an objection will of course be relevant for the decision on the merits, but for the establishment of the jurisdiction it is sufficient that the claimant asserted that the damage occurred and that it occurred in Ljubljana.

169. However, when the court decides the case on the merits, it is not bound by the legal qualification, asserted by the claimant, although such legal qualification was decisive for the establishment of the territorial jurisdiction. Thus, in the above case, the court in Ljubljana is not limited to examine the merits of the case solely on the legal basis of torts, but may – according to the rule of *iura novit curia*– also examine the case from the viewpoint of other possible legal grounds, such as, for example, contractual obligation, although the territorial jurisdiction of the court in Ljubljana was in that case based on rules concerning extra contractual obligation (torts). This principle, undoubtedly, applies with regard to territorial jurisdiction. It, however, cannot apply with regard to international jurisdiction – at least in cases, in which the Brussels I Regulation is applicable.[145] If the court of Slovenia based its jurisdiction on rules concerning torts, it is prevented from examining the merits of the case from the viewpoint of, for example, legal norms concerning contractual obligations.

II. Examination of Delimitation Between Powers of Judicial and Administrative Authorities

170. At all times during the proceedings, the court shall examine, on its own motion, whether the deciding the dispute is within its judicial power. Pursuant to Article 18, CPA, should the court establish, during the course of proceedings, that a different government body (i.e., administrative authority), and not a court, has the power to decide the dispute, it shall declare the lack of judicial jurisdiction and reject (strike out) the action. Thus, in such case, the court does not refer the case to the competent administrative authority, but after the claim is rejected by the court, the party must, if he or she wishes to pursue the case, file a new claim with the administrative authority. This rule of the CPA applies when a party first filed a claim into a court (thus, the position of the administrative authority concerning the question of jurisdiction is still not known). However, the solution is different if a party first addressed an administrative authority and the administrative authority already declared that it had no jurisdiction and that a claim should be pursued before a court. If, in such case, a party subsequently filed the claim in a court and the court believed that the matter falls within jurisdiction of an administrative authority, such court may not simply reject (strike out) the claim, pursuant to Article 17 of the CPA. Because there is already a jurisdictional dispute, (both, an administrative authority as well as a court already declined jurisdiction), the court must refer the matter to

145. The ECJ Judgment, *Kalfelis v. Schroeder*, dated 27 Sep. 1988, C–189/87.

the Constitutional Court. According to Article 160 of the Constitution of the Republic of Slovenia, it is one of competences of the Constitutional Court to decide jurisdictional disputes between judicial and administrative authorities. The decision of the Constitutional Court as to which authority has jurisdiction in such case is binding.

III. Examination of Territorial and Subject Matter Jurisdiction

171. A court may declare ex officio that it has no territorial jurisdiction (venue), only if it finds that another court has exclusive territorial jurisdiction over the dispute concerned. Even in such case, a court may decline jurisdiction only in the phase of preliminary examination of the claim (thus before the claim is served on the defendant). If there is no case of exclusive territorial jurisdiction, the court may examine whether it has jurisdiction only upon a motion of the defendant. Such an objection must already be made in the written reply to the claim thus, the first procedural act taken by the defendant (Article 22 of the CPA). The question of territorial jurisdiction may be a subject of an appeal against final judgment only in case the defendant objected to the jurisdiction already in the proceedings before the First Instance Court and if this court rejected such an objection. This rule applies also in cases of exclusive territorial jurisdiction. Thus, if a defendant does not object the jurisdiction of the court in the first instance proceedings, the question of territorial jurisdiction cannot be (re)examined by the appellate court.

172. Pursuant to Article 19 of the CPA a court must on its own motion (ex officio), examine its jurisdiction over the subject matter of the litigation, however not later than upon the preliminary examination of the action. Also, a defendant may object to the subject matter jurisdiction, but such an objection must already be made in the written reply to the claim (and it must be decided upon at the first hearing). No appeal is allowed against the ruling by which the district court has assumed jurisdiction over the subject matter, but is allowed against the ruling by which the county court assumed jurisdiction over the case, which falls within the subject matter jurisdiction of a district court.

IV. Decision in Jurisdictional Dispute

173. If a court declares (either ex officio or upon the defendant's motion) that it has no jurisdiction and that the case should be transferred to another court, its decision may be appealed against. The case is referred to another court only after the ruling on the lack of jurisdiction becomes final. The court, to which the case has been referred, shall resume the proceedings as if the proceedings were commenced before this court. Procedural acts performed by the court lacking jurisdiction shall not deem to be void only on the ground of having been performed by an incompetent court (Article 23, CPA).

174. The decision, which the appellate court has issued upon the appeal against the decision of the Court of First Instance on the lack of territorial or subject matter jurisdiction, binds the court, to which the case is referred, in respect of the jurisdiction, in case both courts (the court, where the action was filed as well as the court, to which the case was transferred), fall within the jurisdiction of the same appellate court (Article 24, CPA). On the other hand, if the jurisdictional dispute between two respective courts would need to be solved by the Supreme Court of Slovenia (which is, when two courts fall within appellate jurisdiction of different appellate courts),[146] the court, to which the case was transferred, is not bound by the decision of the appellate court and can still initiate a jurisdictional dispute.

175. According to Article 25 of the CPA, jurisdictional disputes concerning subject matter and territorial jurisdiction and the delimitation between courts of general jurisdiction and specialized courts (that are in Slovenia only labour and social courts) are decided by the appellate courts ('higher court', *višje sodišče*) having jurisdiction over the territory of the courts in dispute. Jurisdictional disputes between courts under jurisdiction of different appellate courts are decided by the Supreme Court. A jurisdictional dispute may be decided even if the parties have not made a prior statement concerning jurisdiction. Until a jurisdictional dispute is decided, the court, to which the case has been referred to, is obliged to perform all acts of procedure the postponement of which might be dangerous (Article 26, CPA). No appeal is allowed against the decision on a jurisdictional dispute.

146. For example: Ljubljana County Court declares lack of the territorial jurisdiction and that the case should be transferred to Kranj County Court. The claimant appeals against this decision but the appellate court (Ljubljana Higher Court) confirms the first instance decision. Kranj County Court will be bound by this decision because this court also falls within appellate jurisdiction of Ljubljana Higher Court. However, the solution would be different if Ljubljana County Court declared that Piran County Court has jurisdiction. The appeal against this decision would be decided by the Higher Court of Ljubljana. But if the (claimant's) appeal is dismissed and the case then transferred to Piran County Court, this court will still be able to start a jurisdictional dispute and will not be bound by the decision of the Ljubljana Higher Court. Namely, the Piran County Court falls within appellate jurisdiction of another court (Koper Higher Court). The jurisdictional dispute would be decided by the Supreme Court of Slovenia.

Chapter 2. International Jurisdiction

§1. Rules Applicable in the Absence of a Treaty

I. Sources of Law

176. In cases with an international (cross-border) element, a court examines whether it is vested with international jurisdiction on the basis of the PILPA. The provisions of the CPA concerning territorial jurisdiction (venue) may also be used to constitute international jurisdiction, but only in case no express provision for a certain type of dispute is contained already in the PILPA (Article 29, CPA). Thus, for example, rules of the CPA and the Enforcement of Judgments Act concerning territorial jurisdiction for the granting of provisional measures (such as freezing orders) may also be used as a ground for international jurisdiction. This results from the fact that the PILPA does not contain any provisions concerning international jurisdiction for the granting of provisional measures.[147] However, norms of the CPA concerning territorial jurisdiction for disputes concerning extra-contractual liability (tort) may not be used as a ground for international jurisdiction. Namely, the PILPA does contain provisions, although more restrictive than CPA, about international jurisdiction for such disputes. Thus, for example, a norm of the CPA that a claimant may, in case of an especially grave harmful event, file a claim for damages also in the place of the claimant's residence, may not be used as a ground for international jurisdiction.

II. General Jurisdiction

177. The basic circumstance for international jurisdiction of a Slovenian court is the permanent residence of the defendant (Article 48.1, PILPA). A temporary residence of a defendant in Slovenia is a valid ground for international jurisdiction of Slovenian courts only under the condition that the defendant does not have a permanent residence in any country (Article 48.2, PILPA). The concept of habitual residence does not apply in Slovenian national law. In accordance with modern trends in international civil procedural law, citizenship of the parties plays little importance with regard to the determining of international jurisdiction.[148] There are exceptions in cases concerning:

(1) personal status (e.g., according to Article 78 of the PILPA, a Slovenian court has exclusive power to pronounce a missing Slovenian citizen dead, regardless of the location of that person's permanent residence); and
(2) family cases – concerning the latter usually just as an auxiliary ground (and, usually, a certain additional condition must be fulfilled); for example, according to Article 73 of the PILPA, a Slovenian court shall also have jurisdiction

147. M. Ilešič, A. Polajnar-Pavčnik & D. Wedam-Lukić, *Mednarodno zasebno pravo-, komentar zakona*[*International Private Law: Commentary of the Act*] 82(ČZ Uradni list 1992).
148. *Ibid.*, p. 87.

in disputes over the custody of a child, when the defendant does not have permanent residence in Slovenia, if both parents are Slovenian citizens or if the child is a Slovenian citizen and has a permanent residence in Slovenia.

III. Special Jurisdiction

178. The PILPA provides for several grounds of specific jurisdiction (in the sense of an alternative forum). To mention just some of these:

(i) in matters relating to contracts, if Slovenia is a place of performance of the obligation in question (Article 56, PILPA);[149]
(ii) in matters relating to extra-contractual tort liabilities, if the harmful event occurred (the place where the wrongdoer acted) or the place where the damage was suffered was in Slovenia (Article 55, PILPA);
(iii) for disputes arising out of operations of a branch or an agency or an authorized person, conducting business for a foreign legal entity, if the branch or the agency or this person is situated in Slovenia (Article 59, PILPA);
(iv) for individual labour disputes, when the work is or was performed or should have been performed in Slovenia (Article 57, PILPA);
(v) in pecuniary disputes, if the property, to which the dispute relates, is in Slovenia (Article 58/1 of the CPA);
(vi) in disputes over maintenance payments for children, if a child as a claimant has a permanent residence in Slovenia or if the plaintiff and the defendant are Slovenian citizens or if the plaintiff is a minor and a Slovenian citizen (Article 74, PILPA); similar rules apply also to paternity and maternity disputes (Article 58, PILPA);
(vii) in matrimonial disputes: if:
- both spouses are Slovenian citizens;
- if the plaintiff is a Slovenian citizen with permanent residence in Slovenia;
- if the last joint permanent or temporary residence of the spouses was in Slovenia and the plaintiff still has residence in Slovenia; or if
- both spouses are foreign citizens and their last joint permanent residence was in Slovenia, but only if the defendant does not object to jurisdiction and if the regulations of the country whose citizens the spouses are permit such jurisdiction (Article 68, PILPA).

179. Slovenian law also provides for jurisdiction based on the presence of assets (forum patrimonii) – whereby it is not necessary, that the assets that represent the

149. The jurisdiction for a claim of a seller against a buyer for the payment of the price should be determined in the following way: the claim refers to the contractual obligation of payment; thus it must be established, where the payment should be made; in order to determine, where the payment should be made (whether in the place of the buyer or the place of seller or any other modality), one should consider the applicable substantive law to the contract of sale in question (lex causae). The approach is the same as confirmed by the ECJ with regard to the Brussels Convention (judgment in the case *Schenavai v. Kreischer*, dated 15 Jan. 1987, C–266/85) in the meantime – overwhelmingly – overriden by Art. 5/1(b) of the Brussels Regulation.

ground for jurisdiction have any connection with the dispute (Article 58/2, PILPA). This is a case of an excessive (exorbitant) jurisdiction, although its excessiveness is lessened through an additional condition that the claimant proves as probable that the decision can be executed from this property.[150]

180. Regarding the international jurisdiction in disputes concerning parental responsibility, it must be stressed that in contrast to, for example, Brussels II Regulation, according to which only the residence of the child is relevant, according to PILPA (see Articles 48 and 73, PILPA), the basic factor for international jurisdiction in these cases is the residence of the defendant (which will normally be the other parent); only under certain additional conditions does a residence of child constitute a special jurisdiction. Besides, a Slovenian court also has jurisdiction to decide on custody, maintenance and access rights when such dispute is resolved in the course of divorce litigation – again, regardless of the circumstance, whether the child resides in Slovenia (Article 76, PILPA).

IV. Co-defendants, Counter-Claim, Multiple Claims

181. If one action has been filed against several defendants who constitute a legal community (such as co-owners) or whose obligations are supported by the same legal and factual basis, a Slovenian court shall have jurisdiction over all of them if one of the defendants has permanent residence in Slovenia (Article 49, PILPA). If the main debtor and the guarantor are sued with the same suit, then a Slovenia court has jurisdiction when it has jurisdiction in the suit against the main debtor. A Slovenian court shall have jurisdiction for the counter-claim, but only if it is substantially related to the issue of the original claim. The PILPA does not contain provisions concerning multiple claims and set-off. The theory pleads for a restrictive interpretation: with regard to multiple claims, the existence of international jurisdiction should be examined separately for each of them; with regard to the procedural set-off, it should be permissible only in case the claim, which the set-off is based on, is substantially related to the original claim.[151]

150. Due to the rule of *perpetuatio fori*, it is, however, sufficient that this condition is fulfilled at the time the action is brought and it is not guaranteed that the property will remain in Slovenia during the litigation; besides, it is not clear, to what extent should this property enable the enforcement of the claim – probably it is not necessary that it is sufficient for the fulfilment of the whole claim, but it should be sufficient at least for the repayment of the substantial part of the claim). A. Galič, *International Jurisdiction Based on the Presence of Assets*, in *Dvadeset godina zakona o međunarodnom privatnom pravu: Collection of Papers*277–286(M. Zivkovic ed., Centar za publikacije Pravnog fakulteta 2004).

151. M. Ilešič, A. Polajnar-Pavčnik & D. Wedam-Lukič, *Mednarodno zasebno pravo – komentar zakona*[*International Private Law: Commentary of the Act*] 83(ČZ Uradni list 1992).

V. Exclusive Jurisdiction

182. Some cases, where a Slovenian court has exclusive jurisdiction are the following:

- for actions in rem over immovable property, for disputes concerning disturbance of possessions of immovable property, and for disputes concerning rent of immovable property (Article 64, PILPA);
- in disputes which arise during the founding or cessation of or during status changes in a company, other legal entity or association of natural persons or legal entities, and in disputes over the validity of decisions by their bodies, if the head office of the company, other legal entity or association, is in the Republic of Slovenia (Article 60, PILPA);
- in disputes over the validity of entries in official registers kept in Slovenia (Article 61, PILPA);
- in disputes concerning the applications for, and the validity of patents and trademarks, if the application was submitted in Slovenia (Article 62, PILPA);
- in enforcement procedures if these are carried out in the territory of Slovenia, and in disputes, which arise out of enforcement procedures, carried out in Slovenia (Article 63, PILPA);
- in paternity disputes, if the suit is filed against a child who is a Slovenian citizen and has permanent or temporary residence in of Slovenia (Article 72, PILPA).

183. The PILPA provides also for so-called excluded jurisdiction: 'Courts in the Republic of Slovenia shall have no jurisdiction if there is a link between the matter and a foreign country which, if it existed between the matter and the Republic of Slovenia, would be the grounds for exclusive jurisdiction of courts in Slovenia' (Article 50, CPA). Thus, for example, a Slovenian court would decline to decide a case concerning rights in rem over immovable property in Serbia, although filed against a defendant domiciled in Slovenia.

VI. Jurisdiction Agreement

184. The PILPA contains (unusual) restrictions, that the parties may agree on the jurisdiction of a Slovenian court only if at least one of them is a Slovenian citizen or a legal entity with a seat in Slovenia (Article 52/3). However, a prorogation of a foreign court is permissible if at least one party is a foreign citizen or a legal entity with a seat abroad (Article 52/1).[152] In any case, jurisdiction agreement in favour of

152. It is, however, highly questionable, whether the violation of the latter condition can result in any sanction. There seem to be no obstacles for the recognition of a judgment of a foreign court, for which two Slovenian citizens or legal entities have concluded a jurisdiction agreement, contrary to Art. 52/1 of the PILPA. The only ground, which could be used for a denial of the recognition is the ordre public clause (Art. 100, PILPA), but it is doubtful whether the notion of ordre public (in the context of recognition of foreign judgments) should be interpreted so extensively to enable the conclusion that a jurisdiction agreement of two Slovenian citizens or legal entities in favour of a foreign court violates Slovenian ordre public.

a foreign court is prohibited in consumer disputes and disputes arising out of insurance contracts, if a consumer or the insured, who is a physical person, has a permanent residence in Slovenia (Article 52/2, PILPA). Besides, the jurisdiction agreement is not valid if it refers to matrimonial or paternity disputes or disputes concerning parental responsibilities (Article 52/4, PILPA).

185. Although this would be desirable due to high practical importance, there are no provisions in the PILPA concerning form of jurisdiction agreement. That does not mean that there are no conditions concerning form; rules concerning the jurisdiction agreement (for venue), contained in the CPA, must be used per analogiam.[153] The same solution applies also with regard to the question, when should a jurisdiction agreement be submitted to the court, and how specific should the determination of the elected court be.

186. A tacit (conclusive) jurisdiction agreement is also possible. If a defendant files a reply to the claim (if the Brussels I Regulation is applicable; Article 24) or appears in the first hearing (if the PILPA is applicable; Article 53) without objecting to the jurisdiction, the Slovenian court will become vested with international jurisdiction. Only in case a foreign court is vested with exclusive jurisdiction, must a Slovenian court ex officio proclaim that it has no jurisdiction and must reject (strike out) a claim even before serving it to the defendant.

§2. International Treaties

187. Slovenia is a member of the EU, and therefore, the EU regulations in the field of international (European) civil procedure are directly applicable. Thus, if a case (*ratione materiae*) involves a civil or commercial matter and the claim is filed against a defendant, domiciled in an EU Member State (ratione personae), the Slovenian court will examine whether it has jurisdiction on the basis of the Council Regulation Number 44/2001 on Jurisdiction and Enforcement of Judgments in Civil and Commercial Matters (the Brussels I Regulation). For matrimonial disputes and disputes concerning parental responsibility, international jurisdiction shall be examined pursuant to the Council Regulation Number 2201/2003 concerning jurisdiction and the recognition and enforcement of judgments in matrimonial matters and the matters of parental responsibility (the Brussels II Regulation). Both regulations directly substitute the domestic PILPA. The latter, however, still remains a valid source of law for cases which *ratione materiae* and *ratione personae* fall outside of the scope of the mentioned regulations.

153. M. Ilešič, A. Polajnar–Pavčnik & D. Wedam–Lukič, *Mednarodno zasebno pravo – komentar zakona[International Private Law: Commentary of the Act]* 92(ČZ Uradni list 1992).

188. Slovenia (as it joined the EU only in 2004) has not entered into the Lugano Convention on Jurisdiction and Enforcement of Judgments in Civil and Commercial Matters of 16 September 1988 (which otherwise applies in relation between Member States of EU and European Free Trade Association), but shall be a party to the new Lugano Convention.

189. Certain multilateral treaties, which Slovenia is a party to, contain relevant norms concerning international jurisdiction – such as the Hague Convention of 25 October 1980 on the Civil Aspects of International Child Abduction, Convention of 19 October 1996 on Jurisdiction, Applicable Law, Recognition, Enforcement and Co-operation in respect of Parental Responsibility and Measures for the Protection of Children, and several treaties in the field of transport law (such as The Warsaw Convention for the Unification of Certain Rules relating to International Carriage by Air). Concerning state immunity, the UN Vienna Convention on Diplomatic Relations of 18 April 1961, should be mentioned.

190. Slovenia is a party to several bilateral treaties in the field of legal assistance in civil and commercial matters – some concluded after the independence and some concluded already by Yugoslavia (which bind Slovenia on the basis of succession). These treaties, however, rarely contain rules concerning international jurisdiction.

Part III. Actions and Claims

Chapter 1. Actions

§1. DEFINITION

191. In Slovenian law, the notion of 'an action' (*tožba*) is a purely procedural concept, clearly distinguished from rights under substantive law. An action is a procedural act which initiates the civil proceedings, defines the parties and the subject of the proceedings, and contains a request that the court should render a judgment with the content specified in the prayer for relief.[154]

192. An action is a necessary prerequisite for a civil litigation and it also defines, through seeking a specific relief, the scope of the decision (principle of free disposition, see above, paragraph 31).[155]

193. An action (in the sense of a complaint) should be distinguished from the notion of 'the right to an action' in the sense of the right of access to court, which is understood as a constitutional right to have a civil dispute resolved by the court.[156] It is a generally accepted view that, although it is the purpose of an action to enforce the rights, existing in substantive law, the right to an action does not derive from the private legal relationship between the parties. It is a right of a public-law nature; a right, recognized by the Constitution and directed against (the judicial power of) the state; a right, to which corresponds the obligation of (the courts of) the state to enable for an access to court and, if certain procedural prerequisites are fulfilled, to decide a dispute on merits.[157]

194. Concerning the relief sought, there are three kinds of actions: an action for the performance of an obligation (an action for condemnatory relief), an action requesting a change of a legal relationship and an action for declaratory relief.

---

154. J. Juhart, *Civilno procesno parvo* [*Civil Procedure*] 251(Univerzitetna založba 1961); Wedam Lukić, *Sporni predmet v. civilnem procesu*[*Cause of Action in Civil Procedure*], 53 *Zbornik znanstvenih razprav Pravne fakultete v. Ljubljani*, 1993, pp. 231–273.
155. J. Juhart, *Civilno procesno parvo* [*Civil Procedure*] 252(Univerzitetna založba 1961).
156. Wedam Lukić, *Pravica do sodnega varstva civilnih pravic in obveznosti*[*Right to Judicial Protection of Civil Rights and Obligations*], 56 *Zbornik znanstvenih razprav Pravne fakultete v. Ljubljani*, 305 et seq. (1996).
157. Decision of the Const. Court, Up 107/99, 23 May 2002.

195. An action for performance corresponds to the general concept of civil procedure. The claimant asserts that the defendant has breached a certain obligation, as existing under substantive law, and demands from the court to oblige the defendant to perform something (such as a payment or a delivery of goods, a service or to refrain from doing something). If successful, an action for performance will result in a condemnatory judgment and if the obligation is still not performed, an enforcement procedure may be initiated. The court may impose on a party the performance of an obligation only if such obligation has fallen due until the conclusion of the main hearing. There are only two exceptions to this rule: in a judgment satisfying the claim for maintenance, the court may order the defendant to perform obligations which have not yet fallen due. Besides, the judgment imposing on a party the obligation to deliver or take over the things let on lease may be passed even prior to the lapse of the term of lease (Article 311, CPA).

196. An action for a change of a legal relationship (a constitutive action) is possible when under substantive law, a claimant has a right to achieve a creation, a change or a cessation of a legal relationship (e.g., a dissolution of a marriage) but this right is of such a nature, that it cannot be fulfilled already by a unilateral act (such as withdrawal from a contract or simply by giving a notice of denunciation of a contract). For example, under Slovenian substantive law, a voidable contract cannot be annulled by a unilateral statement of the aggrieved party, but such party must file an action with the court and only through a judgment of a court will such contract be annulled.[158]

197. With a declaratory action (*ugotovitvena tožba*) a claimant may ask a court to establish the existence or non-existence of a right or a legal relationship (thus: not merely to establish certain facts or individual elements of a legal relationship or to solve an abstract legal question); Article 181 of the CPA. An action for a declaratory relief will be granted only if a claimant proves a legal interest for such a relief, i.e., only if rights or legal relationships are disputed, brought in uncertainty and therefore threatened by the defendant. As a rule, a legal interest for a declaratory action will not be recognized if claims from a disputed relationship are already due.[159] Namely, in such case an action for performance is already possible and it is, at least as a principle, accepted, that a legal interest for a declaratory action does not exist if a party can already ask for a condemnatory judgment. The latter namely enables a more effective remedy due to its enforceability.[160]

198. A special form of a declaratory action is a so-called interlocutory declaratory claim (*vmesni ugotovitveni zahtevek*). When the determination of the dispute is dependent upon the prior resolution of the question of whether a certain right or a legal relation exists or not, the plaintiff may claim, in addition to the relief in respect

158. 1 L. Ude et al.*Pravdni postopek – zakon s komentarjem*[*Civil Procedure – Act with the Commentary*]35(GV Založba in CZ UL 2005), *see also* decision of the Supreme Court, II Ips 188/2002, 18 Dec. 2002.
159. Judgment of the Supreme Court, II Ips 17/98, 23 Dec. 1998.
160. Judgment of the Supreme Court, II Ips 652/92, 20 May 1993.

of the cause of action, also the resolution of such question, provided that the court conducting the proceedings has subject matter jurisdiction to determine the latter claim and that both claims may be determined in the same type of procedure (Article 181/3, CPA). The purpose of such claim is to obtain a *res iudicata* effect also with respect to the (non-) existence of the whole legal relationship, not just of the particular claim which the prayer of relief refers to.[161] Namely, if no interlocutory declaratory claim is filed, the question of the prejudicial (preliminary) legal relationship is decided only in the grounds and not the tenor of the judgment and therefore does not gain a *res iudicata* effect.[162]

§2. Admissibility

199. Before a court starts examining the merits of the case, it must establish whether the conditions for the admissibility of the action are fulfilled. These so-called procedural prerequisites (*procesne predpostavke*) can be divided into three groups: those concerning the jurisdiction of the court, those concerning the parties and those concerning the subject matter of the litigation.[163] The majority of procedural prerequisites are taken into consideration ex officio, and just a few may be observed only if the defendant raises an objection (the existence of territorial jurisdiction (venue) in case on a non-exclusive jurisdiction; the payment of a claimant's security for costs (cautio actoris) – when applicable, an arbitration agreement). The procedural prerequisites concerning jurisdiction of the court have already been discussed (see above, paragraphs 137–187). Concerning the parties, the conditions for the admissibility of the action, are the following.

200. Capacity to be a party (*sposobnost biti stranka; ius standi in iudicio*): all physical and legal persons can act as parties in civil procedure (Article 76, CPA). Besides, a statute can vest a certain body, which is not a legal entity, with a capacity to sue (such as: a public prosecutor in certain family law cases). In exceptional cases and with legal effect limited to the case under consideration, the civil court may recognize the capacity to sue also to forms of association which are not legal entities (such as: a contractual association of civil law-societas), if they meet other essential conditions for suing or being sued, especially if they possess assets that can be subject to enforcement (Article 76/3, CPA).

201. Capacity to sue (*procesna sposobnost*): all persons above 18 years of age can represent themselves in their cases, unless their contractual capacity has been withdrawn by a decision of a competent court (Article 77/1, CPA). In the latter case, a custodian as a statutory representative brings an action on behalf of such a person. Children under the age of 15 may act as parties in civil procedure, but must be represented by their statutory representative (parents or custodian), who brings an

161. Decision of the Supreme Court, II Ips 508/95, 16 Oct. 1997.
162. Judgment of the Supreme Court, II Ips 363/2000, 13 Dec. 2001.
163. J. Juhart, *Civilno procesno parvo* [*Civil Procedure*] 17(Univerzitetna založba 1961); L. Ude, *Civilno procesno parvo* [*Civil Procedure*] 95(ČZ UL 2002).

action in the name and on behalf of a child. Children between the ages of 15 and 18 may represent themselves in courts only in disputes, concerning contractual obligations of minor value. This is a consequence of a regulation in substantive law that a person acquires a full contractual capacity at the age of 18, however, contracts of minor value and importance may already be entered by children at the age of 15 without being represented by their parents. Pursuant to Article 77/3, CPA, a minor who has not yet gained full legal capacity shall be capable to litigate to the extent to which his legal capacity is recognized. There are no special rules concerning adults, whose contractual capacity has not been officially withdrawn, but who are – due to, for example, a mental illness – not in a position to effectively pursue their case before the court. However, from a general rule it follows that if a court finds out that a party is in such condition, it shall declare that he or she lacks capacity to sue and a guardian ad litem shall be appointed. A court may seek an expert opinion with regard to the capacity of a party.[164]

202. Standing to sue (legitimatio ad processum): An action may be filed by a person who asserts that he or she personally suffered a direct violation of his or her rights. For an action to be admissible (as a matter of procedural law), it is of course not necessary to prove that the rights of a plaintiff were violated (legitimatio ad causam), but it is necessary to assert such a violation.[165] An action is only admissible if a plaintiff seeks to protect his or her own (asserted) rights and not the rights of a certain third person. From this condition it follows that there are, as a rule, no popular actions (actio popularis) and no class actions in Slovenian law.[166] However, a statute can provide for a possibility to file an action, the object of which is not a protection of rights of the plaintiff but of a certain third person or of an unidentified circle of persons. For example, in the context of environmental protection, anyone can file an action for a cessation of certain acts, which impose imminent harm to the environment, whereby it is not obligatory for the plaintiff to assert any personal interest.[167] Furthermore, an organization for the protection of consumers may file an action for:

(1) declaration that certain general contract terms, which a trader used in contracts, already entered with consumers, are null and void; and
(2) for a cessation of applying these general contract terms in future contracts.[168]

---

164. Decision of the Supreme Court, II Ips 137/99, 22 Dec. 1999.
165. *See*l L. Ude et al. *Pravdni postopek – zakon s komentarjem*[*Civil Procedure – Act with the Commentary*]314(GV Založba in CZ UL 2005).
166. *Ibid.*, p. 313 et seq.
167. Article 14 of the Environmental Protection Act (Zakon o varstvu okolja, ZVO-1), Official Gazette, No. 41/2004.
168. Articles 74–76 of the Consumer Protection Act (Zakon o varstvu potrošnikov – ZVPot – UPB2), Official Gazette No. 98/2004. If such an action is successful, it shall bind the trader, but if it is not successful, it does not prevent individual consumers from pursuing identical cause of action in an individual claim. It must namely be taken into consideration that individual consumers have neither a chance to participate and to be heard in a procedure, based on an action of a consumer protection organization, nor a chance to opt-out from the effects of the judgment. Therefore, it is necessary that a negative judgment cannot bind a consumer.

203. Parties are allowed to conduct their own case in court. The obligation to engage an attorney at law (a solicitor) does not apply, except in proceedings involving extraordinary legal remedies (such as a revision or a motion for a retrial), where they must be represented by an attorney at law (except in case when a party himself has passed a bar exam Article 86/3, CPA). The attorneys at law do not have a full monopoly in the sense that a counsel must be an attorney at law. In county courts (*okrajno sodišče*) a party may be represented by any adult person (unless such, whose capacity to enter contracts was withdrawn). There are however limitations in district courts (*okrožno sodišče*), as well as for appeals procedures. In these courts, a party may still conduct her case by herself, but if she chooses to conduct her case through a representative, a power of attorney may be given only to a person who has a diploma in law and who has passed a bar exam (thus, not necessarily an attorney at law); Article 87, CPA. According to Slovenian law, a representative with power of attorney must be a natural person. A legal entity (except a law firm) cannot be given a power of attorney.[169] This rule applies also with regard to a representative ad litem authorized for receiving service.

204. Procedural prerequisites, concerning the subject matter of the claim, are the following: the claim must not contain the same cause of action that has already been decided between the same parties (*res iudicata*– Article 319, CPA) or that is a subject of another pending litigation (lis pendens – Article 189, CPA). A cause of action is considered not to be identical if the new action either pursues a different relief sought (e.g., first, a monetary claim, second, a specific performance).[170] The prevailing opinion in the case law is that a cause of action is furthermore considered to be different if although the second action contains the same prayer for relief, it is based on a predominantly different set of facts.[171] The decisive moment for the lis pendens effect is not the filing of the claim but its service on the defendant. The filing of a negative declaratory action concerning the nullity of a contract neither prevents a creditor to file a condemnatory action for a performance of this contract nor does it mean that the latter action should be filed at the forum of the negative declaratory action.[172]

205. Furthermore, a plaintiff must possess a legal interest (*pravni interes*) for the action (even beside the prerequisite of standing to sue – which has already been discussed above). The declaratory action is the only kind of action where a claimant must expressly satisfy the court that there exists a legal interest for the action (Article 181, CPA). With regard to action for performance and constitutive action, the existence of legal interest is presumed. However, this presumption is rebuttable.[173] For example, if a creditor already possesses a notary enforceable instrument, he or she may directly initiate an enforcement procedure concerning the

169. Decision of the Supreme Court, Up 179/99, 27 Sep. 2001.
170. Wedam Lukić, *Sporni predmet v civilnem procesu*[*Cause of Action in Civil Procedure*], 53 *Zbornik znanstvenih razprav Pravne fakultete*, 231–273 (1993).
171. For example, Decision of the Ljubljana Court of Appeals, Cpg 179/93, 27 May 1993.
172. *See*, e.g., 2L. Ude et al. *Pravdni postopek – zakon s komentarjem*[Civil Procedure – Act with the Commentary] 223(GV Založba in ČZ UL 2006).
173. Decision of the Supreme Court, II Ips 246/2000, 8 Nov. 2000.

specified obligation of performance. If creditor in such case chose to file an action for performance, such an action would be stricken out (rejected) for the lack of legal interest.

206. The majority of procedural prerequisites are taken into consideration ex officio, whereas just very few of them may only be observed if the defendant raises an objection – the existence of territorial jurisdiction (venue), unless there is a case of an exclusive jurisdiction; the payment of a claimant's security for costs (cautio actoris) – when applicable – and the objection of the concluded arbitration agreement.[174] The court may examine the existence of procedural prerequisites already in the stage of preliminary examination of the claim (thus, even before the complaint is served to the defendant). The lack of procedural prerequisites can result in an immediate striking out of the action (Article 274, CPA) or, if the deficiency can be rectified (such as with regard to errors in capacity to sue or proper representation), in ordering the plaintiff to correct the action appropriately or to take such other measures as are necessary for the resumption of the proceedings with a person capable to sue (Article 273, CPA). If the deficiency is still not rectified, the action is stricken out (dismissed as inadmissible). As a principle, procedural prerequisites must exist during the whole course of proceedings, not just at the time of the filing of an action.

§3. Vexatious Litigation

207. There are no specific provisions about vexatious litigants in Slovenian law. However, the persistent filing of abusive and manifestly ill-founded actions can result in a partial withdrawal of contractual capacity (in the field of capacity to sue without being represented by a statutory representative). The procedure for withdrawal of this capacity is regulated by the Non-Contentious Procedure Act (Articles 44–56) and can be initiated upon a motion of the public prosecutor, the Centre for social work, close relatives or even ex officio.[175] If the contractual capacity is partially withdrawn with effect in the field of capacity to sue, a custodian shall be appointed and he or she shall have the position of a statutory representative – thus any action, brought by a concerned person himself or herself shall need to be approved of by the custodian.

208. It must be stressed that the above-mentioned measure is rarely used in practice. If, however, the above-mentioned measure has not been applied, the court has no possibility in civil litigation to exclude a vexatious litigant. The CPA provides only for a possibility to impose a monetary sanction EUR 1,300 upon a party who deliberately abuses his or her procedural rights (Article 11, CPA) or who files submissions, which are defamatory with regard to court (contempt of court) or other

---

174. L. Ude, *Civilno procesno parvo* [*Civil Procedure*] 98(ČZ UL 2002).
175. *See*, e.g., Decision of the Supreme Court, II Ips 211/94, 7 Sep. 1994.

participants of the proceedings (Article 109, CPA) – which often occurs when vexatious litigants are involved. The original version of the CPA also provided for a possibility of a sanction of imprisonment for up to one month, but such sanction has been declared unconstitutional by the Constitutional Court. Nonetheless, the Constitutional Court confirmed that it is not contrary to the Constitution that a court may impose sanctions for contempt of court. The purpose of such sanctions is not the protection of an individual judge but of the judiciary as a whole. Therefore, it is also not a violation of the right to independent judge, that the sanction may be imposed by a judge, against whom the defamatory submission was directed. In the context of imposing of sanctions for contempt of court, the 'victim' is not an individual judge, but rather the public confidence and the dignity of the judiciary as a whole.[176]

176. The Decision of the Constitutional Court, No. U-I-145/03, 23 Jun. 2005.

Chapter 2. Claims and Defences

§1. Definition

209. In Slovenian doctrine, the notion of a claim can either be understood as an embodiment of an action (a claim in a broader sense) or as a specific prayer for relief as the most essential part of an action (a claim in a narrower sense).[177]

210. A claim (as an embodiment of an action) does not necessarily have to be made on a special form, but it must by law contain certain elements: a reference to the court, the parties' names and permanent or temporary residence, the names of the legal representatives or agents, a prayer for relief concerning the main issue and ancillary claims, the facts supporting the applicant's request, evidence substantiating those facts, the amount in dispute and the signature of the applicant or his attorney (whereby a power of attorney must be attached to the claim); Article 180, CPA.

211. A prayer for relief must always be specific and framed in such a way that if the court finds it to be well-founded it can be verbatim transcripted to the tenor of the judgment and consequently a subject to enforcement.[178] For example, if damages are sought, a particular sum of money must be defined already in the claim.[179] Concerning the statement of facts, the parties must give an exact and concrete statement of facts already in their initial documents (a system of 'fact pleading'). If the claimant, for example, invokes too broad and abstract concepts in his claim or merely drives attention to legal concepts, his claim would be considered as incomplete and it would need to be corrected.[180] As the rule of *iura novit curia* applies, the claimant does not need to make any legal assessment of the claim, but he or she is not prevented from doing so.

§2. Distinctions

I. Main and Ancillary Claims

212. A claim must always contain a main claim, such as: a payment of a certain sum of money, a delivery of a specified object, a sufficiently individualized service or omission in the sense of refraining from doing something, a declaration of (non-)existence of an individualized legal relationship or a right, or a dissolution or a change of an individualized legal relationship. A differentiation of claims with regard to the type of relief sought (declaratory, for performance and constitutive) has already been discussed, see above.

177. J. Juhart, *Civilno procesno parvo* [*Civil Procedure*] 266(Univerzitetna založba 1961).
178. *See,* e.g., Judgment of the Supreme Court, III Ips 23/2004, 29 Sep. 2004.
179. 2 L. Ude et al.*Pravdni postopek – zakon s komentarjem*[*Civil Procedure – Act with the Commentary*]123(GV Založba in ČZ UL 2006).
180. J. Zobec, *Nesklepčnost tožbe in zamudna sodba*[*Unconclusiveness of the Action and Judgment by Default*], 21 Pravna praksa, II (suppl.) (2002).

213. Interest and costs of litigation are considered to be ancillary claims. Also with regard to ancillary claims a principle of free disposition applies – neither interest nor costs can be awarded to a plaintiff unless claimed. The sum of interest should be specified already in the claim (the date, from when the interest should be awarded and – at least in case of contractually determined interest – the rate).[181]

II. Joinder of Claims

214. The plaintiff may join several claims in the same action against the same defendant if all of those claims are based upon the same factual and legal ground (Article 182/1, CPA). If the claims are based upon a different factual or legal ground, they may be joined in one action against the same defendant only if the same court has the power to decide upon each of them and if they may be decided upon in the same type of procedure (Article 182/2, CPA). The plaintiff may join two or more mutually related claims in one action also by petitioning the court to grant to the secondary claim (e.g., a specific performance), if it finds the primary one (e.g., a monetary claim) to be unfounded (Article 182/3, CPA). This so-called eventual claim is an appropriate tool for a plaintiff, who cannot know for sure, what his rights under substantive law are (e.g., if the contract is valid, he can claim the performance of a contract, but if the contract is void, he can, on the basis of the rules governing the unjust enrichment, claim a return of goods, already delivered).[182]

III. Amendment of a Claim

215. The plaintiff may amend the action until the main hearing is completed (Article 184, CPA). The amendment of an action can consist of the change of the cause of action, the increase of the amount of the existing claim, and invoking an additional prayer for relief besides the existing one. A predominant (but far from being settled and firm) position in the case law is that a cause of action is considered to be changed if the claimant relies on a substantially different set of facts (an event) even if the same prayer for relief is retained.[183] On the contrary, the theory predominantly suggests that the cause of action should be deemed to be changed only if the prayer for relief is changed (e.g., a monetary sum is sought instead of a delivery of goods). Therefore, even a substantial change of the factual ground does not, according to this position, constitute an amendment of action if the same prayer

181. However, with regard to the default interest, the formulations of prayers for relief, demanding abstractly just a 'statutory rate' from a specified date, have been accepted in practice and courts do not insist that that a claimant should state a specific rate of default interest in the prayer for relief. Such practice has been developed since the times of high inflation in former Yugoslavia, when a statutory rate of default interest had constantly been adjusted to the inflation. The courts and attor neys are equipped with computer programmes for the calculation of default interest.

182. J. Juhart, *Civilno procesno parvo* [*Civil Procedure*] 213(Univerzitetna založba 1961), 2L. Ude et al.*Pravdni postopek – zakon s komentarjem* [*Civil Procedure – Act with the Commentary*],169.

183. For example, Judgment of the Ljubljana Court of Appeals, Cpg 179/93, 27 May 1993.

of relief is retained.[184] In any case, a mere modification of the legal ground of the claim, or reduction of the amount of claim, or alteration or correction of just some of the factual grounds does not constitute an amendment of a claim. After the action has been served on the defendant, the amendment is subject to her consent; however, the court may, notwithstanding the defendant's refusal to consent, permit the action to be amended when it considers the amendment reasonable and convenient in terms of the definite resolution of the dispute (but not if the increase of the amount sought would result in the need of transfer of the case from the county to the district court).

The defendant is deemed to have consented to the amendment of the action if he or she addresses the merits of an amended claim without having objected to the amendment beforehand (Article 185, CPA). Besides, no consent either of the defendant or of the court is needed, when a amendment of a claim is based on circumstances, which have occurred after the action has been brought and the plaintiff on such grounds claims the delivery of a different thing, or payment of a different sum of money, in respect of the same main subject of dispute (Article 186, CPA), for example if the object initially sought has been destroyed during the course of proceedings and the claimant amends his claim in order to demand a monetary compensation.[185]

IV. Joinder of Parties

216. Several persons may sue or be sued by the same action as co-litigants (*sosporniki*) if, in respect of the cause of action, they form a legal community; or if their rights or obligations are based upon the same factual and legal ground; or if they are joint and several debtors or creditors. If claims of different persons are based only on a similar factual and legal ground, they can act as co-litigants only if the same court has the subject matter and territorial jurisdiction over each of the claims and each of the defendants (Article 191, CPA).

217. Despite of the joinder of parties, each of the co-litigants shall act as an independent party to the litigation; the acts of procedure, which he performs or fails to perform, shall neither benefit nor detriment the other co-litigants.[186] Thus, the mere fact that certain persons are joined as co-litigants does not mean that the judgment shall need to be the same with respect to all of them (Article 195, CPA – so-called ordinary co-litigants; *navadni sosporniki*). However, in certain cases, the nature of the cause of action demands that the case must be decided in an equal manner with

---

184. For example, if the claimant initially requested an annulment of the will stating that there were defects in form because the will was not signed and later relies on different set of facts – for example that the testator was, in the time of making the will, not sane. 2*See* L. Ude et al.*Pravdni postopek – zakon s komentarjem*[*Civil Procedure – Act with the Commentary*], 196.

185. *Ibid.*, p. 208.

186. N. Betetto, *Procesni institut sosporništva glede na učinke*[*Procedural institute of joinder of parties with regard to its effects*], 50 Pravnik, 87 (1995), 2L. Ude et al. *Pravdni postopek – zakon s komentarjem*[*Civil Procedure – Act with the Commentary*]252(GV Založba in ČZ UL 2006).

respect to all co-litigants (so-called uniform co-litigants; *enotni sosporniki*).[187] In such case, also during the course of the proceedings, the procedural acts of each co-litigant shall have an effect to all of them. In case the procedural acts of co-litigants are contradictory, the one most beneficial to all of them shall have the effect (Article 196, CPA).[188] In certain cases, it is a legal obligation that certain persons must be sued jointly (such as: spouses with regard to the obligations stemming from their joint property).[189] This is a case of so-called necessary co-litigants (*nujni sosporniki*). Such an obligation can only exist on the side of defendants and never on the side of the plaintiffs. As no one can be forced to act as a plaintiff, imposing a request that a particular person may not file an action alone, but only jointly with other co-litigants, could result in a violation of a constitutionally guaranteed right of access to court.[190]

218. The plaintiff may bring an action against several defendants also by petitioning the court to grant the claim against the secondary defendant if the claim against the primary one is finally dismissed (Article 192, CPA). This possibility is appropriate in case a plaintiff is not sure who, among several persons, his real debtor is (e.g., who is liable for the damage).[191]

V. Defence on the Merits and Procedural 'Exceptions', Set-Off, Counter-Claim

219. One can differentiate between a defence on the merits which deals with the merits of the plaintiff's claim (usually a denial of these facts) and a specific plea, which is based on facts, not asserted in the plaintiff's claim.[192] This differentiation is only relevant from the viewpoint of the burden of proof: a burden of proof concerning the facts, raised as a specific plea (such as, when a defendant admits that he entered a contract with a plaintiff, but asserts that he has already performed his obligation, or when he admits, that he has not paid for the goods, but asserts that there are serious deficiencies in the quality of the delivered goods) lies with a defendant.

---

187. *See,* e.g., Judgment of the Supreme Court, Sklep II Ips 315/2001, 29 Nov. 2001. For example, if two co-owners of a land (with ideal 50% shares in property) are sued for a declaration that there exists servitude of passage over their land, they are in a position of uniform co-litigants. It follows from the nature of the subject matter that the dispute can only be decided uniformly for both co-defendants: either that the servitude of a right of passage exists or that it does not exist. As the land is not divided in nature, but in ideal shares, it is logically not possible to decide a dispute in such manner that would impose an obligation of allowing a passage on a joint land only on one of co-defendants as co-owners.
188. For example, if a co-defendant A wishes to acknowledge a claim and a co-defendant B objects the claim, only the act of the co-defendant B shall take effect, as it is (from a totally abstract viewpoint) more beneficial for a defendant to object than to acknowledge the claim. *See,* e.g., J. Juhart, *Civilno procesno parvo* [*Civil Procedure*] 313(Univerzitetna založba 1961).
189. Judgment of the Supreme Court, II Ips 564/2004, 18 Jan. 2007.
190. *See,* e.g., Judgment of the Supreme Court, II Ips 476/95, 13 Jun. 1996.
191. *See,* e.g., Judgment of the Ljubljana Court of Appeals, 30 Nov. 2005.
192. L. Ude, *Civilno procesno parvo* [*Civil Procedure*] 225(ČZ UL 2002).

220. In any case, it is advisable for a defendant to carefully examine all factual assertions, forwarded by the plaintiff, as the facts, neither expressly denied nor admitted, can be deemed to be admitted (see above). The defendant is obliged to give a reasoned reply to the claim (Article 277, CPA), an unreasoned reply can be deemed to be non-existent and a default judgment can be entered against the defendant (Article 318, CPA). Thus, except in case of so-called negative facts (when a defendant simply denies entering any kind of relation with a plaintiff) it is not sufficient for a defendant to simply deny the fact, asserted by the plaintiff, but is expected to give his or her own version of the disputed event.[193]

221. It has already been mentioned that most of the procedural prerequisites (conditions for the admissibility of the claim) are examined by the court ex officio (see above). It is, therefore, not obligatory for a defendant to file formal motions, for example, if the same cause of action is already a *res iudicata* or if the plaintiff lacks the capacity to sue. It is nevertheless advisable for the defendant to drive the court's attention to such circumstances. In case the defendant objects to the admissibility of the claim, a court may, if it finds such objection unfounded, simply proceed with the case on merits. Grounds for the dismissal of the defendant's procedural objections are then given in the reasons (motivations) of the final judgment. However, a court can decide upon (a rejection of) the defendant's procedural objection separately, with a separate decision (Article 288, CPA). It is appropriate for the court to issue a separate decision on a procedural objection in case when it considers the decision not to be straight-forward and when it fears that the appellate court (the decision on a rejection of a defendant's procedural objection can be appealed against) could reach a different decision concerning the admissibility of the claim. In such case, it is advisable to issue a separate decision on the question of the admissibility of the claim. If this decision then becomes final, the same question of admissibility cannot be raised again in the appeal against the final judgment on merits.

222. A defence of set-off (*pobotanje, compensatio*) can be pursued in three different ways.[194] First, a defendant may simply proclaim that he or she has already given a statement of a set-off in accordance with a Law on Obligations (Articles 311–318). This equals to any other defence of an extinguished claim (e.g., a defence of accomplished payment). If the court finds such defence to be well-founded, the case is dismissed on merits. In such case, the defence of set-off is purely of a substantive law nature. The second possibility is a so-called procedural set-off. In this case, a defendant does not rely on a set-off, already accomplished as an operation of substantive law, but he or she asserts (usually only as a secondary or reserve argument) that he or she also possesses a claim against a plaintiff and invites the court to proclaim a set-off of both claims. A court will then decide on the existence of a

193. 2 L. Ude et al.*Pravdni postopek – zakon s komentarjem*[*Civil Procedure – Act with the Commentary*]364(GV Založba in ČZ UL 2006).

194. J. Juhart, *Civilno procesno parvo* [*Civil Procedure*] 294(Univerzitetna založba 1961).

defendant's claim with a *res iudicata* effect (Article 319, CPA). If the defendant's assertion proves to be well-founded, the court includes three findings into the operative part of the judgment:

(1) the existence of the plaintiff's claim;
(2) the existence of the defendant's claim; and
(3) the set-off of both claims and a dismissal of the action.

The third possibility for the defendant is to file a counter-claim (*see* below).

223. In case of a procedural set-off as well as a counter-claim, the defendant's claim against the plaintiff shall be decided with a *res iudicata* effect. However, there is a major difference between these two options: the procedural set-off is still merely a tool of defence, and a court cannot, with a *res iudicata* effect, determine that the defendant's claim is higher than the plaintiff's one. Thus, if the defendant's claim exceeds the one of the plaintiff, it is more advisable to pursue such claim through a counter-claim.[195]

224. Until the completion of the main hearing in the court, the defendant may file a counter-claim with the same court: if the counter-claim is in connection with the claim contained in the action; if the claim contained in the action and the counter-claim may be set-off; or if by the filing of the counter-claim the defendant seeks to obtain a judicial resolution of the question of whether a right or a legal relation exists or not, upon which the determination of the plaintiff's claim is wholly or partly dependent (Article 183, CPA). The counter-claim may not be filed if the decision thereupon is to be rendered by a court of different subject matter jurisdiction or in a different type of procedure.

195. L. Ude, *Civilno procesno parvo* [*Civil Procedure*] 230(ČZ UL 2002).

Chapter 3. Sanctions on Procedural Irregularities

§1. Formal Requirements

225. A claim must be made in writing and may be sent to the court by post or delivered directly to its reception office (concerning the obligatory contents of the claim, see above, paragraph 207). The application must be drawn up in Slovenian (except in the border regions, where Italian or Hungarian, respectively, are also official languages, besides Slovenian) and signed by the applicant (or his representative or attorney).

226. If a claim or another procedural submission is intelligible or does not contain all of the matters necessary for the proceeding therewith, the court orders the person submitting the pleading to correct or supplement such submission and sets a binding time limit to do so. If the claim fails to be corrected and/or supplemented as to enable the proceeding therewith, the court rejects it as inadmissible (Article 108, CPA).

227. A due court fee must be paid already at the time a claim is brought into court (except when a claimant requests to be excused from the obligation to pay court fee) and a proof of payment must be attached to the claim. If the court fee is not paid even within an additional period, determined by the court, the claim is deemed withdrawn (Article 105, CPA).

228. Concerning the conditions for the admissibility of an action ('procedural prerequisites') and sanctions for non-compliance see above, paragraph 196.

§2. Time Limits

I. Calculation of Time Limits, Extension, *Restitutio in Integrum*

229. A distinction is drawn between deadlines, determined by law (e.g., deadlines for the filing of appeals, the deadline for making of a defence plea) and those, determined by the judge in accordance with the requirements of an individual case (e.g., the deadline for the rectification of an action or the deadline for the production of a power of attorney).[196] This distinction is important with regard to the possibility of extension of deadlines: only deadlines, determined by the judge, but not those, determined by statute, are extensible (Article 110/3, CPA). In any case, a motion for the extension of a deadline must be submitted before the initial deadline has expired (Article 110/3, CPA).[197] The shortening of deadlines, determined by statute, is neither possible by the decision of a judge nor by a consensus of parties.[198]

196. *Ibid.*, p. 199.
197. The case law is not settled with regard to the question, how the court should react if the party fulfils a procedural act (e.g., production of power of attorney or rectification of the claim) after the

230. The starting point for a calculation of deadlines is generally the first day after the moment at which the service of the document setting the deadline takes effect (Article 111.2, CPA). The time taken by the postal service is not included in the procedural deadlines. This means that where a procedural deadline is concerned, an action is brought in time if it is posted on the last day of the period allowed (date as postmarked), even if it does not reach the court until a long time after the deadline (Article 112, CPA).

231. Time limits are calculated in calendar days (thus, not only working days). Non-working days have no bearing on the beginning of a deadline (thus, a calculation of a time limit can start already on a Saturday). However, if the period is due to expire on a Saturday, Sunday or a public holiday, it does not expire until the first following working day (Article 111/4, CPA).

232. Most of the deadlines, determined by the CPA, are calculated in days. However, there are also certain deadlines, expressed in months or years. In such case, the deadline expires on the day in the last week or month, which corresponds in name or number to the first day of the period in question (Article 111/3, CPA). If there is no such day in the last month of the period in question (if, for example, a one-month deadline begins on 30 January), the period ends on the last day of the last month (28 February).

233. As a general rule, a failure to comply with an element of the legal proceedings results in a preclusive effect. If a defendant fails to make a defence plea, a judgment by default may be rendered (if certain other conditions are fulfilled, see below, paragraph 294; in this chapter, see also sanctions applied against parties who do not attend the court hearing).

234. Reversion to the previous state of affairs (*vrnitev v. prejšnje stanje, restitutio in integrum*) is a legal remedy against the consequences of a failure to appear in court or to take part in a legal act subject to a deadline. It can be used in cases where the party or its representative has failed to comply owing to an unforeseen or unavoidable event (such as: an unforeseeable illness, a traffic accident; but not, for example, a traffic jam, that could be counted with,[199] omissions, resulting from an inadequate organization of work in attorney's office,[200] a state of illness on the day of a court's hearing, which, although severe, was not unforeseeable).[201] This appeal

deadline, set by the court, but before the court reacted to the default (in the aforementioned examples, by striking out of an action). It seems that a strict interpretation is prevailing nowadays: the party shall be deemed to be in default and the sanction can be imposed even though the party nevertheless had accomplished the required procedural act before the court reacted to the default. *See*lL. Ude et al.*Pravdni postopek – zakon s komentarjem*[*Civil Procedure – Act with the Commentary*],457.

198. J. Juhart, *Civilno procesno parvo* [*Civil Procedure*] 211(Univerzitetna založba 1961).

199. For example, Decision of the Ljubljana Court of Appeals, Cpg 788/2001, 9 Aug. 2001.

200. For example, Decision of the Supreme Court, I Up 544/2001, 7 Nov. 2001.

201. For example, Decision of the Const. Court, Up 184/94, 2 Feb. 1999.

must be submitted within fifteen days of the removal of the obstacle (but in any case within six months from the moment of default).

II. Preclusion of Facts, Evidence and Procedural Objections, Submitted in Default

235. The most important sanction for the inactivity or delayed activity of the parties in litigation is that the court can refuse to take delayed submissions into consideration – a rule that facts must be pleaded and evidence offered until a certain point in the proceedings or they will otherwise be precluded. A certain system of preclusions was introduced in Slovenia by the CPA-1999. According to Article 286, CPA, the parties can assert new facts and evidence until (including) the first session of the main hearing (according to the Yugoslav CPA-1976, there was no limitation and the parties were free to come out with new facts and evidence till the end of the last session of the main hearing and, except in commercial cases, even in appeal). At later hearing sessions, the parties shall be allowed to present new facts and new evidence only if at the opening session they were prevented from presenting them by reasons beyond their control. A notion of 'reasons beyond their control' should be interpreted with a degree of flexibility.[202] A proper excuse is not only a circumstance that a party subsequently got knowledge of certain fact or evidence, but also a circumstance that it was only after the course of foregoing proceedings that certain facts and evidence appeared relevant for the case. A too restrictive approach to preclusions can namely constitute a breach of the right of the parties in litigation to be heard.[203] Besides, a system of preclusions ought not to be too rigid also in order to avoid a reintroduction of '*Eventualmaxime*'. If a party is rigidly demanded to state all facts and evidence, even those which could only eventually become relevant if the legal evaluation of the case goes into a certain direction, already in the first stage of proceedings, the pleadings of the parties would become too complex and unclear.[204]

236. Although the CPA limited the unrestricted right to assert new facts and evidence to (the end of) the first session of the main hearing (see above) it remained halfway. The problem of preparatory written submissions during the litigation remained entirely unsolved. If these submissions contained new facts and evidence, they may be presented even just a short time before the first session of the main hearing or even at this session (which shall often cause a need for adjournment). The system of preclusions as described above also did not solve the problem of preparatory submissions, which the parties file during the time between the sessions of

202. *See*, e.g., A. Butala, *Pravdni postopek brez nepotrebnega odlašanja*[*A Litigation Without Unnecessary Delay*], 25 Podjetje in delo, 1160 (1999); N. Betetto, *Ustavna procesna jamstva v dokaznem postopku*[*Constitutional Procedural Guarantees Concerning Evidence*], 22 Pravna praksa, 18 (2003).

203. Z. Trampuš, *Materialno procesno vodstvo in sodna poravnava*[*Substantive Procedural Guidance and Court Settlement*], 28 Podjetje in delo, 1549 (2002).

204. D. Wedam Lukić, *Vloga sodišča in strank pri zbiranju procesnega gradiva*[*The Role of the Judge and Parties Concerning the Collection of Procedural Material*], 24 Podjetje in delo, 990 (1998).

the main hearing. The 2008 Amendment of the CPA strengthened the system of procedural sanctions for delays in litigations. In order to enable the other party a right to be heard and to organize its case, a party is obliged to, whenever possible, file new written submissions in sufficient time for them to be served on the other party in an adequate time limit before the main hearing, so the main hearing would never need to be adjourned for the reason that the other party must be given a reasonable time period to prepare a response (Article 286a/4, CPA). Besides, a judge can now set binding time limits for the filing of the preparatory submissions with further comments or clarifications (Article 286a/1, CPA). This can contribute to the goal that procedural material should be clarified before the main hearing; the standpoints of the parties are clearer and more complete, and it is clarified which facts are really at dispute and which questions the main hearing should be concentrated at.[205] If a court set the time limits for the filing of new preparatory submissions and this time limit is not met, new submissions made after the time period has expired are admissible only if the court is convinced that admitting them will not delay the resolution of the dispute or if the party provides an adequate justification for the delay in presenting them.

237. The amendment of the CPA in 2008 also introduced a provision on a presumed waiver of the right to object to a procedural error. Pursuant to Article 286b of the CPA, a party who knows that any provision of the CPA has not been complied with and yet proceeds with litigation without stating his or her objection to such non-compliance without undue delay, or, if a time limit is provided, therefore, within such period of time, is deemed to have waived his or her right to object. Thus: an appeal against a final judgment cannot be based on such procedural violation. The only exception applies with regard to grave procedural errors, which the appellate court examines ex officio (such as: *res iudicata*, lis pendens, lack of capacity to be a party, lack of capacity to sue, etc.).

205. Of course, there are numerous reasons (*inter alia*, new legal standpoints in the case, the results of the evidence …) which justify the filing of new submissions not only at the first, but also at subsequent sessions of the court, but this should be solved through a flexible interpretation of the notion of 'guilt'. The system is flexible – enabling a judge to adapt each litigation to its characteristics and to determine the time framework. As litigations can differ strongly – some are easily solved, some involve difficult questions of law, some involve difficult questions of facts and a time consuming evidence procedure – a flexible system is more appropriate than a rigid system of time limits imposed by law.

Part IV. Proceedings

Chapter 1. Pre-action and Pre-trial Proceedings

§1. No Pre-action Proceedings

238. In Slovenian law, there are no formal requirements for the plaintiff before the filing of an action. There are no cases of mandatory pre-action mediation and no obligation to formally communicate with the opponent (e.g., via the pre-action protocols). Moreover, there are very limited possibilities of access to relevant information before the start of a civil procedure (the pre-action stage). Slovenian legislature has so far failed to learn anything from one of the most interesting developments in recent years which is that the law of civil procedure has been gradually extending to the phase when the prospective litigants only start preparing to bring the lawsuit. If access to relevant information is enabled even before the commencement of proceedings, it may prevent an escalation of the conflict and may enable the parties to re-evaluate their positions and to engage in informed settlement negotiations. This can often result in avoiding litigation altogether. In such a manner, the principle that litigation should be the last resort is most clearly promoted. In Slovenia, however, this area has remained entirely underdeveloped. So far the issue has remained constrained to the question of access to information concerning debtors' assets, which however predominantly benefits creditors, who already obtained an enforceable judgment. Moreover, the recent introduction and rigid application of personal data protection legislation, has resulted in ever more obstacles for access to information in the pre-action stage.

There exists a possibility for a party to ask the court to assist the parties in reaching settlement before bringing a lawsuit (so-called: praetorian settlement attempt; *pretorična poravnava*, *see* Article 309 of the CPA), this instrument, however, is almost never used in practice.

§2. No Formal Distinction between Pre-trial and Trial

239. In Slovenian civil procedure, there is no formal distinction between pre-trial and trial. The preparatory measures concerning the main hearing (see below) could only roughly be equated with a pre-trial stage. The preparatory measures should, in principle, assure that the litigation, whenever possible, should be terminated in one single main hearing (Article 298/2, CPA). However, in reality, the litigation usually consists of a number of consecutive hearings.

§3. A Preparatory hearing Prior to the Main Hearing

240. The CPA amendment of 2017 reintroduced the Preparatory hearing as the intermediary stage between the pleadings stage and the main hearing. The purpose of the preparatory hearing is twosome: on the one hand it is aimed at promoting settlement, on the other hand it should be a stage in proceedings where the judge with the parties actively prepare for the main hearing should the settlement attempt not be successful. The issues such as which evidence should be taken, which facts are relevant and in dispute, what is a preliminary legal basis of the dispute, the tentative scheduling of hearings etc. A preparatory hearing followed the receipt of a reply to an action and is held prior to the trial (i.e., the main hearing).

Chapter 2. Proceedings in First Instance

§1. Adversary Proceedings

I. Ordinary Proceedings

A. *Introduction of the Claim*

1. Filing of a Claim with a Court

241. The plaintiff must file a claim with a court (in sufficient copies for the court and for the defendant(s). Thus, when bringing an action into court, a plaintiff does not need to prove that the action has already been served on a defendant (in a formal sense – it even cannot be). The file then gets its case number and the court examines the admissibility of the action and whether formal requirements concerning its content are fulfilled. If inadmissible, an action can already be stricken out at that moment (Article 274, CPA) and if incomplete, it can be returned to the plaintiff for correction (Article 105, CPA). Only then, the court effects service on the defendant.

2. Domestic Service

242. Pursuant to Article 132, CPA, documents may be served on addressees by post, by a court official, at the court or by an authorized bailiff, who conducts the service of documents as a professional activity on the basis of a special authorization from the Ministry of Justice. In practice, the service through post is by far most common. The service through post is cost-free (the costs for service are included in court fees). However, if a party wishes the service to be effected through an authorized bailiff, the cost for such service must be paid in advance. It also needs to be mentioned that a service of documents is a matter for the court. The Slovenian law does not provide for a possibility of direct service between parties. There is only one exception: since the Amendment of the CPA in 2008, it is possible, if both parties are represented by attorneys at law, that the service of documents during the litigation may be affected directly between attorneys (Article 139a, CPA). This possibility cannot be used for the service of a claim, but only in later phases of the litigation. Slovenian legal system recognizes two forms of service of documents – ordinary service under Articles 140 and 141 CPA and personal service under Article 142 of the CPA. The most important documents must be served personally (such as: a claim, a judgment, an appeal, a subpoena). Other documents are served in person only in case the court deems it necessary because the documents enclosed arc in the original or for any other precautionary reasons. Otherwise, ordinary service is used. The difference between ordinary and personal service is only evident in case the addressee is not found at home or at the workplace at the attempt of service. In case of ordinary service, a process-server may hand a document to any adult member of the household (who are obliged to accept it), or, in case of a service at the workplace, to a person, authorized for the acceptance of postal documents in the establishment (who is obliged to accept it) or a person employed at the same place as the addressee (who may decline to accept the document) or (most commonly used) simply leave it in the addressee's mailbox. If, however, the document must be served personally, the process-server must first, pursuant to one of the aforementioned methods, leave a notice for the addressee, informing him or her that the judicial document will be left at a post-office and that it can be personally picked by the addressee within fifteen days. If the addressee does not follow the instruction, the document shall be deemed to be served in the moment of the expiration of the aforementioned time limit (and then delivered in a manner of an ordinary postal service to the addressee).

243. , The postal service to the mailbox is admissible only if it is affected at the real dwelling of the addressee.[206] It is not sufficient that a certain address is entered in an administrative register; the addressee must really live at this address.

244. On the contrary, a service to a legal entity, which is a subject of registration in a company register, can be affected at the address, entered in such register – even if it is evident for a process-server that the legal entity in question does not really exist in such an address (Article 142, CPA).

245. Where the party has a legal representative or an authorized representative, the document is served on that person (Article 142, CPA).

246. If the address of the defendant is unknown and all reasonable attempts to find out the real address have failed, the claimant can ask the court to appoint a temporary representative (as a rule: an attorney at law or a public notary; Article 82/4, CPA) to the defendant. The service is then effected on the temporary representative. In fact, litigation through such temporary representative often equals to an only fictitious possibility of defence. If, namely, the temporary representative cannot establish a contact with the defendant, he will rarely be in a position to effectively pursue the defendant's case. As this impedes the party's constitutional right to be heard, the court should construe this possibility in a restrictive manner.[207]

3. Foreign Parties and Service Abroad

247. According to Articles 146 and 147 of the CPA, upon filing of the action, the plaintiff who is abroad and who is not represented by an attorney at law in Slovenia, must appoint a person authorized to accept the service in Slovenia on his behalf. If the plaintiff fails to appoint such person upon the filing of the action, the court appoints to the plaintiff, and to his expense, a temporary representative authorized to accept the service, and through such representative orders the plaintiff to

206. Decision of the Supreme Court, II Ips 72/2002, 27 Jun. 2002.
207. *Ibid.*, p. 356.

appoint a person authorized to accept the service in a specified period of time. If the plaintiff fails to appoint an authorized person in a given time period, the court dismisses the action. A similar system applies also with regard to the defendant. The claim must, nevertheless, be served directly on a defendant abroad, but together with a service of a claim, the defendant is ordered to appoint a representative, authorized to accept service, in Slovenia. If the defendant fails to do so, a court will appoint him or her a temporary representative, authorized for accepting service, and affect all the subsequent services on him (and this temporary representative will then try to inform a party of the effected service through an ordinary post or another means of communication).

248. As Slovenia is a member of the EU, service to persons in other EU Member States is effected in accordance with the EU Regulation Number 1393/2007 on the service in the Member States of judicial and extrajudicial documents in civil or commercial matters, repealing Council Regulation (EC) Number 1348/2000 (applicable since 13 November 2008). The regulation establishes a system of decentralized service through transmitting (in Slovenia: all courts) and receiving (in Slovenia: all district courts, *okrožna sodišča*) agencies. If the document to be served is in a language other than the official language of the state addressed or the language that the recipient understands, he or she may refuse to accept it.

249. Besides, the Regulation also allows a direct postal service, whereby Member States could impose conditions for such service. Slovenia declared that the documents to be served by post in Slovenia must be written in or accompanied by a translation into Slovenian language or the language of the Member State, where the document is sent from, if the addressee is a national of that state, otherwise the recipient of service may refuse to accept the document. Of course, when a Slovenian court wishes to serve a document by post to a recipient in another EU Member State, it needs to adhere to conditions, which that state notified with regard to postal service. The important advantage of the Service Regulation is the use of standard forms.

250. Slovenia is also a party to the Hague Convention of 15 November 1965 on the Service Abroad of Judicial and Extrajudicial Documents in Civil or Commercial Matters. There are also some (though not many) bilateral treaties, which simplify the cross-border service of judicial documents (such as with Croatia and Macedonia), usually enabling the court, which needs to transmit the document, to contact directly the Ministry of Justice of the state addressed (and then the service is effected according to the rules of national law). If nothing of the above-mentioned applies, a service abroad is affected through diplomatic channels (Article 135, CPA). Courts in Slovenia generally serve documents of foreign courts by inviting the party on whom the document must be served to come to the court, where he or she is formally notified that the court is not obliged to receive documents that are not translated into Slovenian language (however, the invitation also contains a clause that in case the addressee does not come to court, the document will be sent to him or her by post, and that in such case he or she will no longer be able to refuse to accept it if it was not in Slovenian language).

251. If a defendant resides abroad and a service abroad could not be accomplished, a plaintiff may ask the court to appoint the defendant a temporary representative in Slovenia (Article 82, CPA). A service is then affected on such representative. A temporary representative will then again try to establish a contact with the defendant, but the service is deemed to be effective already from the moment the document was served on a temporary representative.

4. No Summary Judgment

252. Prior to the main hearing, a court may only strike out a claim for procedural reasons (if it is inadmissible, including the situation, when an action was not formally in order and it was returned to the plaintiff for correction, but the latter failed to correct it). This can occur not only before the action is served to the defendant, but also after the defendant filed the defence plea (and possibly drove the attention to certain procedural obstacles). However, Slovenian law does not provide for a possibility of a summary judgment on merits. Even if manifestly ill-founded, a claim must be served to the defendant and if contested, a public main hearing must take place. The same applies in a case, when it follows from a defence plea, that the defendant has no real prospect of success in the litigation.

B. Progress of Proceedings

1. Procedural and Substantive Preparation of a Trial

253. Except the defendant's obligation to file a defence plea within thirty days from the service of the claim (under a possible sanction of a default judgment), there is no obligatory written preparatory procedure.

254. In the preparatory stage of proceedings, according to Slovenian CPA, a court may address and solve only preliminary procedural questions (such as objections to jurisdiction, lis pendens, *res iudicata*, standing, deciding on a intervention, on securing of evidence, on interlocutory injunctions; on the joinder and severance of claims, on the exemption of a party from the payment of the costs of the proceedings; on the security for the costs of the proceedings; on the appointment of an expert; on the measures for the correction of pleadings; on the validity of the power of attorney; and on all the other issues respecting the direction of the proceedings (Article 270, CPA). But, these measures are not directed towards a substantive preparation of a trial (with the exception of the appointment of the expert witness – but even this does not mean that expert evidence will be available before the trial).

255. Especially before the CPA amendment in 2008, there were serious deficiencies in the preparatory stage of civil litigation. A judge did not have sufficient powers to assure a timely gathering of evidence and assertions and clarifications of relevant facts and legal contestations. A partial improvement was reached with the CPA amendment in 2008. A judge is now given powers to determine the binding time limits for the parties with regard, for example, to the submitting of written observations, comments or clarifications on their factual assertions, the evidence offered or already taken and the legal standpoints. In this manner, a judge can, at least to a certain extent, assure that procedural material (factual assertions and evidence offered) shall be gathered before the commencement of main hearing (about the sanction of preclusion: see above, paragraph 232).

256. The CPA-1999, which, after receiving the claim and the defendant's answer to the claim, directly envisaged the calling of the main hearing (and thus the commencement of the procedure for the taking of evidence), was, despite being in principle inclined to in-court settlement, in fact disinclined to the possibility of a successful preliminary examination of the possibility to settle.[208] The amendment of the CPA in 2002 introduced the instrument of a settlement conference (*poravnalni narok*) as a special stage in the civil procedure (Article 305a–305c, CPA), whereas the CPA amendment of 2017 replaced the settlement conference with the Preparatory hearing (but otherwise did not change much as to the dual purpose of this conference/hearing – attempt to promote settlement as well as prepare for the main hearing should the settlement attempt not be successful). A preparatory hearing followed the receipt of a reply to an action and is held prior to the trial (i.e., the main hearing). It is conducted by the judge (the same judge as throughout the whole procedure at the First Instance Court) who, by means of his or her active role in accordance with the principles of case management, tries, together with the parties, to achieve a consensual resolution of a dispute.[209] A preparatory hearing must be scheduled prior to oral hearing. However this cannot have any real positive effects for the organization of the main hearing if the main hearing is scheduled to take place immediately after the preparatory conference (i.e. that it is all one hearing – its first part the preparatory hearing, the second part the (first session of the) main hearing). Understandably, in such case – which is, as experience in Slovenia shows –, the rule, it can hardly serve the purpose of an effective preparation of a trial.

2. Limited Scope of Disclosure of Evidence

257. The CPA does not provide for a special procedural stage, aimed at disclosure of evidence. The CPA provides only for a very narrow scope of the duty to produce documents (Article 227). Only documentary evidence will, at least to a certain extent, be available already before the main hearing. In their initial pleadings (the claim, the defence plea) parties are obliged to assert facts and to adduce evidence. Only the documentary evidence, which is quoted in the claim (and the defence plea), is expected to be enclosed (if in a possession of the party) – thus documents

208. N. Betetto, *Poravnalni narok*[*A Settlement Conference*], 28 Podjetje in delo, 1562 (2002), *see* in detail:. Galič, A., *Alternative Dispute Resolution in Slovenia*, 1 Slovenian L. Rev. 41 (May 2004).
209. N. Betetto, *Poravnalni narok*[*A Settlement Conference*], 28 Podjetje in delo, 1563 (2002); Z. Trampuš, *Materialno procesno vodstvo in sodna poravnava*[*Material Procedural Guidance and Court Settlement*], 28 Podjetje in delo, 1558 (2002).

which will support the party's claim. But there is no obligation to disclose (or at least mention) documents, which the party possesses or knows about and might support the case of her opponent. Names and addresses of witnesses need to be given – but there is neither an obligation to produce preliminary witness statements nor to state what presumably the content of the witness statement shall be. Since the amendment of the CPA in 2008, there exists a limited possibility of submitting written witness statements, but this is predominantly considered to be a part of the taking of evidence and not a tool of disclosure of evidence (see below, paragraph 369370).[210]In addition, the parties have, in principle, an unlimited right to state new facts and evidence also until the end of the first main hearing. This further frustrates the goal of the production of evidence. However, since the CPA amendment in 2008, the judge has the power to make observations and to put questions in writing to the parties even before the main hearing and requests from them to offer further evidence (Article 286.a CPA). If a party does not react, such party may be precluded from stating such evidence in the later stages of the procedure.

3. Determination of the Trial (Main Hearing) Date

258. Courts are not obliged to fix the date of the main hearing in with the parties. Nevertheless, since the CPA amendment in 2017, the court must, after giving the Parties the right to comment, adopt a 'procedural plan' in the preparatory stage of proceedings (during or immediately after the preparatory conference). It is advisable that dates for exchange of briefs as well as for the main hearing are fixed with the procedural plan. Usually, the date of a main hearing is not fixed long in advance (it will rarely be fixed more than thirty days in advance).[211] It is also not unusual for the court to fix a date of a main hearing already together with the serving of the claim to the defendant (whereby it must be considered that a defendant must always be given a thirty-day period for the filing of a defence plea). But this is advisable only in cases, when it cannot be expected that the court will need to carry out any other preparatory measures for the trial.

4. Trial (Main Hearing)

259. The notion of a trial is not used in Slovenian civil procedure. Rather, it is spoken about a main hearing (*glavna obravnava*). The main hearing is considered to be a single event even if it consists of several sessions.[212] The main hearing is always held in the court's building (Article 114, CPA), in a conference hall, just exceptionally in the judge's chamber (in certain commercial cases, when no witnesses are to be examined and no public is expected to attend). Since the CPA

210. N. Betetto, *Predvidene novosti v ZPP glede dokaznega postopka*[*The Foreseen Novelties in CPA Concerning Evidence*], 33 Podjetje in delo, 1073 (2007).
211. N. Betetto, *Pospešeni pravdni postopek*[*An Accelerated Litigation*], 29 Pravna praksa, 3 et seq. (2004).
212. L. Ude, *Civilno procesno parvo* [*Civil Procedure*] 281(ČZ UL 2002).

amendment in 2008, it is possible to organize a main hearing in a way of a videoconference, but only if the court is technically equipped (Article 114a, CPA). The main hearing is usually not tape-recorded. The records are made in such manner that the judge dictates to the recording clerk what to enter in the record (Article 124, CPA). With regard to, for example, witness statements, the whole statement is not dictated for the record, but the judge, after hearing a part of a witness statement, summarizes it and dictates it to a clerk. A witness and parties can object to the content of the judge's summary of the statement. With regard to the statements of the parties and their attorneys, a judge can give permission to the party or their attorney to directly dictate what should be entered into a record.

260. Parties are not obliged to appear in court in person (unless the evidence of examination of a party as a witness should be taken, see below, paragraph 377), they can always appear through an attorney at law (about the limitations, concerning the possibility to issue the power of attorney to persons other than attorneys at law, see above, paragraph 200). However, in the First Instance Court (as well as in appellate courts), parties can present their own case by themselves and they are not obliged to be represented by an attorney at law.

261. The main hearing is opened by the presiding judge who shall declare the subject matter to be heard and ascertain if all summoned persons have appeared; in the case of non-appearance, the judge shall verify whether they have been duly summoned and whether they have justified their non-appearance (Article 282, CPA). A judge may, but is not obliged to, discuss with the parties the plan of progress of the trial and a time-frame for its accomplishment.[213] In theory, the main hearing then proceeds with the plaintiff's and the defendant's opening speeches (Article 283, CPA). In practice, the parties usually just drive attention to their prior written submissions. Even if a party wishes to make new submissions on the main hearing, the principle of orality is not strictly enforced; parties or their attorneys are not prevented from reading statements, prepared in advance. After possible clarification of certain procedural issues, a judge shall need to make a determination, which facts are in dispute and which are relevant for the case. A so-called evidence decree is then issued, defining which evidence will be taken and with regard to what facts in dispute. As already explained above, the judge is bound by the prayer for relief sought and also by the factual frame asserted by the parties and can only take evidence proposed by the parties (the principle of free disposition and adversarial principle, see in detail above, paragraphs 31–35). Nevertheless, the judge takes an active role in the litigation and has not only the power but also a duty to ask questions and to provoke the parties to clarify and, if necessary, to supplement their factual assertions and evidence.[214] The judge also needs to comment on legal issues and to drive

---

213. *See* M. Dolenc, *Materialno procesno vodstvo v. luči odločb Ustavnega sodišča[Material Procedural Guidance in the Light of Jurisprudence of the Constitutional Court]* Pravosodni bilten, št. 1, str. 70 (2007).

214. *See* J. Juhart, *Zbiranje procesnega gradiva[Production of Facts, Evidence and Legal Basis]*, 12 *Pravnik*, 223 et seq. (1957); Z. Trampuš, *Metode racionalnega vodenja postopka[Methods of Rational Case-Management]*, 2 Pravosodni bilten, 49 (1999), *see also* the Decision of the Const. Court Up 130/04, 24 Nov. 2005.

attention to legal grounds, which parties might have overlooked, but the judge intends to rely on (which, in accordance with the principle of *iura novit curia*, the judge is entitled to). The judge must make sure that all the disputed issues are discussed and addressed. This is an expression of the so-called material procedural guidance (see in detail, above, paragraph 36). However, this activity must not result in an appearance, as if a judge was favouring one party.[215] The main hearing must be conducted in a contradictory manner, with respect of the parties' right to be heard. The parties have a right to make comments with regard to factual assertions, evidence and also points of law. There is no explicit requirement to enable the parties to make summations (final speeches) at the end of the trial, but it stems already from their constitutional right to be heard that a right to make a final comment on the results of evidence should be respected.

262. The trial also serves the purpose of trying to reach a settlement. The 2008 Amendment of the CPA emphasized to a greater extent the obligation of the court – throughout the whole course of proceedings to be more active at the encouraging of settlements.[216]The court must evaluate whether there exists such possibility of dispute resolution, and actively assist the parties in reaching such (Article 306c, SiCPA) and this applies throughout the entire proceedings (e.g., a suitable time to try to reach a settlement could also be after the procedure of the taking of evidence is completed). A judge may actively advise the parties on how to reach a settlement, and in practice, a judge often does not hide his or her views as to what content of settlement would be appropriate for the case.[217] But even when the judge actively cooperates at the reaching of a settlement, it is imperative that the settlement observes the principle of self-determination.[218] If a settlement is reached (in the form of a written protocol, signed by the parties and the judge), it has an effect of *res iudicata* and an effect of direct enforceability.

263. Article 298/2 of the CPA provides that litigation, whenever possible, should be terminated in one single main hearing (trial). However in reality, litigation usually consists of a number of consecutive ('piecemeal') hearings, many of which are empty in substance; the time intervals between sessions are often long (rarely less than a fortnight). It can realistically be assessed that an adjournment of a hearing is sometimes a result of a too poor preparation of a trial and a lack of proper study of the case – both on a side of a judge as well as of parties' attorneys. If a hearing is adjourned and the next session needs to be called, its time should, as a principle, be fixed already at the end of the previous one (Article 115, CPA). Sometimes, however, this cannot be done, for example, if the report of an expert must be waited for. In such case, the court will determine a new date of the hearing after it gains the report and a formal service to the parties will be needed.

---

215. 2 L. Ude et al. *Pravdni postopek – zakon s komentarjem*[*Civil Procedure – Act with the Commentary*]595(GV Založba in ČZ UL 2006).

216. Z. Trampuš, *Materialno procesno vodstvo in sodna poravnava*[*Material Procedural Guidance and Court Settlement*], 28 Podjetje in delo, 1561 et seq. (2002).

217. *Ibid.*

218. Wedam Lukić, *Vloga in odgovornost sodnika v civilnem pravdnem postopku*[*Role and Responsibility of a Judge in Civil Procedure*], 29 Podjetje in delo, 1667 (2003).

264. An adjournment of the hearing must be distinguished from a suspension of proceedings (Articles 205–208, CPA). The dissolution of a legal entity always results in a suspension of proceedings, till the legal successor is invited to take over the procedure. A suspension of proceedings is also a result of an opening of bankruptcy proceedings (till the bankruptcy administrator takes it over). However, upon the death or incapacitation of a party who is a physical person, a procedure is not suspended if that party had an attorney. In such case, the procedure goes on with the attorney representing the parties' successors (although their identity might not be known yet). One other example of a suspension of procedure is, when a court decides that it will not resolve a preliminary question, which falls within the jurisdiction of another state authority, but will wait for the outcome of another procedure, in which it shall be adjudicated upon such question with a *res iudicata* effect. Upon the suspension of the proceedings, all time periods prescribed for the performance of acts of procedure are suspended.

5. No Avocat General, Amicus Curiae or Opinion by the 'Ministère Public'

265. In Slovenian civil procedure, there is no such concept as an avocat general or ministere public or a similar body that could submit its impartial legal opinion to the court. Nobody can appear in a court as amicus curiae. A concept of a 'technical assessor', which would assist the judge at the understanding of technical issues and the evidence, given by an expert, also does not apply.

C. Judgment

1. Deliberation and Delivering the Judgment

266. When the panel considers that the case in dispute has been examined to a sufficient degree so that it can be decided upon, a judge shall announce the conclusion of the main hearing (Article 291, CPA). Since almost in all cases, a case is decided by a single judge, there is practically never a need for a special stage of deliberation in the First Instance Court. In exceptional cases, when a case is decided by a panel of judges (such as in labour disputes), a law provides that the deliberations of judges are held in private. A protocol concerning deliberations and votes of members of a panel is sealed. Thus, neither the parties nor any other persons can find out how the judges voted in the case. Also from a judgment itself, it is not evident if a certain member of a panel voted against the decision. Moreover, no dissenting opinion can be given. The above-mentioned rules apply also with regard to proccedings in appellate courts, but since the 2017 amendment of the CPA no longer for proceedings in the Supreme Court. As of this reform, judgments of the Supreme Court contain information as to how individual judges in the panel voted. Separate opinions – both concurring as well as dissenting – are possible (Article 381.a CPA).

267. In the First Instance Court, the judge or the panel may deliver a judgment already at the end of the main hearing. When the judgment is announced, the presiding judge shall read in open court the ordering part of the judgment and give a brief statement of the reasons (Article 322, CPA). In written form, a judgment should then be delivered within thirty days (Article 325, CPA): However, in practice, it very rarely happens that a judgment is delivered orally already upon the termination of the main hearing. Judges very often apply the provision of Article 321/3, CPA, according to which the court may, in more complex cases, decide that the judgment be rendered in writing. In such event, rather than being announced, the judgment shall be served on the parties in writing after the completion of the main hearing. According to the mentioned provision, this should be done within thirty days – but this time limit is often exceeded (whereby there are no procedural sanctions for this delay). It should be stressed, that in case the judgment is not pronounced orally upon the termination of the main hearing, it is only delivered in writing. There is no separate hearing, which would serve as a pronunciation of the judgment. It is questionable whether this system is in line with the requests of a public trial, as guaranteed by Article 6.1 of the ECHR (though, the interested public may always seek an insight into a judgment at the court depositary office).

2. Different Kinds of Judgments

268. A judgment on the merits decides upon the relief claimed in respect of the cause of action, and determines the lateral claims (Article 310, CPA). Besides on the basis of the hearing of the case in dispute, the judgment on the merits may also be based on the declarations of the parties in accordance with the principle of free disposition (see above, paragraph 32) – judgment by acknowledgment (Article 316, CPA) and judgment by abandonment of the claim (Article 317, CPA). If a settlement is reached, it becomes directly effective by the parties signing the settlement protocol and no judgment (such as: judgment by consent) is rendered.

269. Slovenian law does not provide for 'procedural judgments'. If a court determines that the action was inadmissible for procedural reasons, the action is not rejected (stricken out) in a form of a judgment, but in a form of an order (a decision –*sklep*); Article 329, CPA.

270. A judgment may be rendered on the ground of contradictory proceedings or on the basis of the defendant's default (a judgment by default, see below, paragraph 192). A judgment may be final, disposing of all main and ancillary claims. A court can also render partial judgments when only a part of the claim is already ripe for final determination (Article 314, CPA). Concerning the relief granted, one can, in the same manner as with regard to different types of actions (see above, paragraph 192), differentiate between judgments ordering a performance (a condemnatory judgment), declaratory judgments and judgments establishing a change (a formation, a cessation) in a legal relationship (a constitutive judgment).

271. A special kind of a judgment is a so-called interlocutory judgment (*vmesna sodba*) – Article 315, CPA. A court may render an interlocutory judgment, when it finds it appropriate to decide first on the issue of liability and reserve the decision on the amount of damages (or purchase price etc.) for the time after the decision on liability becomes final. An interlocutory judgment may be appealed against, and while the appeal is pending, the court may not continue the proceedings with a determination of the amount of damages. But when the interlocutory judgment becomes final, it binds the court in the subsequent stages of procedure – thus, when determining the amount of damages (but it has no binding effect for possible later litigations, based on the same occurrence, for example, when further damages are sought in a second action).[219] The court will render an interlocutory judgment on its own motion, if it finds it appropriate. It may be appropriate to render an interlocutory judgment when the defendant disputes both the liability and the amount sought, and when the case is of such nature that the question of liability is not straightforward (and it is therefore useful to wait for this determination to be confirmed by the appellate court) and the evidence proceedings concerning the amount of damages would be lengthy and costly.[220]

3. Formal Aspects of the Judgment

272. Judgments are rendered and announced in the name of the people (Article 321, CPA). It has already been mentioned that in practice, in most cases the judgment is not pronounced orally (not just a detailed reasoning, but also the decision upon the cause of action) and is delivered to the parties in writing only after the termination of the trial.

273. A judgment contains an introductory part, an ordering (dispositive) part (*izrek*), a statement of ground (*obrazlozitev*), and a legal instruction (pravni pouk) on the right of appeal (Article 324, CPA). The introductory part of the judgment contains the:

– name of the court, in case of a decision in a panel of judges;
– the names of the members of the panel;
– the names as well as the residences of the parties and their representatives and/or attorneys;
– a brief description of the matter of dispute;
– the day on which the main hearing was completed; and
– the day on which the judgment was rendered.

The ordering part of the judgment contains the decision by which the court satisfies or dismisses particular claims relating to the main claim and lateral claims, and the decision on the existence or non-existence of the claim pleaded to be offset. The statement of ground first indicates the claims raised by the parties and repeats

219. Judgment of the Supreme Court, II Ips 791/95, 11 Jun. 1997.
220. J. Juhart, *Civilno procesno parvo* [*Civil Procedure*] 426(Univerzitetna založba 1961).

the main factual assertions of the parties. Thus, in the first part of the statement of ground, the court only summarizes the positions taken by the parties. In the second part, the court then gives reasons with regard to the questions, which facts were not in dispute, and which were disputed, furthermore it refers to evidence, its relevance and evaluation. The court must state which facts it established and how it applied the law to the case. In accordance with the constitutional right to be heard, the court must, in the judgment, address all relevant points raised by the parties. Although case law is not a formal source of law, it is common for the court to refer to case law, especially that of the Supreme Court. Positions of the doctrine are rarely cited, but even this is becoming more frequent nowadays. A judgment must also contain an instruction with regard to the time period within which the appeal may be taken, the name of court with which the appeal is to be filed and the necessary contents which an eventual appeal must contain. A judgment is signed by the (presiding) judge and stamped.

4. Notice and Service

274. Judgments are served on the parties in the same manner as the action – thus, practically always by the post (in a manner of personal service, see above, paragraph 239). If a party has an attorney, the judgment is served only to the latter. If a party changes her address during the trial, the party is obliged to notify the court about the new address (Article 145, CPA). If the party fails to do so, all further process (including the judgment) is to be served upon her by affixing it on the court notice board.

5. Interpretation and Rectification of Judgments

275. Slovenian law does not provide for the possibility that a court could give an interpretation of a judgment and its meaning. In fact, it is considered to be inappropriate for the court to comment on its judgment (also, for example, with regard to the media). Arguments in the reasons stated in the judgment itself should be sufficient.

276. If there are contradictions in the judgment to the extent that it is not clear what the judgment imposes or in case of clear contradictions between the tenor and reasons of the judgment, this can be a ground for an appeal, which will result in quashing the judgment and ordering of a retrial.

277. The judge may nevertheless at any time, upon a party's motion or ex officio, correct mistakes in writing and computing, shortcomings in form, and discrepancies between the copy and original of the judgment (correction of judgment,

Article 328, CPA). This correction of the judgment can, however, never amount to a rectification of substantive errors, even if these are evident.[221]

278. The correction of a judgment must be distinguished from a 'supplementary judgment' (Article 325, CPA). A judge, upon a motion of a party, can deliver a supplementary judgment if the judge, by mistake, overlooked certain claims or parts of a claim and failed to determine them in the original judgment. Also, if a party files an appeal, arguing that a judge forgot to decide a certain claim or a part of it, such appeal is deemed to constitute a motion for the rendering of a supplementary judgment (Article 327, CPA).

6. *Res Iudicata*

279. The aim of the principle of finality is not only to assure a reestablishment of legal certainty and peace, but also to assure an effective right of access to court. As stated by the Constitutional Court, it is an integral part of an effective judicial protection that a party can rely upon that at a certain moment, the judicial determination of a dispute is final and cannot be questioned any more (e.g., in proceedings concerning the enforcement of a judgment).[222]

280. The 'formal aspect of *res iudicata*' is that a judgment can no longer be subject to challenge by an appeal (Article 319, CPA) and that the proceedings between the parties are concluded.[223] A judgment that is already a *res iudicata* can, however, still be subject to attack by a so-called extraordinary legal remedy. Under Slovenian law (unlike, for example, in German or Austrian law), a revizija (a further appeal on points of law which is decided by the Supreme Court) is also considered to be an extraordinary legal remedy – thus directed against a judgment which already is a *res iudicata.* Other extraordinary legal remedies are: a motion for reopening of procedure, a request for a protection of legality (a legal remedy, invoked by a public prosecutor), and an action for annulment of a settlement in court.

281. According to the position of the Slovenian doctrine, a settlement in court has an effect of a *res iudicata.*[224] Thus, if an action brought concerns the same cause of action as has already been determined by the virtue of a settlement in a court, such an action shall be rejected as inadmissible because of the *res iudicata* effect.

282. The substantive aspect of *res iudicata* binds in two directions. A *res iudicata* is one of the so-called negative procedural prerequisites. A final judgment is conclusive upon the parties in any subsequent litigation involving the same cause of action. If the court finds that the litigation has been initiated in respect of a claim that has already been finally determined, the action is rejected as inadmissible

221. Decisions of the Supreme Court, II Ips 62/99, 14 Apr. 1999, and Cp 2/2002, 6 Mar. 2002.
222. Decision of the Const. Court, Up 206/02, 16 Apr. 2002.
223. J. Juhart, *Civilno procesno parvo*[*Civil Procedure*] 445(Univerzitetna založba 1961).
224. L. Ude, *Civilno procesno parvo* [*Civil Procedure*] 294(ČZ UL 2002).

(Article 319 of the CPA). This is a so-called negative effect of the material aspect of *res iudicata* (*ne bis in idem*). As the effect of *res iudicata* serves not only the individual interests of parties but also the general interest of legal certainty and peace (as well as the preventing of unnecessary burden for courts), the court may invoke this procedural bar on its own motion (ex officio). In practice, it is, however, highly unlikely that a court will know about the fact that a certain cause of action has already been finally decided if neither of the parties drives the court's attention to that circumstance.

283. Besides the negative affect of *ne bis in idem*, a *res iudicata* substantially produces also a positive effect: what is finally decided is considered to be correct (*res iudicata pro veritate habetur*) and therefore it binds the court and the parties (*res iudicata facit ius inter partes*).[225] A prior judgment can therefore be used as the basis for a subsequent action, especially when the first one is a declaratory judgment. For example, if in the first proceedings (between A and B) a court delivers a declaratory judgment, proclaiming that a contract between A and B is null and void, but B afterwards, in spite of that decision, brings an action for a fulfilment of this contract, the court will dismiss the second claim on the merits. In such case, the first judgment has a substantive effect on the second action. Since the claim in the second action is not the same as that in the first, the court shall judge the latter on its merits, but it cannot approve the claim. Concerning the second action, the court and the parties are bound by a final decision, included in the dispositive part of the first judgment, that the contract is null and void.

284. The effect of *res iudicata* is limited in three different directions, and it needs to be differentiated between subject matter (objective), personal and inter-temporary boundaries of *res iudicata*.[226]

285. Concerning the subject matter boundaries: A prior judgment only presents a bar for a new action if it concerns the same parties (or their successors) and the same cause of action. The term 'cause of action' in this regard refers both to the claim (the prayer for relief) and its factual basis.[227] Thus, even if a prayer for relief, included in the second action, is the same as in the action, already dismissed on merits, a new action shall nevertheless be admissible if it relies on different factual circumstances as those alleged in the first action. If the factual basis of the second action forms an independent historical event, which was not invoked in the first proceedings, the second action shall be admissible.[228] Thus, a new action is admissible

---

225. *Ibid.*, p. 312, J. Juhart, *Civilno procesno parvo* [*Civil Procedure*] 448(Univerzitetna založba 1961).
226. *Ibid.*
227. D. Wedam Lukić, *Sporni predmet v civilnem procesu*[*Cause of Action in Civil Procedure*], 53 *Zbornik znanstvenih razprav Pravne fakultete v. Ljubljani*, 266 (1993); L. Ude, *Civilno procesno parvo* [*Civil Procedure*] 215(ČZ UL 2002).
228. An example: In the first action, a plaintiff (a heir at-law) requests an annulment of a last will based on alleged deficiencies in form (e.g., there was only one witness present, instead of two, as demanded by law). The action is dismissed. Afterwards, the same plaintiff brings a new action against the same defendant, requesting anew that the same last will should be annulled. But in this action, he relies on the alleged duress (allegedly, a couple of days before the testator made his last

if it either concerns a different prayer for relief or if it is based on a significantly different factual basis (hence the notion of a 'two-fold subject matter theory'; in German: *zweigliedrige Streitgegenstandstheorie*).[229] If, however, the second action is based on predominantly the same historical event, the conclusive effect of the first judgment will include not only the facts, which were actually litigated, but also the facts, which could have been litigated.

286. Concerning the question whether the prayer for relief, included in the second action, is the same as in the first action, it is worth mentioning that according to Slovenian law, there is no 'one-shot' rule: thus, a creditor is not obliged to include all different claims arising out of a certain legal relationship in one single action. For example, a person, injured in an accident, may join all claims, concerning material and immaterial damages in one single action, but he or she is also free to first sue for the repayment of material damages (such as: expenses for medical treatment or loss of income) in one action and claim the immaterial damages (such as for pain and suffering) later in the second action.[230] The same applies to the case when a seller requests a payment of a purchase price in two parts – the first part in a first action and the remaining part in the second action. It is therefore quite possible that the same legal relationship gives rise to more than one action between the same parties.

287. Concerning the objective boundaries, it is important to take into account that the binding force of a judgment applies only to the judgment order (dispositive part of the judgment) and not to its grounds (reasons). There is only the claim-preclusion effect and no collateral estoppel (issue preclusion) effect of a final judgment.[231] Therefore, although the second action concerns the same parties and the same legal relationship (the same factual event), the court dealing with the second action is not bound by the legal views and factual findings, expressed in the grounds (reasons) of the first judgment.[232] The same applies with regard to the question of

---

will, one of the beneficiaries threatened him with certain harm if he failed to appoint him as his heir). The new action would be admissible as it relies on a considerably different factual basis as the first action.

229. D. Wedam Lukić, *Sporni predmet v civilnem procesu*[*Cause of Action in Civil Procedure*], 53 *Zbornik znanstvenih razprav Pravne fakultete v. Ljubljani*, 239 (1993).

230. J. Juhart, *Civilno procesno pravo* [*Civil Procedure*] 452(Univerzitetną založba 1961).

231. *Ibid*., p. 453, L. Ude, *Civilno procesno parvo* [*Civil Procedure*] 315(ČZ UL 2002).

232. An example: the injured person brings an action concerning material damages, suffered in connection with a certain traffic accident. The court finds that the defendant's acted wrongfully and that he failed to observe traffic regulations and the plaintiff succeeds. Later, between the same parties another action is brought with regard to immaterial damages (suffer and pain) resulting from the same accident. In this proceedings, the plaintiff will anew need to prove all the facts concerning the accident. The findings of the court (facts, interpretation of law) in the first proceedings have no binding effects – as they are included only in the reasons of the judgment and therefore not included in the *res iudicata* effect.

the preliminary question of the existence (validity) of a legal relationship, the performance of which (thus not just a declaration of its existence or validity) is a subject matter of an action.[233] But the parties have a possibility to assure that a question of a preliminary legal relationship shall be decided with a *res iudicata* effect if a plaintiff files a so-called interlocutory declaratory claim or if a defendant files a counter-claim for a declaration of a (non)existence of a preliminary legal relationship (see above, paragraph 196).[234]

288. The court's findings about the objections, invoked by the defendant, are not covered by the *res iudicata* effect. The only exception is if the judgment is passed on a claim against which the defendant has brought a plea in the set-off. In such case, the decision as to the existence or non-existence of a claim, invoked in a manner of a set-off plea, shall become final (but only to the extent necessary to extinguish the plaintiff's claim.[235]

289. Concerning the personal boundaries: A prior judgment only presents a hindrance for a new action if it concerns the same parties (*inter partes*).[236] A judgment cannot have a binding effect upon anyone who was not a party to the proceedings and who as such had no opportunity to be heard.[237] The principle of mutuality of estoppel is strictly adhered to. A judgment rendered between two parties not only cannot go to the detriment of a third person, but also not to the benefit of a third person.[238] A judgment also binds the parties' successors, in case of actions in rem

233. An example: a landlord brings an action for a payment of a rent for February 2007. The defendant objects that the lease contract is null and void. The courts reject this objection and the plaintiff succeeds. As the plaintiff later discovers that the tenant was also behindhand with the rent for March 2007, he files another action, now requesting the payment of the rent for this month. Although the second action concerns the same lease contract and although in the first judgment the court has already found that this contract is valid, the question of the validity of the contract will need to be addressed independently again. It must be taken into account that the issue of the first action was not a declaration of the validity of the contract, but its performance. The question of the validity of the contract was decided only as a preliminary question and therefore included only in the reasons (grounds) of the first judgment. Therefore it is not covered with the *res iudicata* effect.

234. Judgment of the Supreme Court, II Ips 363/2000, 13 Dec. 2001, J. Juhart, *Vmesna ugotovitvena tožba[Interlocutory Declaratory Action]*, 13 Pravnik, 296 (1958).

235. For example: A brings an action against B for the payment of EUR 1,000. B files a set-off plea, claiming that he has a claim against A in the value of EUR 1,500. If the court finds that this claim actually does exist, it will first make a declaration in the dispositive part of the judgment that the B's claim exists – but only to the extent of EUR 1,000 – and then proclaim a set-off. Thus, in such manner the defendant cannot achieve a *res iudicata* decision concerning the remaining EUR 500. He could achieve such an effect only by the filing of a counter-claim concerning the whole amount (and then proclaim a set-off for a part of it) instead of invoking the defensive set-off plea).

236. J. Juhart, *Civilno procesno parvo* [*Civil Procedure*] 456(Univerzitetna založba 1961); L. Ude, *Civilno procesno parvo* [*Civil Procedure*] 316(ČZ UL 2002), *see* in detail: A. Galič, *Načelo kontradiktornosti in subjektivne meje pravnomočnosti[Right to be Heard and Procedural Privity]*, 59 *Zbornik znanstvenih razprav PF v. Ljubljani*, 69 et seq. (1999)

237. Decision of the Const. Court, Up 39/95, 16 Jan. 1997.

238. An example: In case of a traffic accident, in which many passengers in the bus were injured, one of them brings an action against the bus company and it succeeds in establishing the liability of the bus company. Then another injured passenger brings an action against the same company, concerning the same accident. He will need to prove independently that the liability of the defendant exists and will not be able to rely on the findings against the defendant, contained in the first judgment.

also the person who acquired the object in dispute from the party after the commencement of the proceedings (Article 190, CPA).[239] It is also generally recognized that judgments concerning personal status (e.g., judgment concerning a divorce or an establishment or challenge of a parenthood status) have an *erga omnes* effect.[240] An extra partes effect of a judgment applies also to persons who are known as uniform co-litigants (see above, paragraph 214). Moreover, a judgment concerning the challenge of claims in the context of bankruptcy proceedings has an effect upon all creditors.[241]

290. Concerning the inter-temporary boundaries of *res iudicata*: the judgment refers to the state of affairs at the end of oral hearings. Thus, the *res iudicata* does not prevent a new action which is based on some essential facts, which occurred after the termination of the main hearing in the proceedings, in which the first judgment was rendered.[242]If the judgment is against the defendant, the latter will be able to invoke objections against the fulfilment of the obligation in the course of subsequent enforcement proceedings but only if these objections are based on facts, which came into existence after the termination of the main hearing.[243]

7. Penalty in Case of Non-compliance (if Available)

291. Once a judgment is delivered, it is considered to be purely in the interest of a claimant, whether it will be complied with. A plaintiff can proceed with an enforcement of the judgment, or, in case of non-monetary claims, she can also apply for a civil penalty (‘*astreinte*’), usually ascertained in daily or monthly amounts, which should be paid to the plaintiff in case of non-compliance. However this civil penalty, although directly enforceable is not a sanction of a public-law nature, but a right to the benefit of the plaintiff.

II. Provisional Proceedings

292. There are no provisional proceedings in Slovenian law, except for the proceedings concerning requests for protective measures (*začasna odredba*; ‘provisional order’). These are not regulated by the CPA but by the Enforcement and

239. 2 L. Ude et al., *Pravdni postopek – zakon s komentarjem*[*Civil Procedure – Act with the Commentary*]228 et seq.(GV Založba in ČZ UL 2006).
240. L. Ude, *Civilno procesno parvo* [*Civil Procedure*] 317(ČZ UL 2002).
241. *Ibid.*
242. If, for example, a claim is rejected because it was not due during the first lawsuit, this will not prevent a claimant to bring the same claim anew when the claim later eventually falls due.
243. If, for example, the court establishes that the defendant did not perform his or her obligation and renders a judgment in favour the plaintiff, the defendant will, due to the *res iudicata* effect, be precluded from questioning the correctness of the judgment in the course of enforcement proceedings. He or she will, however, not be prevented from objecting to an enforcement based on the alleged fact that he or she subsequently – thus, after the termination of the main hearing – already performed the obligation.

Provisional Measures Act (EJPMA). For a provisional order to be granted, a plaintiff must satisfy the court that the existence of his claim is at least probable. In addition, an actual danger must be present that the enforcement of the future judgment would become impossible or more difficult due to the defendant's hiding, disposing of or destroying of his or her property and thereby putting an enforcement of the future judgment at risk. The most common provisional orders are the orders for the temporary freezing of bank accounts and prohibitory order against the sale of the movable or immovable property (concerning the latter, the order is remarked in the land register). It must be stressed that in Slovenian law, a provisional order does not have an effect in rem. A creditor, who acquires a provisional order, does not enjoy priority in case of the debtor's bankruptcy or priority over another creditor, who acquires an attachment of the same property in the framework of enforcement proceedings.[244]

293. With regard to the securement of non-pecuniary claims, a danger of an irreversible harm or violence can also form a basis for the granting of a provisional order. In such case, a provisional order is of a regulatory character as it attempts to temporarily regulate the relationship between the parties and to defer the other party from infringing on the plaintiff's rights any further and thereby retaining a status quo in cases, when a harm, incurred during the proceedings, would be irreversible and when even a final positive judgment on the merits would therefore not adequately protect the claimant's position. However, the position of the defendant must be also taken into account when deciding upon a motion for a regulatory provisional order. The applicable test is that such measure, if granted and implemented, may not be irreversible and it may not put the defendant in a position where even the ultimate winning of the case would not assure an effective protection of his or her rights and interests.[245]

294. Instead of establishing the existence of a danger, the plaintiff may also achieve the provisional order if he or she furnishes a sufficient security for the defendant's impending disadvantages. But in any case, an order for security may also be made upon request of a defendant. Namely, if a provisional order at a later stage of the proceedings proves to be unjustified from the start (practically: if the defendant ultimately wins the case on the merits) the plaintiff is liable for all damages suffered by the defendant as a result of the provisional order. In order to secure this possible future claim for damages, the defendant may, already at the time, when a provisional order is granted, request the court to order the plaintiff to provide an adequate security (Article 275 EJPMA).[246]

295. Temporary orders can be issued (and, in fact, they commonly are) without an oral hearing and without having heard the other party, who has the opportunity to file an objection against the order within fifteen days (which, however, does not

244. M. Šipec et al., *Začasne odredbe*, [*Protective Measures*], 200(GV Založba 2001). Decision of the Const. Court, Up 275/97, 16 Jul. 1998.
245. *See* M. Šipec et al., *Začasne odredbe*[*Protective Measures*]277(GV Založba 2001).
246. *See,* e.g., Decision of the Const. Court, Up 201/01, 6 Nov. 2003.

prevent the enforcement of the provisional measure). Then, the First Instance Court shall re-examine the measure and may revoke or modify it. A request for a temporary order may be made already at the time of the filing of the claim. In such case, the court, which has the jurisdiction to decide the case on the merits, also has the jurisdiction to decide upon the request for a temporary order. If, however, the request for a temporary order is made even before the commencement of the litigation (whereby a court would set a time limit, in which a claimant ought to bring an action) or after the termination of the litigation (but before the enforcement proceedings), a court, which has the jurisdiction for the enforcement of the judgment, has the jurisdiction for the dealing with the request for a provisional order (Article 266, EJPMA).

296. Slovenian law does not provide for a possibility to grant provisional payment orders (or to order the defendant to pay the requested sum or a part of it even before the final resolution of a dispute) except for the temporary order for the payment of alimonies (maintenance) in favour of a child or a spouse, which the court can grant during a proceedings concerning parental responsibilities or divorce proceedings, respectively.

§2. Default Proceedings

297. A judgment by default (*zamudna sodba*) is a sanction against a defendant who fails to defend a claim by filing an answer to a claim within thirty days (Article 318, CPA). If a (sufficiently grounded) answer is filed, there can be no judgment by default in the later stages of proceedings. If statutory conditions for a judgment by default are fulfilled, the court renders it ex officio – no motion of the plaintiff is necessary. In addition to the obvious procedural prerequisite for the judgment by default that a claim had to be properly served on the defendant (and the warning of a possible default judgment must be included in the writ), there is also a substantive condition for rendering a judgment by default: the court must be satisfied that the facts alleged in the claim are legally sufficient to justify the remedy claimed (*sklepčnost tožbe*; German: *Schlüssigkeit der Klage*).[247] Thus, the passivity of the defendant in fact constitutes a presumption that they have admitted all the facts asserted in the claim (which means that there is no need to take evidence regarding

247. According to Slovenian law, in case of a defendant's default the question of evidence is not addressed at all – an obstacle for a default judgment only exists if the evidence offered by the claimant is evidently contrary to the factual allegations (such as, for example, in a case when a claimant alleges that he lent a defendant a sum of EUR 1,000 but in a written contract, which is offered by a claimant as evidence it is stated that only EUR 500 are to be borrowed). But the case has no power to deny rendering a default judgment if it finds evidence offered just insufficient or unconvincing (such as for example if in the above mentioned case, a claimant alleges that he lent EUR 1,000 to a defendant and he offers no documentary evidence (such as a written contract), but only proposes the evidence to examine parties. Such evidence is rather unconvincing, but it is not the case that there is an obvious contradiction between the evidence on file and the claim. So, a default judgment would be rendered.

these facts).[248] Thus, the court is not authorized to deny the rendering of a default judgment on the grounds that plaintiff's allegations do not seem probable or that the evidence the plaintiff offered is insufficient – the factual assertions of the plaintiff are all considered to be admitted. But the court must then still find that the claim, based on these facts, is legally justified in substantive law. If that is so, a judgment on default is entered, if not, the case is dismissed on merits. This, however, is not a default judgment as it is directed against the claimant and the claimant was not in default.[249] Before the court, in case of the defendant's default, dismisses the claim on merits, it has a duty to give the plaintiff an opportunity to remedy the action (by supplementing the factual assertions), unless it is clear that the claim cannot have a basis in substantive law even if additional facts were supplemented.

298. The judgment by default binds the defendant in the same manner as if it had been entered after a contested trial. Unlike in, for example, German law, where a defendant can get rid of the effects of default and have a judgment by default set aside by a simple objection, in Slovenia, this can only be reached through an appeal (invoking violations of substantive or procedural law, but not incorrect findings of facts – logically, as the judgment by default is based on a presumed admission of facts) or a motion for the restoration of the previous state of affairs (*restitutio in integrum*), but for the latter the defendant needs to satisfy the court that his or her failure to file a defence plea was due to reasons beyond his or her control (see above, paragraph 232).

299. As already mentioned, the defendant can avoid the judgment by default by filing a written defence plea. Defaults or non-appearances of either of the parties at later stages of litigation cannot lead to a default judgment. There can be no judgment by default (or a dismissal for failure to prosecute) against a defaulting claimant although it is the claimant who initiated litigation and foremost from him it should be expected to actively take care for the further development of the litigation. An improvement in this regard was made by the CPA amendment in 2008, when a system of sanctions against the party (a claimant or a defendant), who failed to attend the first oral meeting in the litigation, was introduced. The legislator acknowledged that it is of a great importance both for the case management as well as for the stimulating of settlements if the parties attend the (first session of) the main hearing and that at least a limited sanction should apply against the party who fails to attend. The sanction is harsh): if the claimant fails to attend, the claim is automatically dismissed (with *res iudicata* effect). If the defendant fails to attend, a judgment by default may be entered against him or her under the same conditions as have already been described above (Article 282, CPA). Thus, even if the defendant had previously filed a defence plea and adduced evidence (maybe with quite firm and convincing reasons against the claim), this shall remain totally ignored if

248. J. Zobec, *Nesklepčnost tožbe in zamudna sodba*[*Unconclusiveness of an Action and Judgment by Default*], 21 Pravna praksa, 5 (suppl.). (2002)

249. Procedures involving only one party are, however, common in certain non-contentious procedures – for example a procedure for an entry into a land or companies register, procedure for deprivation of a contractual capacity or procedure for compulsory commitment of psychiatric patients.

the defendant later fails to attend the settlement conference or the first session of the main hearing. The sanction is therefore very harsh – especially if it is taken into account that (unlike in e.g., German law) it is not possible for the parties to get rid of the effects of the default by filing a simple objection (see above).

§3. Ex Parte Proceedings

300. A prerequisite for civil litigation is the existence of a dispute between two parties. As the regulation of civil procedure is based *inter alia* on a principle of equality of arms, and as the right to be heard is one of the fundamental procedural guarantees, it is understandable that there are no real ex parte proceedings in civil litigation.[250] An exception is a procedure for provisional orders, but even this is not a real exception as the right of the other party to be heard is guaranteed through a possibility to file an objection and have a measure re-examined. A similar system applies with regard to the procedure for the issuing of a payment order (*plačilni nalog*), see in detail, below, paragraph 379.

§4. Collective Claims

301. The law allowing collective actions (*Zakon o kolektivnih tožbah*) for compensatory relief was adopted in 2017 and entered into force in 2018. Ad hoc organizations (established at the occasion of a specific collective harm; although they have to be registered with a status of a legal entity) as well as permanent Non-governmental organizations (NGO's) active in the area, where collective claims can be brought (e.g., consumer organizations) can bring claims, as well as the State attorney (but not individual class members for the benefit of the whole class). The law does not have a universal scope of applicability; a collective claim is only possible in specifically enumerated sectors. The scope however is broad: the law allows for recovery of mass monetary claims arising out of the breaches of consumer law, labour law, financial instrument market law and antitrust law as well as a recovery of environmental damage. Both opt-in and opt-out procedures are allowed, whereby the decision which model shall apply in proceedings at hand is in the court's discretion and is taken after the certification hearing. However, the opt-out system may not apply if typical individual claims do not exceed EUR 3,000 and it may not apply to persons, not domiciled in Slovenia. The procedure is structured as follows: (1) certification, where the court determines whether the claimant organization can fairly and adequately protect the interests of the class and whether the collective action is the best option to manage the multiple claims (assessing, inter alia, issues of the size of the class and of existence of prevailing common questions of law and fact in individual members' claims, and, (2) notification phase and opting-in or opting-out, (3) assessment of the merits (both individual assessment as well as aggregate damages are possible, the decision is taken by the court, (4) in case of

250. *Niederoest-Huber v. Switzerland*, Reports of Judgments and Decisions, judgment dated 18 Feb. 1997, Judgments and Decisions, 1997-I, No. 29.

aggregate damages; distribution of funds (a public notary is appointed as damages administrator). The court maintains a closer control of proceedings and exercises oversight as to class representative's safeguarding of the interest of the class. A collective settlement is only possible with the court's approval. 'Loser pays' rules applies as to the costs. A peculiarity of the Slovenian collective claims model is that lawyers' contingency fees are admissible (up to 15% of the damages; this is in line with the Slovenian Lawyers Act). As an additional option contingency fee may be increased up to 25% if the lawyer takes the risk not only to work for free if the action fails but also to cover all costs. It is foreseen that this regime would represent a realistic stimulus for attorneys to take the risk of financing certain collective claims. Also a genuine third party funding is admissible, but safeguards concerning transparency and prevention from abuse are in place.

The law also foresees, following the Dutch model, a special procedure of so called collective settlement, where the court is called to approve (following a similar scrutiny as applies to collective actions, foremost the representativeness of the claimant organization) a settlement concluded by a representative claimant (an ad hoc organization or an existing NGO, e.g., a consumer organization) and a defendant.

In addition to the recovery of mass monetary claims, the Collective Claims Act also regulates, in a comprehensive manner and applicable to all sectors, referred to above (plus breaches of anti-discrimination law) claims for injunctive relief.

Chapter 3. Review Proceedings

§1. Appeal

302. It is always possible to appeal (*pritožba*) against the decision of a district (*okrožno*) or a county (*okrajno*) court, which terminated the proceedings at the First Instance Court (a judgment on merits or a decree on the striking out of an action for the lack of procedural prerequisites), regardless of the value of dispute. This comes as a matter of right as it is expressly guaranteed by Article 25 of the Slovenian Constitution. It is not possible to waive the right to appeal before the judgment of the First Instance Court is rendered. A party may waive the right of appeal only after the judgment is announced or, if it has not been announced, after it has been served on her (Article 334, CPA).

303. The time limit for an appeal is thirty days from the day of service of the copy of the judgment. A timely institution of an appeal has a suspensive effect which means that it prevents the judgment from becoming enforceable and *res iudicata* in respect of the part subject to the appeal. The appeal must contain the designation of the judgment subject to appellate attack; the statement as to whether the judgment is challenged in whole or in a specific part; the grounds of the appeal; and the signature of the appellant (Article 335, CPA). The appeal must be filed with the court which has passed the judgment of the first instance (Article 342, CPA). The First Instance Court may strike out the appeal if it is inadmissible, incomplete or belated, whereby the time limit for an appeal is fifteen days (the decision of the First Instance Court to strike out an appeal may be appealed against). Otherwise, the First Instance Court serves a copy of the appeal on the opposing party who may submit a replication within thirty days. Then the appeal and the replication are sent to the appellate court ('Higher court'; *višje sodišče*). If the appellant asserts that civil procedure provisions have been violated during the first instance proceedings, the first instance judge can (although it very rarely happens in practice) give explanations in respect of the references to such violations and, if necessary, conduct inquiries to establish the truth of the statements contained in the appeal. Since the CPA amendment in 2002, which took account of the case law of the ECourHR,[251] in such case the parties need to be informed about these explanations and have a right to comment on them (Article 346, CPA). Thereby, the parties' right to be heard is respected.

304. When the files relating to the appeal reach the court of second instance, the reporting judge prepares a report on the appeal to be considered by the appellate panel (Article 346, CPA). The case is, in the majority of cases, decided by the panel of three judges. However the CPA amendment of 2008 has introduced a rule that in certain cases (appeal in small claims cases or appeal against certain interlocutory procedural orders) an appeal can be decided upon by a single judge. But the case

251. *See*: L. Ude, *Civil procedure* 324 ff.(ČZ UL 2002).

may still be recommitted to a panel of three judges if the case presents special factual or legal difficulties, or raises an issue of fundamental significance.

305. The grounds for appeal in the Slovenian CPA (Article 338) consist of errors in substantive law, errors in procedural law and errors in the findings of facts (except in small claims matters; Article 458 CPA).[252] Errors of procedural law can be divided into two groups: the first are known as 'absolute violations of procedure', which are exclusively listed (such as a violation of the right to be heard, violations regarding the jurisdiction, the disqualification of judges, violations regarding the capacity and representation of parties, violation of the rules on public trial, violation of the right to use one's own language, violation of rules concerning *res iudicata* and lis pendens or the circumstance that the judgment is affected by shortcomings for which it cannot be reviewed, in particular if the ordering part thereof is incomprehensible, inconsistent, or in contradiction with the reasons for the judgment, or if the judgment fails to contain reasons or fails to contain reasons in respect of ultimate facts or if such reasons are vague or self-contradictory). These violations cause a nullity of a judgment in the sense that the appellate court must crush the judgment, appealed against, regardless of the question whether this violation of procedure resulted or could have resulted in the erroneous final decision on the substance (Article 339.2 CPA). Regarding all other possible violations of procedure (known as 'relative violations of procedure'), such test of the appellate court must be invoked (Article 339.1 CPA). With regard to the errors in findings of facts, it is important to mention that the appellate court can only consider evidence and facts, asserted already during the trial in the first instance (Article 337.1 CPA). Points which were not risen already in the first instance may be considered only in case of an exceptional circumstance when a party proves that they could not without fault assert such a fact or offer such evidence during the proceedings in the first instance (Article 337.2 CPA). The plea in set-off which has not been raised in first instance proceedings may not be raised in the appeal and neither can the original claim be amended or additional claims added. Regarding procedural errors, a party will be precluded to invoke it if he or she was already aware of this violation during the proceedings in the first instance and if he or she could have already at that time invoked that violation and demand the Court of First Instance to redress it (Article 286b, CPA). It is therefore considered that a party has waived the right to appeal for procedural errors, which were known to them already during the proceedings in the First Instance Court, but did not raise objections at that stage. This rule does not apply only with regard to such procedural errors, which the appellate court may invoke ex officio (see below).[253]

252. J. Zobec, *Reforma pritožbenega postopka*[*Reform of Procedure on Appeal*], inV. *dnevi civilnega prava* 23 et seq.(L. Ude ed., Institut za primerjalno pravo 2007).

253. *See* M. Dolenc, '*Racionalizacija instančnih postopkov v. pravdnih in gospodarskih zadevah*' [*A Rationalization of the Appeals Procedure in Civil and Commercial Matters*], 31 Podjetje in delo, 1030–1039 (2005).

306. A judgment on the basis of acknowledgement and a judgment on the basis of relinquishment may be attacked on the ground of severe violation of civil procedure provisions and on the ground that the statement on acknowledgement and/or relinquishment of claim has been made in error, under duress or due to deception (Article 338, CPA). As the judgment by default is based on the presumption that the defaulting defendant admitted all the facts, asserted by the claimant, this judgment cannot be appealed against on the basis of erroneous or incomplete findings of facts.

307. The court of second instance may not modify the judgment to the detriment of the appellant if the appellant is the only person to have lodged the appeal (Article 359; CPA); *nulla reformatio in peius*. The appellate court examines the judgment only in respect of those parts which are subject to attack; if the appeal fails to indicate such parts of the judgment, the review shall be confined to that part of judgment in respect of which the party lost the litigation (Article 350, CPA). The appellate court examines the judgment of the Court of First Instance within the limits of reasons stated in the appeal. However, if an appeal is filed, the Court of Appeals may ex officio examine the correctness of the application of substantive law and may ex officio inquire into certain 'absolute procedural errors' such as: violation of the rules concerning *res iudicata* or lis pendens, or if a person incapable to sue participated as a party to the proceedings, or if a legal person, as a party to the proceedings, was not represented by a person authorized by law to represent it, or if a person incapable to litigate was not represented by a statutory representative, or if the court was improperly composed or if a judge who did not attend the main hearing participated in the rendition of the judgment or if the court based its judgment on inadmissible dispositive acts of the parties.

308. At least until the implementation of the Amendment of the CPA in 2017, appellate courts almost always decided in session in camera without the parties and their representatives being present; the taking of evidence only exceptionally took place. In the session in camera the appellate court may dismiss the appeal which it finds unfounded. It may also strike out (reject) the appeal if it is inadmissible, incomplete or belated, if the Court of First Instance has failed to do so beforehand (Article 343, CPA). The critical point regards the question of what the powers of the appellate court are in case it finds the appeal to be well-founded.[254] It may, in the session in camera, alter the judgment of the First Instance Court only in case where the First Instance Court correctly and completely established all the relevant facts but applied the substantive law erroneously. In such case, the appellate court may render a binding and final judgment. The appellate court also has powers to make a different evaluation of documentary evidence in the file. Yet, the appellate court, sitting in session in camera, has no powers to alter the evaluation of oral evidence (witness statements and also the findings of an expert), made by the First Instance Court, because such powers would contravene the principle of immediacy (see above, paragraph 46). The appellate court may alter the evaluation of the oral evidence only if it fixes an open (appellate main) hearing and rehear the witnesses.

---

254. *See* A. Cvetko, A. Galič, K. Kralj &J. Novak, *Komentar Zakona o delovnih in socialnih sodišči-h*[Commentary of the Law on Labour and Social Courts] 147 et seq. (GV Založba 2005).

But in practice, this happens very rarely. Only in exceptional cases (when the appellate court finds that some evidence that has already been taken in the first instance needs to be repeated) the appellate court has an obligation to decide in an open hearing (Article 355 CPA). But in case, when there was some procedural error of the Court of First Instance or in case of erroneous or incomplete findings of facts (the latter concerns the case when a Court of First Instance omitted at all to address the question of the existence of certain facts, although these were asserted by a party), the appellate court, before the CPA amendment in 2008, could make no final determination of the issue, but usually just annulled the judgment and remanded a case for a retrial to the Court of First Instance – which necessarily results in a further delay of litigation and more (and never foreseeable costs). This often triggered a 'vicious circle or remittals'. There were numerous attempts for reform that appellate courts should (following the German model) be given more powers finally to determine the case by deciding in a public appellate hearing. Through such reform, the number of cases in which appellate courts annul decisions and remand them for a retrial should be diminished and the powers of appellate courts to decide in a public hearing (with taking of evidence and other procedural steps) should be broadened.[255]However such proposals faced a strong opposition from the side of the appellate judges and certain academics who have – in my opinion in an exaggerated and disproportionate manner – emphasized on the constitutional right to an appeal. The reform of the CPA in 2008 made certain steps in the direction of assuring that the cases will be decided on merits by appellate courts, The appellate court is principle obliged to fix an open hearing, with an aim to take evidence, which, although proposed by the parties, was not taken by the First Instance Court and to establish the facts, which, although asserted by the parties, were not addressed by the First Instance Court (the latter is usually a result of an erroneous application of substantive law, which resulted in the court's opinion that specific facts were not legally relevant) or to remedy procedural errors. The appellate court may in such case take the missing evidence or correct the procedural errors (where possible) on its open hearing and then determine the case finally. Only in exceptional cases may an appellate court decide in a session in camera and annul the judgment and order a retrial. The decision for either of these options remains in the hands of the appellate courts and cannot be appealed against. Nevertheless, the experience shows that this legislature's attempt was futile; the number of cases, where appellate courts schedule an open and public hearing for hearing an appeal has remained almost zero. The latest reform – the CPA amendment of 2017 – again focuses on proceedings in appellate courts and strives to achieve that the number of remittals will diminish. It still remains to be seen, whether this legislative change will have any significant effect in the practice of appellate courts.[256]

If the appellate court quashes the judgment and remits the case for a retrial, it may also order the case to be heard by a different judge (Article 356, CPA); but in practice, this rarely happens. The Court of First Instance must carry out all acts of procedure and determine all questions in dispute which have been pointed out in the

255. *See* J. Zobec, *Reforma pritožbenega postopka* [*Reform of Procedure on Appeal*], in*V.dnevi civilnega prava* 23 et seq.(L. Ude ed., Institut za primerjalno pravo 2007).
256. *See* L. Ude, *Civilno procesno parvo* [*Civil Procedure*] 337(ČZ UL 2002).

decree of the court of second instance (Article 362, CPA). It is, however, not bound by the legal opinion, expressed in the decision of the appellate court (Article 11, Courts Act). Thus, it may insist on its legal position (and, of course, risk that an appeal against its judgment will be successful again).

§2. REVISION (REVIZIJA: THE FURTHER APPEAL ON POINTS OF LAW)

309. The *revizija* in Slovenian legal system is a further appeal on points of law, similar to the remedy of the same name (Revision) in e.g., German or Austrian law and can also be compared to the cassation in e.g., French or Italian law.[257] It enables for access to the Supreme Court and thereby strives to achieve that this court will be able to effectively fulfil its constitutionally determined role of the supreme judicial authority, responsible for the unifying of case law. In Slovenian law, a revision is considered to be an extraordinary legal remedy. It neither prevents the enforceability of the judgment it is directed against, nor its becoming *res iudicat*a (Article 369, CPA). However, if the revision is well-founded, the attacked judgment can be altered or set aside. The grounds for revision consist of errors in substantive and procedural law; most of the so-called absolute violations of procedure may be invoked and only those 'relative violations of procedure' which were committed in the proceedings in the appellate court. Findings of facts cannot be subject to review in the Supreme Court. The differentiation between questions of facts and questions of law is, however, in certain aspects, difficult. For example, a question whether established facts can be subordinated to a certain legal standard (general clause), such as 'due care of a reasonable person', 'activity with an elevated degree of risk' (in connection with the issue of strict liability) or 'appropriate time-limit' are considered to be questions of law (and therefore can be subject to review in the Supreme Court). Also the determination, whether the awarded damages for the established suffering correspond to a standard of a 'just satisfaction' is a question of law.[258] With regard to future damages, resulting from the harmful event, the determination of the court, that their coming into existence can be expected on the 'basis of a regular course of events' (which is a legal precondition for awarding compensation for future damages) is considered to be a question of law.[259] The question, whether one event gave rise to another in the sense of natural science, is a question of fact, however the question whether a legally relevant causal link is thereby established, is a question of law.[260] However, the determination of the contractual will

257. For example, Judgment of the Supreme Court, II Ips 354/98, 11 Mar. 1999.

258. Judgment of the Supreme Court, II Ips 781/94, 6 Dec. 1995.

259. J. Zobec, *Ugotavljanje (obsega) škode – pravno ali dejansko vprašanje? [Determination of (the Extent) of Damage – Question of Law or Question of Fact]*v: . *Dnevi civilnega prava* 81 et seq.(L. Ude III. ed., Inštitut za primerjalno pravo 2005).

260. L. Ude, *Dejstva in pravo – razlikovanje dejanskih in pravnih vprašanj[Facts and Law – Distinction between Questions of Law and of Fact]*v: *Dnevi civilnega prava* 121(L. Ude III. ed., Inštitut za primerjalno pravo 2005).

(in the sense of the goal, which the parties wished to achieve by entering the contract) is considered to be a question of fact.[261] The Supreme Court examines the judgment only in respect of those parts which are subject to attack and only within the limits of reasons stated in the revision. Unless the party himself is a lawyer, who has passed the state legal exam, both the petition for the leave to file a revision, as well as then the revision must be filed by an attorney at law. If this condition is not fulfilled, the application is rejected as inadmissible without first returning the matter to the applicant for rectification.

310. With the CPA amendments in 2008 and 2017, the system of the revision has been considerably reformed.[262] Previously, the decisive admissibility criteria for the revision was solely the amount in dispute (whereby this was set rather low, causing that the access to the Supreme Court was widely available, which resulted in backlogs in the Supreme Court). Already with the 2008 reform (and more comprehensively with the 2017 amendment of the CPA), the legislator has changed the criteria of admissibility of the revision with the result that the revision now amounts to a remedy, the availability of which depends rather on the discretion of the Supreme Court. The importance of the role of the Supreme Court at the unifying of case law and the giving of guidance for the application of law is emphasized. Moreover, the requirements for the filing and support of a revision have been changed. After the 2008 reform, the revision is admissible only if a leave has been granted by the Supreme Court. The Supreme Court is supposed to give such permission, if the case raises a question of law of fundamental significance, or if the development of law or the preservation of uniformity of case law requires a decision by the Supreme Court. The criterion of amount in dispute has been retained partially with the 2008 and abolished entirely with the 2017 CPA amendment. Thereby the legislative goal of this remedy has obviously shifted – previously the interest of particular parties was in focus and an access to the Supreme Court was admissible if the matter was of sufficient significance from the viewpoint of the parties (the amount in dispute). Since the 2008 reform, this remedy serves predominantly the interest of jurisprudence as a whole. Whether the leave to file a revision should be granted, depends on the significance of the case from the objective point of view, and this significance should, in any case, go beyond the particular case. It is concerned with the question of preserving or achieving the uniformity of case law or with achieving that the highest judicial authority will have an opportunity to resolve an important legal question and thereby contribute to the development of law. The fact that the appellate court may have decided the case erroneously is not, therefore, a sufficient ground to grant leave. This way, the Supreme Court is able to concentrate its resources to the questions of general importance. Thereby, the Courts of Appeal are the highest instance for most civil litigations, whereas the role of the Supreme Court

---

261. *See*, e.g., L. Ude, *Reforma revizije in zahteve za varstvo zakonitosti*[*A Reform of Remedies of Revision and Protection of Legality*], 33 Podjetje in delo, 1078 et seq. (2007); A. Galič, *Za reformo revizije v pravdnem postopku*[*In Favour of a Reform of Remedy of Revision in Civil Procedure*], 26 Pravna praksa(2007).

262. F. Testen, *V prokrustovi postelji*[*In the Procrustean Bed*], 26 Pravna praksa, 6 (2007).

is that of creating precedents.[263]The introduction of the described system proves that the legislator recognizes case law as an important legal source, which has not always been the case in the civil law legal traditions. This applies both to the view of the development of law through case law as well as to the view of ensuring the uniformity of case law. The regulation according to which the court may autonomously, in accordance with the above-mentioned criteria, decide whether it will allow revision or not, can strongly contribute to making case law more uniform and firm.[264] By introducing such filtering criteria, legislature has implicitly recognized – and the Slovenian Constitutional Court has even explicitly confirmed – that the role of the Supreme Court is predominantly that of *creating precedents*– thus, in view of the benefit foremost for the justice system as a whole and all future litigants.[265] In summarizing the goal of the reform, the Slovenian Constitutional Court, went on to establish the following:

> When the Supreme Court takes positions on relevant legal issues within the scope of interpretation it has as the supreme authority of the third branch of power, it co-creates the law. It co-shapes the criteria that in similar cases in the future will serve as ex ante guidelines for courts and the addressees of legal rules in general. In such a manner it enhances the predictability of legal rules and, by extension, legal certainty.[266]

311. The reshaping of the role of the Supreme Court was not achieved smoothly and without resistance in Slovenia. The new system introduced in 2008 was soon confronted with severe, although often demagogical and increasingly populist criticisms. It is obvious that a large part of the legal community – especially some practicing lawyers, however some academics as well – have difficulty accepting the shift in the Supreme Court's role from the above-mentioned private purpose to a public one. They as well have a difficulty to detach themselves from the perception that the access to a Supreme Court is a matter of right, even a constitutionally protected right. It has been argued that access to justice was unreasonably restricted, and that litigants would become exposed to judicial arbitrariness.[267] Potentially the most lethal indication of the inability to accept the new public role of the Supreme Court was evidenced in demands that the Supreme Court's rulings denying leave should contain full reasons as to why the statutory conditions for the leave were not fulfilled. It was argued that the constitutional right to be heard is only effective if the court is obliged to reason its decisions (which is also a vital safeguard against arbitrariness). Only then can a party establish whether it was effectively 'heard'. These demands however were incompatible with the rule that the Supreme Court's decision denying leave to appeal does not need to be reasoned. Pursuant to Article 367.c

---

263. *See also* M. Pavčnik, *Argument sodnega (pravnega) precedensa*[*Argument of Judicial (legal) Precedent*], 30 Podjetje in delo,1032 et seq., 1036 (2004).
264. *See,* e.g., L. Ude, *Reforma revizije in zahteve za varstvo zakonitosti*[*Reform of Remedies of Revision and Protection of Legality*], 33 Podjetje in delo, 1085 (2007).
265. Decision of the Slovenian Constitutional Court, U-I-302/09 of 12 May 2011: 'This regulation of an appeal on a point of law affirms the role of the Supreme Court as *a precedent court.'*
266. Decision of the Slovenian Constitutional Court, U-I-302/09, 12 May 2011.
267. Ude, Rijavec, 2008, p. 87.

of the Slovenian CPA, in the event the Supreme Court (in a panel of three judges) denies permission to appeal (i.e., to file a *revizija*), it is sufficient to briefly state that the case does not fulfil the selection criteria as determined in Article 367.a CPA. Hence the 'battle for reform' did not end with the implementation of the new legislation.

312. In an influential and well-reasoned decision, rendered in 2011 the Slovenian court rejected the view that the omission of reasoning in the Supreme Court's rulings denying a leave to appeal amounts to a violation of the right to be heard or the requirement that judicial decisions should not be arbitrary.[268] In order to reach this result, the Constitutional Court first thoroughly explained that the goal of the reform was to strengthen the public purpose role of the Supreme Court. Thereby, the Constitutional Court did not shy away from explicitly stating that this role consists in creating precedents. The Supreme Court's decision on the issue of leave does not pursue individual interests. On the contrary, this decision is public in purpose. Following that pattern, the Constitutional Court went on to state that the procedure on the issue of leave, which is preoccupied with the question of whether the case raises issues of public importance, does not per se really concern the civil rights of the applicant.[269] Rather it is 'a *sui generis* preliminary procedure' in which a party 'attempts to raise an issue of public interest which go beyond the specific case and interests of the parties to the specific proceedings […]. Its consequence is a decision that does not significantly affect a party's individual position'.[270] Only once leave to appeal is granted and the applicant then files an appeal on points of law does the procedure in the Supreme Court need to comply with all the requirements concerning access to court and a fair trial, including the obligation of the court to reason its decision on the merits.

313. But the Constitutional Court did not stop at that point. It also affirmed that the omission of reasoning in decisions rejecting leave to appeal is actually an inherent element of the new system. Only in this manner can the goal of reducing the workload of Supreme Court judges be achieved.[271] Thereby, the Constitutional Court stressed that the lessening of the Supreme Court's workload is not the goal per se. It is a precondition for fulfilling the expectation that the Supreme Court's judges will fully concentrate their research, discussions, and deliberations and thus create well and thoroughly reasoned judgments in cases which they have accepted for review. Even more important is the Constitutional Court's finding that the option of only stating the formal reasoning of orders dismissing leaves to appeal is necessary to ensure the precedential dimension of the Supreme Court's mission.[272] What is crucial, as the Constitutional Court reiterates, is that manageability and clarity with regard to the number of cases are inherent to the nature of precedent.[273]

268. Decision of the Slovenian Constitutional Court, U-I-302/09, 12 May 2011.
269. *Ibid.*
270. *Ibid.*
271. *Ibid.*
272. *Ibid.*
273. *Ibid. See also* the Constitutional court's decision No. Up-349/11-7 of 14 Feb. 2013.

Only if the number of cases is manageable and it is possible to maintain an overview in terms of substance is it reasonable to expect that the cases will indeed serve as *ex ante* guidelines. The Constitutional Court further suggested that the omission of reasoning also explicitly shows that a decision of the Supreme Court to deny leave to appeal in a particular case should not be considered as expressing an opinion as to whether in its view the lower courts were right or wrong.[274]

314. The omission of substantive reasons[275] in the Supreme Court's decisions denying leave to appeal is an inherent part of this reform. To require otherwise would thus amount to a frustration of the reform. Therefore the Slovenian Constitutional Court is, in my opinion, perfectly right in finding that '*the requirement to provide reasoning on the merits of orders rejecting leave to appeal would undermine the purpose of the regulation of the appeal to the Supreme Court and consequently the significance of that Court would be weakened*'.[276] Thus, a system that allows for the omission of reasoning in Supreme Court decisions rejecting leave applications is not only constitutionally acceptable, but also preferred or outright necessary – but only if one is willing to accept that the Supreme Court can better (and should) perform its tasks on the level of creating precedents and thus of pursuing the public purpose of judicial decision-making.

315. The party may, within thirty days from the day, when a judgment of the Court of Appeals was served on her, file a petition to grant a leave to revision. The petition must be addressed directly to the Supreme Court and must briefly, but concretely, state the reasons, which could justify the granting of the leave to revision. If the appellant invokes that the judgment of the appellate court departs from the case law of the Supreme Court, it must concretely identify the file numbers of the Supreme Court judgments, which the attacked judgment allegedly departs from. In the similar manner, the appellant is expected to prove that the decision in his case departs from the case law, which has been uniformly established on the level of appellate courts, concerning questions of law, not yet resolved by the Supreme Court. The Supreme Court decides upon the petition in a panel of three judges. If the Supreme Court rejects to grant the leave to file a revision, it does not need to give extensive reasons for such decision, it is sufficient to briefly state that the case does not fulfil the admissibility criteria as defined by the CPA. The decision of the Supreme Court not to grant the leave to file a revision cannot be appealed against. If, however, the Supreme Court grants the leave to file a revision (which may be restricted just to certain issues raised by the appellant), the party then has fifteen further days, in which he or she must file a revision with detailed reasons. The revision is filed with the Court of First Instance, which shall, if the revision is admissible and complete, send both the revision and the previous petition for leave to file it to

---

274. *See also*: The Explanatory memorandum to the draft amendment of the Civil Procedure Act, 2008, p. 157.
275. More precisely: very short reasons, summarizing the appellant's arguments (which can show the appellant that his arguments were not overlooked) and then referring, in generic terms, to the statutory provisions on selection criteria with a short conclusion that these are not fulfilled.
276. Decision of the Slovenian Constitutional Court, U-I-302/09, 12 May 2011.

the opponent, who may submit the replication in fifteen days. The file is then sent to the Supreme Court. The Supreme Court decides about the revision in session in camera, in a panel of five judges.

§3. Other Extraordinary Appeals

I. Request for the Protection of Legality

316. This extraordinary legal remedy (*zahteva za varstvo zakonitosti*), which is decided about by the Supreme Court, may be filed by the supreme state prosecutor against a final judgment on the grounds of an alleged violation of substantive or procedural law. This role of the state prosecutor in civil procedure has been considerably diminished since the 2008 reform, which reshaped the remedy of revision (see above), and its role is closely connected with the above-described system of revision.[277]When *revizija* is excluded already ex lege in certain types of proceedings and claims (such as judgments in small claims proceedings, decisions in bankruptcy proceedings, certain non-contentious matters, and in proceedings concerned with enforcement of judgments and provisional and protective measures), in such types of cases it is beneficial that there exists another tool that enables the Supreme Court to take a stand on important legal questions and to safeguard the uniformity of case law. Therefore, this extraordinary legal remedy in hands of a state prosecutor was retained, but restricted to cases, where the revision is excluded already by statute. The criteria for filing of the request for the protection of legality are the same as for the granting of leave for filing of a revision (see above).

317. Parties, who know that a revision is not admissible in their case, often approach the state prosecutor with a plea to file the request for the protection of legality. But they have no right to appeal against the 'notification' of the state prosecutor informing them that this extraordinary appeal will not be filed. The decision on whether this extraordinary appeal shall be filed remains totally in the hands of the state prosecutor.[278] However, if the request for the protection of legality is filed, it can have a substantial effect on the parties' position (if the Supreme Court finds that the request is well-founded and that the judgment, which it is directed against, is based on an erroneous application of substantive law or that a grave procedural error occurred, the Supreme Court can alter the judgment or set it aside and order a retrial). It is not, unlike in certain other legal systems that provide for a similar role of the state prosecutor or an attorney general, restricted to rendering a declaratory decision which does not affect the outcome of the particular case but merely serves as a guidance for future cases. It is highly questionable whether the Slovenian system is in line with the guarantees, contained in the Article 6 ECHR. The critical point does not concern the right of both parties to be heard – they both are served with the state prosecutor's request for the protection of legality and may respond to it. It is the right of access to court that might be infringed by the rules

277. *See,* e.g., L. Ude, *Civilno procesno pravo* [*Civil Procedure*] 343(ČZ UL 2002).
278. Judgment of the Supreme Court, II Ips 23/2007, 1 Feb. 2007.

that the outcome of the proceedings before the Supreme Court may affect the determination of the parties' civil rights and obligations, but the decision, whether the access to the Supreme Court is possible, depends neither on the parties nor on the court, but on the decision of the state body which is not a part of judiciary (the State Prosecutor).In the light of these considerations, the system was changed and the role of the State Prosecutor further diminished with the 2017 amendment of the CPA. Since then, this public prosecutor's appeal does not affect the rights of the litigants in the case at hand any longer. The decision taken following the public prosecutor's appeal has a mere declaratory effect (except in cases, where revizija is excluded already by law). Thus, its goal is exclusively in creating a precedent with an effect pro future, without affecting the rights of the parties in the case, where it was brought.

II. Reopening of Proceedings

318. In exceptional circumstances, proceedings, which were already finally closed, may be reopened upon a motion by a party. The circumstances that justify the reopening of proceedings (*obnova postopka*) come in different categories, such as:

- certain grave procedural errors, the existence of which becomes known only after the finality of the judgment (e.g., that a judge has participated in the rendition of judgment who should have been disqualified for one of so-called absolute reasons for disqualification or that for any unlawful reason, particularly in the respect of the service of process, a party has been denied the opportunity to be heard, or the violations concerning a party's capacity or representation);
- it becomes known that the judicial decision was based upon a false statement of a witness or an expert, or a forged document or upon a document certifying false facts; – or if the judicial decision was rendered due to a criminal offence committed by a judge or a lay judge, a party's statutory representative or attorney, the opposing party, or by any other person (such circumstance can only be proved with a final judgment, rendered in criminal procedure, except if it is impossible to pursue a criminal procedure, due to, for example, the death or immunity of the offender);
- the judgment was based upon some other judicial decision or upon a decision of some other authority that was later finally reversed or annulled or abrogated; and
- the party either learns of new facts or finds or becomes able to adduce evidence, which, if they had been submitted and used in the earlier proceedings, could have resulted in a more favourable decision for her.

319. The appearance of new facts and evidence is practically the most often used ground in the motions for the reopening of proceedings. But, nevertheless, these motions are rarely successful, because for the proceedings to be reopened, it is not sufficient to prove that such facts and evidence, if presented earlier, could lead to a different decision, but it is also necessary to demonstrate that the applicant had not been able to become aware of and allege such reasons already in the earlier proceedings without fault (Article 396, CPA). If, with a sufficient degree of diligence, a party could have become aware of such facts and evidence or become able to adduce evidence already in the previous proceedings, the motion for reopening will not be successful.[279]The new facts, which the motion for reopening of proceedings is based on, must have already existed at the time before the termination of the main hearing in the previous proceedings (just their existence has at that time not yet been known to the applicant).[280] This follows from the rules on inter-temporary limits of *res iudicata* (see above, paragraph 287). The motion for the reopening of the proceedings cannot be based on facts, which came into existence after the termination of the main hearing in the first proceedings. Such facts can, if they are in favour of the plaintiff (e.g., after the claim has been dismissed because the obligation has at that time not yet been due, but it becomes due afterwards), enable him to file a new action, and if they are in favour of the defendant (e.g., the obligation has subsequently been performed and the claim therefore extinguished), form a basis for a defendant's objection in the proceedings, concerned with the enforcement of judgment.[281]

320. The motion to reopen the proceedings shall be filed within the period of three months, but in any case not later than within five years, after the finality of the judgment. The latter time limit does only not apply in the case of subsequently discovered procedural violations concerning the party's capacity and representation and violations of the right to be heard (Article 396, CPA). The motion to reopen the proceedings must be filed with and is then decided by the court which has rendered the judgment in first instance (Article 397, CPA). Because the motion for the reopening of the proceedings is an extraordinary legal remedy, a party must be represented by an attorney at law (see above, paragraph 128).

321. Unlike in certain other Member States of the Council of Europe, a judgment of the ECourHR (which is always only declaratory in nature), which declares that a certain human right had been violated in the proceedings in a domestic court, does not form a ground for the reopening of domestic civil proceedings in Slovenia (such is the case only in criminal procedure (Article 416, Criminal Procedure Act).

III. Action for Annulment of a Court Settlement

322. A court settlement (see above, paragraph 259) has an effect of *res iudicata* and no ordinary remedies are available against it.[282] It can, however, be attacked by an action for annulment. It must be filed within three months after the learning of the grounds for annulment but, in any case, not after five years have lapsed since the day when the court settlement was concluded (Article 393, CPA). It is decided

279. Judgment of the Supreme Court, II Ips 147/2000, 20 Sep. 2000.
280. J. Juhart, *Civilno procesno parvo* [*Civil Procedure*] 439(Univerzitetna založba 1961).
281. L. Ude, *Civilno procesno parvo* [*Civil Procedure*] 345(CZ UL 2002).
282. *See*, e.g., Decision of the Supreme Court, III Ips 10/2006, 17 Oct. 2006.

upon by the court in which the settlement concerned was concluded. The action for annulment of a court settlement may be brought if the court settlement was concluded in error, under duress or due to deception. A court settlement may furthermore be annulled if it was concluded with participation of a judge who should have been disqualified for one of so-called absolute grounds for disqualification or who was excluded from the proceedings by a court decree or if the court settlement was concluded by a person incapable to sue or if there were errors concerning the proper representation of the party (Article 394, CPA).

Part V. Incidents

Chapter 1. Third-Party Intervention and Third-Party Notice

323. A person who claims an legal interest in respect of the subject of litigation between other persons may join the litigation on the side of the party (usually the defendant), Article 199, CPA (*stranska intervencija*). A legal, not just economic interest must be established.[283] This is the case, when the defendant, if defeated in litigation, would be able to pursue certain claims against the intervening party (e.g., in litigation concerning the defects of the purchased goods between the consumer and the seller, the producer has a legal interest to join the defendant (the seller) in this litigation.[284] Namely, if the consumer succeeds in his action against the seller, it is quite possible that the seller will be able to seek further redress from the producer. The intervening person may argue and accomplish procedural acts in favour of the party which he or she has joined, unless these acts are refuted by this party or are in contradiction with this party's arguments.[285]

324. A party may inform a third person of the ongoing litigation and invite such person to intervene (*litis denuntiatio*); Article 204, CPA. The third person, duly notified of the litigation, may join in as an intervenor, but he or she is not obliged to. However, the purpose of the third-party notice is to assure that the findings of the court in the first litigation shall be binding upon the intervenor in the possible subsequent second litigation, in which a defendant from the first litigation will pursue a claim against the notified person.[286] The effect of third-party notice is that in this subsequent procedure, the notified third party will be precluded from arguing that the notifying party had not defended himself efficiently in the first litigation (*exceptio mali processus*).[287] However, this so-called effect of intervention (*intervencijski učinek*) is extinguished if the intervener's arguments in the first litigation were refuted by the notifying party or were in contradiction with the party's arguments (and therefore had to be disregarded by the court).[288]

283. *Ibid.*
284. 2L. Ude et al.*Pravdni postopek - zakon s komentarjem* [*Civil Procedure - Act with the commentary*]272(GV Založba in ČZ UL 2005).
285. *See,* e.g., Judgment of the Supreme Court, II Ips 150/2004, 2 Dec. 2004.
286. 2 L. Ude et al.*Pravdni postopek - zakon s komentarjem* [*Civil Procedure - Act with the commentary*]283(GV Založba in ČZ UL 2005).
287. *See* Judgment of the Supreme Court, II Ips 409/2001, 17 Apr. 2002.
288. 2 L. Ude et al. *Pravdni postopek - zakon s komentarjem* [*Civil Procedure - Act with the commentary*] (GV Založba in ČZ UL 2005),274.

Chapter 2. Withdrawal and Discontinuance of Action

325. As a result of the principle of free disposition (party control over the initiation), the plaintiff may withdraw the claim (*umik tožbe*) at any stage of the proceedings in the first instance (Article 188, CPA). After the termination of the proceedings in the first instance, an action can no longer be withdrawn. However, after the defendant has filed a defence plea, their consent must be obtained in order for the withdrawal to be effective. A silence on the side of the defendant is considered as implicit consent. The consent of the defendant is necessary, as the withdrawal of an action has no *ne bis in idem* effect and is therefore not necessarily in the interest of the defendant. Pending the time limit, in which the defendant may give their consent concerning the withdrawal of an action, the claimant may not revoke their statement of withdrawal of an action.[289] There is no settled case law, whether an out-of-court agreement (sometimes included in an out-of-court settlement) of the parties that the claimant shall withdraw the claim, is binding upon the court. However, at least the traditional doctrine of Slovenian civil procedure was not in favour of such so-called procedural contracts.[290] A withdrawal of an action must be distinguished from a voluntary dismissal (*odpoved zahtevku*). The latter produces a *res iudicata* effect (the same as the acknowledgment of the claim and the in-court settlement).

326. An example of discontinuance of an action by operation of law is the case when a claimant dies and the claim concerns a non-inheritable right.[291] The same applies to the case when, after the proclamation of bankruptcy, no legal successor is nominated for a legal person and to the case when due to succession the claimant and the defendant are merged into one single entity.

289. Judgment of the Supreme Court, II Ips 544/2001, 30 May 2002.
290. 2 L. Ude et al.*Pravdni postopek – zakon s komentarjem*[*Civil Procedure: Act with the Commentary*]218(GV Založba in ČZ UL 2005).
291. L. Ude, *Civilno procesno parvo* [*Civil Procedure*] 292(ČZ UL 2002); S. Triva, V. Belajec & M. Dika, *Gradjansko parnično procesno parvo* [*Civil Procedure*] 241(Narodne novine 1986). In the latest case law, an opposing view can be found: that the case concerns non-inheritable rights is not relevant. Heirs of the deceased claimant steps into his position as a claimant, but as the case concerns non-inheritable rights, the judgment will be in favour of the defendant. Judgment of the Supreme Court, II Ips 136/2003, 29 Feb. 2004.

Chapter 3. Suspension and Stay of Proceedings

327. The proceedings are suspended (*prekinitev postopka*), for example, upon the death or incapacitation (withdrawal of the capacity to enter contracts) of a party who does not have an attorney; upon the death or cessation of power of a statutory representative of the party who does not have an attorney; if a party, which is a legal person, ceases to exist or is prohibited to operate business (Article 205, CPA). Thus, the death of a party (or their legal representative) does not necessarily result in a suspension of proceedings, but only in case that the party was not represented by an attorney at law. However, a cessation of a party which is a legal entity always results in a suspension of proceedings. There are other cases, in which proceedings are suspended; such as coming into effect of legal consequences of bankruptcy proceedings, or if the court is prevented from operation due to the state of war or other reasons (Article 205, CPA). The same is the case if the court decides that it will not decide upon a certain preliminary question alone, but rather wait for the outcome of another proceeding, where such question is decided as a main issue. A suspension of litigation (for maximum of three months) also follows if both parties agree to try to resolve their dispute through an out-of-court or court-annexed scheme of ADR (Article 305b, CPA). Litigation is also suspended in a case when a court opines that the law, which it should apply, violates the Constitution. In such case, the court may not simply ignore the law and apply the constitutional provisions directly; there is no possibility of a judicial review. The court is obliged to suspend the proceedings and refer the matter of constitutionality to the Constitutional Court (whereas, if the court opines that a certain bylaw or governmental order violates the Constitution, it may ignore it and apply the law directly). The court is obliged to suspend the proceedings and refer the matter to the Constitutional Court only if the court believes that the law violates the Constitution. It is, however, not obliged to act in such manner if one of the parties (or even both parties) believes that the law is unconstitutional, but the court does not agree with such opinion.[292]

328. Upon the suspension of the proceedings, all time periods prescribed for the performance of acts of procedure shall be suspended (Article 207, CPA). During the suspension of the proceedings, the court may not perform any act of procedure. Nevertheless, if the proceedings are suspended after the main hearing has been completed, the judge may render a decision on the basis of the conducted hearing. The proceedings, which have been suspended, are continued when they are taken over by an heir, administrator of the estate, a new statutory representative, bankruptcy liquidator, or by successors of a legal person, or when the stated persons are invited by the court to take over the proceedings (Article 208, CPA).

329. Suspension must be distinguished from stay of proceedings (*mirovanje postopka*). The proceedings are stayed if both parties have agreed thereupon (Article 209, CPA).

292. Judgment of the Supreme Court, Sodba I Up 982/2006, 22 Jun. 2006.

330. Legal consequences of the stay of proceedings are the same as those of the suspension of proceedings, except that upon the stay of proceedings the statutorily prescribed time limits are not suspended. The proceedings are stayed until any of the parties' moves for the continuation thereof. But, such move cannot be made until three months have lapsed since the day when they were stayed. If none of the parties has moved for the continuation of the proceedings within four months from the day when they were stayed, the action is deemed to be withdrawn (Article 210, CPA)

Chapter 4. Challenge of Judges

331. Article 23 of the Slovenian Constitution guarantees a right to an independent and impartial tribunal. In order to assure compliance with this constitutional provision, the CPA provides for grounds and procedure for disqualification of a judge (*izločitev sodnika*). Certain circumstances per se constitute a ground for a disqualification – iudex inhabilis (Article 70/1-5, CPA) such as, if a judge is a party to the civil proceedings, a representative or an attorney of a party, a co-debtor or recourse debtor of a party or was heard as a witness or an expert in the same proceedings. Also, a judge who is employed by a party, or is a partner in a commercial company (except public limited company) which is a party to litigation or is a close relative, spouse a guardian, adoptor or adoptee to a party, their statutory representative or attorney, is disqualified per se.[293] And so is also a judge, who participated in the same proceedings before a lower court.[294]

332. The list of grounds for disqualification is not exhaustive. According to Article 70/6 of the CPA, a judge must be disqualified also 'if other circumstances raise doubt about his or her impartiality' (iudex suspectus). Concerning the latter, an objective test of reasonable doubt applies and it is not necessary to establish a real bias on the side of the judge. It is sufficient that there are ascertainable facts which may raise legitimate doubt as to the judge's impartiality, since justice must not only be done, it must also be seen to be done.[295] Circumstances, which justify the disqualification, are, for example, close friendship or animosity between a judge and a party or her representative or attorney, a distant family relationship,[296] a financial interest in the outcome of the case (e.g., if a judge is a share-holder of a public limited company, which is a party in a dispute). However, expressing a scientific opinion (e.g., in legal periodicals)[297] or expressing an interpretation of a certain legal question in a judgment in another case on a legal matter which may be relevant for the proceedings does not serve as reason for disqualification from the proceedings.[298] Also, an active procedural guidance of a judge, who during the trial does not hide his or her legal views about the case (e.g., with a goal to stimulate settlement) does not as such constitute a ground for disqualification.[299] However, the judge, who actively expresses his views during the litigation, must make sure

293. Thus, if a judge's spouse is an attorney, who represents a party in a given case, the judge is disqualified. But the judge is not per se disqualified if his spouse, who is an attorney, represents a party in another case. However, such a circumstance may form a basis for a disqualification of a judge for 'other circumstances, raising doubt about his or her impartiality'. Decision of the Const. Court, Up 290/98, dated 30 Jan. 2001.

294. Not only a judge, who participated at rendering of a judgment in a lower court, is disqualified, but also a judge, who participated in the case at any stage (and was later, for example, promoted to a post of a judge in an appellate court). Decision of the Supreme Court of Slovenia, II Ips 281/2002, dated 6 Feb. 2003.

295. Decision of the Const. Court, Up-365/05, dated 6 Jul. 2006.

296. Decision of the Supreme Court, Cp 5/2006, dated 18 May 2006.

297. Decision of the Const. Court, Up 270/01, dated 19 Feb. 2004.

298. Decisions of the Supreme Court of Slovenia, Cp 2/2006, dated 23 Feb. 2006 and 9/2006, dated 18 May 2006.

299. L. Ude, *Civilno procesno parvo* [*Civil Procedure*] 144(ČZ UL 2002).

that he retains an impression that his conclusions are not categorical and unchangeable, and that they are based on a current state of presented facts and law.[300]

333. If a judge realizes that there are grounds for disqualification per se, he or she must discontinue forthwith any activity in the case (Article 71, CPA). Only in case he or she believes that the disqualification should be based on 'other circumstances that raise doubt as to his or her impartiality', a judge may continue to conduct proceedings until the matter of disqualification is decided upon (except rendering the final decision in the case).[301] If a judge is disqualified on such ground, the acts of procedure which he has performed after having learnt of the existence of such ground shall have no legal effect. The above-mentioned rules apply in case a party files a motion for a disqualification of a judge (Article 74, CPA). A party must seek the disqualification of a judge or a lay judge as soon as he or she learns of a reason for disqualification, but no later than by the end of the hearing or, when no hearing was held, by the time the decision is rendered (Article 72, CPA). The latter is practically important foremost with regard to disqualification of judges in appellate courts and in the Supreme Court. The procedures in these two courts are usually purely written, with the courts deciding appeals in sessions in chambers, without parties being able to attend. In order to effectively achieve disqualification, a party must therefore seek disqualification until the beginning of the in camera session (although in advance, a party cannot yet be certain, if a certain judge of the appellate court or the Supreme Court will actually be a member of panel, deciding the particular case).[302]

334. The motion for disqualification is decided upon by the president of the court. If the motion for disqualification involves the president of the court, it is decided upon by the president of the superior court;[303] if the disqualification of the president of the Supreme Court is requested, it is decided upon by the general session of the Supreme Court (Article 73, CPA). No appeal lies against the decree granting the motion for disqualification. The decree dismissing the motion for disqualification of a judge in the First Instance Court cannot be separately appealed against; however, an incorrect dismissal of motion for disqualification can be invoked in the appeal against the final judgment. However, a decree dismissing the motion for disqualification of an appellate court's judge can be immediately appealed against (Article 73, CPA).

300. D. Wedam Lukić, *Vloga in odgovornost sodnika v civilnem pravdnem postopku*[*The Role and Responsibility of the Judge in Civil Litigation*], 31, Podjetje in delo, 1670(2004).
301. Decision of the Const. Court, Up 365/05, 6 Jul. 2006.
302. Decision of the Const. Court, Up 132/03, 25 Feb. 2004.
303. In practice, it is not uncommon for certain parties to persistently repeat motions for disqualification even in the same proceedings, with an obvious purpose of delaying the progress of litigation. Depending on the circumstances, such acts can be qualified as an abuse of right and can be rejected as inadmissible and it is not necessary to interrupt the procedure and refer the matter to the president of the court. *See* Judgment of the Supreme Court, No. II Ips 306/99, dated 13 Jan. 2000 and Decision of the Supreme Court, Su 29/2004, 14 Jan. 2005.

Part VI. Legal Aid and Legal Costs

Chapter 1. Legal Aid

335. As the Constitutional Court of Slovenia stated on numerous occasions, the financial burden of litigation must not form an insurmountable obstacle for the access to court for a poor party. This is a consequence of not only the right of access to court but also of the right of equality before the law and the prohibition of discrimination with regard to financial status (Article 14 of the Constitution).[304] In Slovenia, free legal aid is comprehensively regulated in the Free Legal Aid Act (2001).[305] A person is entitled to free legal aid if, in view of the financial position of the applicant and his or her family, the applicant would not be able to cover the costs of legal proceedings without jeopardizing the financial position of him or her and that of her family. The detailed criteria concerning the calculation of financial eligibility are determined in the Act. Legal aid includes further legal advice (besides the 'initial legal advice');[306] representation in court proceedings through an attorney at law and partial or full exemption from payment of the costs of proceedings (court fees, costs of experts, witnesses, interpreters, costs of translation and so on). Only a natural person and certain categories of non-profit NGOs that operate in public interest can qualify for free legal aid; however, this is not the case, for example, for a commercial company or an NGO that does not pursue purposes in public interest. The amendment of the Act in 2004 introduced a new chapter on legal aid in cross-border cases within the EU in order to implement the EU Directive 2002/8/EC of 27 January 2003 to improve access to justice in cross-border disputes by establishing minimum common rules relating to legal aid for such disputes. Residents of other EU Member States are guaranteed the same level of access to free legal aid as Slovenian residents. The same goes for foreigners, domiciled in Slovenia and for stateless persons. Nationals of non-EU states (unless they are domiciled in the EU) can obtain free legal aid under the condition of reciprocity or under the conditions and in cases laid down in international treaties binding the Republic of Slovenia.

304. Decision of the Const. Court, No. Up 103/97, 26 Feb. 1998.
305. Free Legal Aid Act (*Zakon o brezplačni pravni pomoči*- ZBPP – Official Gazette of the Republic of Slovenia No. 48/2001), Act amending the ZBPP (Official Gazette No. 50/2004).
306. Initial legal advice is provided by the staff of the Legal Aid Service Departments, established at every district court. Everybody is entitled to benefit from initial legal advice and it is not necessary to establish any financial criteria. However, the reach of this service is very limited; it covers just a preliminary explanation of possible legal steps, without giving any firm legal opinion.

336. The application for free legal aid is decided upon by the president of the district court (Legal Aid Authority), whereas the draft decision is prepared by the Legal Aid Services Department of the court. The rules of the Administrative Procedure Act apply.[307] It is not possible to appeal against the decision of the president of the court, but an unsuccessful applicant may bring an administrative complaint before the Administrative Court of the Republic of Slovenia. The application, duly completed using the prescribed form, must be accompanied by documents proving the criteria concerning income and property of the applicant and his or her family. Besides the financial criteria, the Legal Aid Authority also checks whether the case is not manifestly ill-founded. In this manner, the legislation pursues the aim that indigenous litigants should not be stimulated to pursue unreasonable claims in courts and that through this restriction more available funding will remain for cases which contain some merits.[308] However, the Act does not sufficiently emphasize on the participation of the applicant at the covering of the costs of litigation (and thereby stimulating a critical assessment of the chances of success); there are only limited possibilities to grant free legal aid in a form of repayment of costs in instalments or in a form of postponed payment of costs. If granted, free legal aid may be conditioned with the request that the party first tries to settle the case through a certain ADR mechanism before pursuing the case in court (Article 28 of the Free Legal Aid Act). Free legal aid may also be restricted to certain phases of procedure. For example, only for a detailed legal advice or only for the procedure at the First Instance Court, whereas for the appeal and for the revision to the Supreme Court, another decision must be obtained at a later stage.

337. Legal aid is provided by attorneys at law and (except representation in courts) also by private bodies, licensed by the state and by NGOs, which obtained permission for such activity. Since the Free Legal Aid Act amendment of 2004, a person, whom legal aid was granted to, can choose an attorney at law from the list, submitted by the Chamber of Attorneys. For the accomplished services, attorneys at law are remunerated according to the 'Attorneys' Tariff' (*Odvetniška tarifa*). Thus, at least for the time being, for the attorney at law, representing a client on the free legal aid basis, the enumeration is the same as in case of providing services for ordinary clients.[309]

338. If circumstances concerning the financial status of the applicant change during the procedure, the decision granting the legal aid may be revoked. The same applies for the case if the Legal Aid Authority finds out that the applicant misrepresented his or her financial position (which is also a ground for criminal prosecution). If the applicant succeeds in the litigation, the state has a right to claim costs, incurred through free legal aid, from the opponent. If costs cannot be recovered

307. B. Tratar, *Predpisi o pravni pomoči z uvodnimi pojasnili*[*Rules on Free Legal Aid with Introductory Notes*]10 et seq. (ČZ UL 2001). L. Ude, *Civilno procesno parvo* [*Civil Procedure*] 251(ČZ UL 2002).

308. Judgment of the Supreme Court, I Up 366/2005, 23 Mar. 2005.

309. However, this system will change in the future and there will be a different (lower) fee for lawyers, concerning services to clients, obtained through the free legal aid scheme, (pursuant to the new Lawyers' Fee Act, which will be in force since 1 Jan. 2009).

from the opponent, the state can still claim the repayment of the costs from the person, who obtained free legal aid, if due to the success in the litigation, his or her financial position has considerably improved. It must be stressed that the granting of free legal aid does not affect the relation between the applicant and the other party in civil proceedings.[310] Therefore, if the opponent wins, he or she is entitled to claim costs from the losing party – free legal aid beneficiary – and the free legal aid does not cover that risk. Thus, the beneficiary of the free legal aid faces the risk that he or she will, despite the grant of full free legal aid, need to pay all the costs of the opponent in case if the latter wins the case. The system that the other party cannot claim costs from the free legal aid schemes can, however, prove to be very unfavourable for the other party as well. Namely, the opponent of the beneficiary of the legal aid has a right to claim repayment of the costs from the losing party, but the losing party is obviously in a bad financial position (otherwise, such party would not be entitled to free legal aid). There is therefore a considerable factual risk that the claim for repayment of costs will remain practically unenforceable.

339. Provisions on the exemption from costs in civil litigation were previously also contained in the CPA. Before the adoption of the Free Legal Aid Act in 2001, these norms were the only basis for the free legal aid. After the implementation of a comprehensive system of the Free Legal Aid Act, there was no more need to retain a parallel system of exemption from costs in the CPA. However, the provisions of the CPA still applied till they were finally abolished with the Amendment of the CPA in 2008. Nevertheless, the provisions on the exemption from court fees are retained in the Court Fees Act. Thus, a litigant who wishes to apply for an exemption from this part of the overall costs of litigation, has two options: either to apply for free legal aid pursuant to the Free Legal Aid Act (whereby this application is decided upon by the president of the district court in the place for the domicile of the applicant) or to apply for an exemption from court fees pursuant to the Court Fees Act (whereby this application shall be decided by the trial judge; Article 12).[311] The reason for this double option is that the court fees are usually just the minor part of the overall cost of proceedings – far lower than attorneys' fees and costs for expert evidence. It is therefore considered to be reasonable to enable the application for exemption from court fees to be decided directly by the trial judge, with a less formal and strict evaluation of financial status of the applicant as would be the case in the system of the Free Legal Aid Act.[312] Besides granting an exemption from court fees, the court may also postpone ordering the party to pay the fee until the decision is passed, or allow the payment by instalments (Article 11, Court Fees Act). Concerning the substantive differences between both possible options, it might be worth mentioning that pursuant to the Court Fees Act (Article 11/3) also a sole trader, a commercial company or any other legal entity may be exempted from court fees for those motions, which are admissible only if the court fee is paid already at the time of filing them; such as the claim and the defence plea (Article

310. 2 L. Ude et al.*Pravdni postopek – zakon s komentarjem* [*Civil Procedure: Act with the Commentary*]93(GV Založba in ČZ UL 2005).
311. Zakon o sodnih taksah, Official Gazette, No. 37/2008.
312. L. Ude, *Civilno procesno parvo* [*Civil Procedure*] 252(ČZ UL 2002).

105a, CPA).[313] A legal entity may be exempted from such costs if it can satisfy the court that it cannot cover these costs without detriment to its operations. The same as in the system of the Free Legal Aid Act, an exemption from court fees, granted pursuant to the Court Fees Act, does not affect the relation between the parties. Thus, if the applicant loses in the litigation, he or she will be obliged to repay the costs (including court fees) of the successful party (Article 173, Court Fees Act).

313. The Amendment of the CPA in 2004 introduced the provisions on the partial exemption of court fees for legal entities following the Decision of the Const. Court, U-I-255/99, 5 Jun. 2003.

Chapter 2. Legal Costs

340. The costs of proceedings include the expenses incurred during or due to the litigation (Article 151, CPA). The major costs incurred in litigation are attorneys' fees, court fees and costs caused by the taking of evidence, including the expert's fee (as determined by the law). Each party must advance the payment for costs incurred by procedural acts performed or caused to be performed by them. In certain cases, a failure to assure the advance payment of certain costs has direct procedural effects. For example, the court fee for the claim must be paid already at the time of the filing of the claim; if the claimant fails to pay the court fee even after the court ordered him or her to do so, the claim is deemed withdrawn (Article 105a, CPA).[314] Also, the party moving for the taking of a piece of evidence must pay in advance the amount necessary to cover the costs which are envisaged to be incurred in the production of such evidence. If the party fails to do so, the motion for taking such evidence is deemed withdrawn (Article 153, CPA).

341. The major principle concerning the costs in litigation is that the losing party must reimburse them to the winning opponent. If the party only partially succeeds in the litigation, such party is entitled to an appropriate (proportionate) amount of costs. In such case, the court may also order that each party bears his or her own costs (Article 154, CPA). Considering the calculation of the proportion of success, different methods are used by the courts. Sometimes, only the proportion between the amount sought and the amount granted is taken into account (e.g., if the claimant demanded EUR 1,000 damages and the court ordered the defendant to pay EUR 500, the claimant will be considered to have succeeded 50% and will be entitled to the reimbursement of half of his or her expenses – and on the other hand the defendant will be entitled to reimburse from the claimant half of his or her expenses). However, especially in cases concerning immaterial damages, courts often apply a different approach (which usually proves to be more favourable to the claimant) and differentiate between the success concerning the issue of liability and the success concerning the degree of damage. If in the above-mentioned case, the defendant denied both his liability as well as the degree of damage, and the court found that the defendant is fully liable, but that the amount of damages sought is excessive, the calculation of reimbursement of costs would be the following: concerning the issue of liability, the claimant succeeded 100% and concerning the amount of damages she succeeded 50%; as both issues have an equal weight, it can be concluded that in total, the claimant succeeded 75% and is therefore entitled to three-quarters of his or her costs (whereas the defendant is entitled to a reimbursement of a quarter of his or her costs).[315]

314. There is however no such sanction for the belated payment for court fee for the defence plea or for an appeal, although also these court fees are due already in the time of performance of procedural act. The obligation to pay the court fee for the defence plea or for an appeal can be enforced ex officio also after the termination of the litigation.

315. For example, Judgment of the Supreme Court, II Ips 205/2003, 18 Mar. 2004; *in favour of this approach also*: 2 L. Ude et al.*Pravdni postopek – zakon s komentarjem* [*Civil Procedure: Act with the Commentary*]30(GV Založba in ČZ UL 2005).

342. The winning party is not automatically entitled to reimbursement of his or her costs. At deciding which costs are to be refunded, the court takes into account only the expenses which were necessary for the litigation (Article 155, CPA). The court may, for example, find that the lawyer's fee for the filing of a certain written preparatory submission cannot be considered a necessary expense as it either contained nothing new or relevant for the case or – this being practically more important – if the attorney, if acting with due care, could have included the arguments, contained in such written preparatory submission, already in the claim, the defence plea or an earlier written preparatory submission.[316] By having the possibility to deny the reimbursement of such costs, the court can, at least to a certain extent, contribute to the concentration and acceleration of the proceedings. Also, for example, if a party decides to be represented by two attorneys at law, only costs of the representation of one of them shall be considered necessary for the litigation.[317]

343. Another rule that represents an exemption of the principle of success is that irrespective of the outcome of the litigation, the party shall refund the opposing party the costs arising due to the default of, or the accident occurring to, the former (Article 156, CPA). For example, if it is the party (or a party's attorney at law) who is responsible for an adjournment of the court hearing, the costs incurred through such an adjournment shall be borne by that party; thus, if a party files an extensive written preparatory submission at the court hearing, instead of sending it to the court on time in advance and thereby enable the other party to receive it before the hearing, and it is therefore necessary to adjourn the hearing in order to enable the opponent to comment on it.[318] The same rule applies also in case an adjournment of a hearing cannot be attributed to any lack of due care on the side of the party, but it is still a result of circumstances in this party's sphere (e.g., if a party is involved in a car accident while going to the court hearing and the hearing therefore needed to be adjourned).

344. Special rules apply for certain specific procedural situations. If a claimant withdraws the claim, he or she must reimburse the defendant's costs, unless the withdrawal of the claim followed immediately after the defendant has satisfied the claim (Article 158, CPA). In case of an acknowledgment of the claim, the costs must be paid by the defendant. However, if the defendant did not provide any cause for the bringing of the action and has acknowledged the claim in the defence plea or at the main hearing, before becoming engaged in the trying of the main subject of dispute, the costs of the proceedings must be reimbursed by the plaintiff (Article 157, CPA). If the litigation is brought to end by a conclusion of a court settlement, each party shall bear their own costs of proceedings, unless otherwise agreed upon by the settlement (Article 159, CPA).

---

316. Decision of the Ljubljana Court of Appeals, I Cpg 10303/99, 25 Oct. 2000.
317. 2 L. Ude et al. *Pravdni postopek – zakon s komentarjem* [*Civil Procedure: Act with the Commentary*]37(GV Založba in CZ UL 2005).
318. Decision of the Ljubljana Court of Appeals, I Cp 514/2000, 12 Apr. 2000.

345. The party must request the refunding of costs until the completion of the last session of the main hearing, whereby the request must be specified. Only if a decree on the discontinuation of the proceedings is passed without an accomplishment of a main hearing (due to, for example, the withdrawal of action), the refunding of costs may still be requested afterwards (within fifteen days from the receipt of the decree on discontinuation; Article 163, CPA). The motion for the refunding of costs is determined in the judgment or decree by which the proceedings are completed (whereby the costs are usually calculated not by the judge but by the legal advisor) and the decision on costs can be appealed against in the same manner as the decision on the main claim.

346. The amount of both the court fees as well as the attorney fees depends on the amount in controversy, and they are calculated according to the tariff. The tariff of court fees is determined in the Court Fees Act. In ordinary proceedings, court fees must be paid for each instance of proceedings (so, including access to the Supreme Court, up to three court fees; Article 18, Court Fees Act).[319] If an action is withdrawn before the main hearing, if an action is stricken out as inadmissible, or if a settlement is reached, the parties are entitled to retribution of 50% of the court fee for the claim (Article 32, Court Fees Act).Lawyers' fees are calculated in accordance with the Attorneys' Tariff.[320] The Attorneys Tariff, currently in force, has been adopted by the Attorneys Chamber of Slovenia (with approval of the Minister of Justice). In accordance with Article 19 of the Attorneys Act, the Attorneys' Tariff is passed by the Attorneys Chamber of Slovenia and is subject to approval by the Minister of Justice. The amount of the attorney fees depends on the amount of controversy.[321] If an attorney is a specialist (this title is obtained from the Attorneys

---

319. For example, if the amount in controversy is EUR 1,000, a claimant must pay the following court fees (EUR 41 for first instance proceedings and EUR 41 for appellate proceedings). In the case concerning EUR 1,000,000, court fees would amount to the following: EUR 1,719 for first instance proceedings, EUR 1,719 for appellate proceedings and (if filed) EUR 573 for the motion for leave to a further appeal on points of law to the Supreme Court (with further EUR 1,146 for filing of this further appeal, if leave is granted).
320. Odvetniška tarifa, Official Gazette, 67/2003.
321. For example, if the amount in controversy is EUR 1,000, a claimant would pay the following attorney fees (which are also the lowest possible): EUR 100 for the claim, EUR 100 for the first written preparatory submission, EUR 75 for every following written preparatory submission, EUR 100 for the first session of the main hearing, EUR 50 for the every consecutive session of the main hearing, where the merits of the case are discussed and EUR 25 for the court session, which ends without going into the merits of the case (in any case, if the hearing lasts for more than half an hour, an attorney is entitled to around EUR 25 for every following half an hour) and EUR 125 for the appeal; thus in total around EUR 500 [plus 20% value added tax (VAT)] in a rather straightforward case (with only two preparatory submissions and two not excessively long hearings, where the merits of the case are discussed and with only one case that a hearing was adjourned). If the amount in controversy was EUR 50,000, the final amount of the attorney fees in a similar case would be around EUR 5,000 (plus 20% VAT). It, however, needs to be stressed out that the above example – with few written preparatory submissions, with few court hearings, without a further attempt of access to the Supreme Court (revision) or to the Constitutional Court (constitutional complaint) – is rather improbable and that a litigant should count with a higher cost risk. Besides, there is also a possibility that the Court of Appeals might quash the judgment of the First Instance Court and remit the case for a retrial, which results in almost doubling of costs. In order to evaluate the overall financial risk of the litigation concerning the attorneys' fees, the above mentioned

Chamber) in a field of law, applicable to the dispute, and if it was, due the complexity of the case, necessary to use the specialist knowledge, such attorney at law is entitled to a higher remuneration. A characteristic of the Slovenian system of the reimbursement of attorney fees currently in force is that an attorney at law is entitled to reimbursement for every single procedural act performed (thus, the plaintiff for the claim, for every following written preparatory submission, for attendance of every single hearing separately …) and not (like, for example, in German law) for a certain phase of proceedings as a whole. The problem with this system is that it does not stimulate an attorney to strive for a concentrated trial and for efficient progress of the proceedings. However, the attempts to change the system are always faced with a stiff opposition from the side of the Attorneys Chamber. In the (contractual) relationship between an attorney at law and a client, they can agree on the use of other criteria for the payment and not for the application of the Attorneys' Tariff. They can agree on a contingency fee ((*pactum de quota litis*), which cannot exceed 15%) or a payment of an hourly rate on the basis of the time actually spent working on the case (still very uncommon in practice of Slovenian attorneys) or a payment pursuant to rates, higher than those in the Attorneys' Tariff. Only if no special agreement is made between the party and the attorney, the Attorneys' Tariff applies. Therefore, it does not restrict the autonomous position of attorneys as private entrepreneurs if attorneys' fees shall in the future be determined by the law. The real importance of the Attorneys' Tariff is namely only that the court's determination of reimbursable fees is subject to the calculation method under the Attorneys' Tariff, irrespective of the actual agreement between the winning party and its attorney (Article 155, CPA). Thus, for the court it will be irrelevant if the winning party agreed to pay its attorney, for example, a double fee, and the losing party will be ordered to reimburse only the amount that corresponds to the fee as prescribed by the Attorneys Tariff. The same is the case if the lawyer worked on contingency fee. The winning plaintiff will still be able to reimburse costs concerning the representation through a lawyer from the losing defendant, but only in amount calculated in accordance with the Attorneys Tariff. Thus, the Attorneys fees in fact do not affect the internal relation between the attorney and his client, but only the question what amount of the fees, paid to the attorney, shall the party be able to reimburse from her opponent (if she wins the case).

347. With regard to the issue of financial risk of litigation it is possible, but in practice still uncommon, for Slovenians to have legal expense insurance.

348. Foreign claimants must, upon the defendant's request, provide security for the defendant's costs (cautio actoris), as regulated by the International Private Law and Procedure Act. This obligation does not apply to citizens of a EU Member State or to citizens of states, which do not impose an obligation to secure costs to

amounts should in any case be doubled – because if the party loses the party will not only bear the costs of own representation but also those of the representation of the opponent.

Slovenian citizens. In any case, no obligation to secure costs can be imposed in labour disputes and in matrimonial, paternity or maintenance suits (Article 91, PILPA). The Slovenian law does not provide for any possibility that a defendant may request security for costs from a Slovenian natural or legal person.

Part VII. Evidence

Chapter 1. Burden and Standard of Proof

349. The rules governing the burden of proof derive from substantive law.[322] Substantive law determines which facts are in favour of a certain party and, therefore, need to exist in order to establish a claim or a defence.[323] The creditor needs to assert, and ultimately prove, the facts, necessary for the coming into existence of the claim, whereas the debtor needs to assert the facts which cause the possible extinguishing of the claim (e.g., an assertion that the debt has already been paid off) or the facts that constitute so-called independent objections (e.g., in a dispute concerning a reclamation of the plaintiff's property, based on the plaintiff's ownership right, the defendant admits that the plaintiff is an owner, but asserts that he or she nevertheless has a valid title to retain the possession as a lessee).[324] Thus, the burden of proof (onus probandi) rests upon the party who raises an issue (more precisely, who is obliged to raise an issue – onus proferendi).

350. There are also some explicit rules concerning shifting of the burden of proof. For example, in a tort case, a claimant must establish the facts concerning the harmful act, the causal link and the damage. However, Article 131 of the Code of Obligations imposes a presumption that the wrongdoer is liable, and therefore, it is the defendant who must prove the lack of his or her fault in a case concerning the damages. In general, if there is a statutory presumption, the party whom a burden of proof rests upon only has to demonstrate and prove the facts on which the presumption is based. For example, the Prevention of Restriction of Competition Act provides that it is presumed that a company has a dominant position, if its market share exceeds 40%. Statutory presumptions can be rebutted if the law does not provide otherwise (Article 214/3, CPA). Thus, in the above-mentioned case, it is sufficient for the claimant to prove that the defendant has a market share, exceeding 40%, but if such fact is established, the party against whom that presumption operates may

322. Judgment of the Supreme Court, II Ips 405/2000, 29 Mar. 2001.
323. J. Zobec, *Dokazno breme v pravdnem postopku*[*Burden of Proof in Civil Procedure*], Pravnik(1996).
324. *See* Judgment of the Supreme Court, II Ips 27/2000, 28 Jun. 2000. J. Juhart, *Civilno procesno parvo* [*Civil Procedure*] 351(Univerzitetna založba 1961).

still invoke and prove facts so as to counter the effect of presumption (thus in the above-mentioned case: prove that in spite of such a market share, there is no dominant position).[325]

351. The notion of standard of proof describes the amount and quality of evidence required to discharge a burden of proof. In Slovenia, the standard of proof, as it is defined by Article 216, CPA, is very high. Pursuant to this rule, the judge should decide according to the burden of proof if he or she cannot reliably establish the existence/non-existence of the disputed fact. The judge must be (practically) convinced (persuaded) about the existence of a certain fact, if not, the judge should find against the party whom a burden of proof for this fact rests upon (thus, even if the court finds it more probable – but still not with a degree beyond a doubt of a reasonable person – that this fact actually exists).[326] In the doctrine as well as in case law, the harshness of the high standard of proof (combined with a very limited scope of pre-trial production of evidence and a very limited access to evidence in the possession of the opponent) is sometimes rectified by shifting a burden of proof. This is the case if the claimant (e.g., in a medical malpractice case) establishes a prima facie proof (*res ipsa loquitur doctrine*); typically with regard to establishing a causal link and the liability.[327] This applies in case where a fact to be proved is a typical occurrence in the normal course of events. The *res ipsa loquitur* establishes a de facto presumption (as a contrast to statutory presumptions, contained in certain norms of substantive law, see above).[328] Besides, some authors try to relax the standard of proof and propose a solution that a standard of proof in a civil case should not, as Article 216 of the CPA could imply, be practically identical as the one in criminal cases (beyond reasonable doubt); therefore a clearly overwhelming degree of probability should be sufficient in a civil case.[329] But in any case, a mere decision on the preponderance of probabilities is definitely not sufficient. A preponderance of evidence as a standard of proof is sufficient only with regard to certain procedural decisions and prerequisites (such as standing to sue and legal interest) and with regard to the issuing of protective measures.[330]

---

325. L. Ude, *Civilno procesno parvo* [*Civil Procedure*] 260(ČZ UL 2002).
326. Judgment of the Supreme Court, II Ips 492/2002, 8 Jul. 2004: 'Convinced of the existence of material fact beyond doubt of any reasonable person'.
327. For example, Judgment of the Supreme Court, II Ips 712/2004, 16 Feb. 2006.
328. 2 L. Ude et al.*Pravdni postopęk – zakon s komentarjem* [*Civil Procedure: Act with the Commentary*]338(GV Založba in ČZ UL 2005).
329. *Ibid.*
330. L. Ude, *Civilno procesno parvo* [*Civil Procedure*] 117(ČZ UL 2002).

Chapter 2. The Object of Proof

352. Only facts need to be proved, whereby the taking of evidence is restricted to the facts that are in dispute and relevant to the case. Legal norms do not need to be proved. The rule *iura novit curia* applies also with regard to foreign law. The court may invite parties to present sources of foreign law to the court. However, if they fail to do so, the court is still obliged to find the substance of foreign law on its own motion – if necessary through diplomatic channels with the assistance of the Ministry of Justice. Laws of science, logic and general experience do not normally need to be proved. However, sometimes an expert must be appointed to provide the relevant information.[331]

353. Facts that are admitted are deemed to exist (Article 214/1, CPA). A party (including his or her attorney) may revoke the statement of admission. In such case, the court determines, in view of the reasons for the withdrawal and all circumstances of the case, whether the facts shall be deemed to be admitted or disputed (Article 214/2, CPA). There is an ongoing debate, whether the court is bound to accept an obviously false admission, but the prevailing view is that also such admissions must be accepted as an expression of a party autonomy and free disposition.[332] According to Article 214 of the CPA the admission of facts is not binding for the court only in case a party is believed to have admitted to the facts with intention to perform a dispositive act which the parties are not entitled to perform (prevention from abuse of process; see above, paragraph 32).

354. Till the amendment of the CPA in 2008, it was questionable whether also the facts that were neither disputed nor admitted may be deemed to be admitted.[333] Now, the CPA explicitly provides that only facts that have been disputed need to be proved. In addition, a denial of facts must be substantiated; the party must in principle offer his or her version of disputed events. A statement of non-knowledge may resolve the party of the effect of presumed admission only if it concerns the facts that are not in the sphere of this party (Article 214/2, CPA).[334]

355. A judge may not rely on his or her private knowledge of certain facts.[335] A judicial notice may only be invoked with regard to notorious facts (generally known facts; Article 214, CPA).

---

331. 2 L. Ude et al.*Pravdni postopek – zakon s komentarjem* [*Civil Procedure: Act with the Commentary*]82 (GV Založba in ČZ UL 2005).
332. *See* J. Juhart, *Zbiranje procesnega gradiva*[*Production of Facts, Evidence and Legal Basis*], 12 *Pravnik*, 217 et seq. (1957).
333. *Ibid.*, p. 212 et seq. and L. Ude, *Civilno procesno parvo* [*Civil Procedure*] 228(ČZ UL 2002).
334. N. Betetto, *Predvidene novosti v ZPP glede dokaznega postopka*[*The Foreseen Novelties in CPA Concerning Evidence*], 33 Podjetje in delo, 1068 (2007).
335. L. Ude, *Civilno procesno parvo* [*Civil Procedure*] 259(ČZ UL 2002).

356. Circumstantial facts also can be an object of proof. These are the facts that are not immediately relevant for the case, but have bearing on the probability or improbability of the facts at issue. Rules concerning direct evidence also apply to circumstantial evidence.

357. When the liability of a party is established, and only the quantum (the amount in question) remains in dispute, a court may, in exceptional circumstances, use judicial discretion to establish the missing facts. The court may act in such manner if unreasonable difficulties would ensue the determination of these facts through means of evidence; for example, the cost of evidence would be entirely disproportionate to the value of the claim (Article 216, CPA).[336] In such case, judicial discretion is applied to establish the facts (e.g., the amount of damages) and not to interpret the law (e.g., the notion of 'just satisfaction').[337]

---

336. Judgment of the Supreme Court, II Ips 38/2002, 15 Jan. 2003.
337. Decision of the Supreme Court, II Ips 82/2005, 25 Jan. 2007.

Chapter 3. Admissibility of Evidence

358. Means of proof are statutorily limited to the following: inspection of person or object (view), documents, witness testimony, expert testimony and party testimony. In a regular civil case, a court may only take evidence, relied on and adduced by the parties (see above, paragraph 35). Evidence is produced in respect of all facts relevant for the adjudication of the case in dispute, and it is the court who decides which evidence will be produced for the determination of the ultimate facts (Article 213). So, the court may not take evidence which was not proposed by the parties, but can refuse to take evidence, although it was proposed by the parties if it finds that evidence irrelevant, i.e., that it is meant to prove the facts, which are not relevant for the case (Article 287, CPA).[338] Otherwise, there are few restrictions on the admissibility of evidence. According to the case law of the Constitutional Court, a party has, in principle, a constitutionally protected right to have all the adduced evidence taken. It is a part of the constitutional right to be heard that a party may not only state the facts but also propose evidence. To this right of the party corresponds an obligation of the court to take all the proposed evidence unless there are constitutionally justifiable grounds for refusing it.[339] The court has no general discretion to exclude evidence which is uneconomical or unfeasible to achieve.[340] Only if the circumstances involved give rise to reasonable belief that evidence will not be able to be produced in the expected period of time, or if evidence must be produced abroad, the court may determine how long will it wait for the evidence to be produced (otherwise, it shall continue with the case irrespective of such evidence; Article 219, CPA). There is no rule against adducing a statement made outside court as evidence of the facts contained in that statement (hearsay evidence). However, hearsay evidence will usually have less weight than direct testimony, and this will be taken into account by a final evaluation of evidence.

359. The judge may exclude evidence which is obviously unsuitable,[341] but in general, the court may not refuse evidence, proposed by a party, on the grounds that it has already come to an adverse decision on the existence of the disputed facts. In general, the court may not make a beforehand evaluation of evidence. For example, the court may not refuse to hear a witness, proposed by the defendant, on the grounds that it is unreliable or biased and that whatever she would say, could not overturn the judge's conclusions, made on the basis of evidence adduced by the other party. The principle of free evaluation of evidence presupposes that the evidence is first taken.[342]

360. Evidence may be rejected on the grounds that it was not submitted on time (see above, paragraph 233). The court may also refuse evidence if the party did not

338. Decision of the Const. Court, 12/97, 25 Mar. 1999.
339. Decision of the Supreme Court, II Ips 438/99, 24 Feb. 2000, Decision of the Const. Court, Up 266/01, 25 Apr. 2002.
340. N. Betetto, *Ustavna procesna jamstva v dokaznem postopku*[*Constitutional Procedural Guarantees Concerning Evidence*], 22 Pravna praksa, 18 (2003).
341. *Ibid.*
342. Decision of the Const. Court, Up 121/00, 18 Sep. 2001.

demonstrate with a sufficient accuracy why the proposed evidence would be beneficial to the case (e.g., what the content of a certain document is or why the party believes that the proposed witness can testify on certain events).[343] Furthermore, the court must exclude evidence, aimed at the proving of facts, which would contravene the *res iudicata* effect of a prior judgment, which the court is bound about. The same goes for the collateral estoppel, produced by criminal conviction in relation to the later civil litigation, arising from the same set of facts (see above, paragraph 17).

361. In case a party submits very extensive and complex documentary evidence (e.g., a company's files); she may be ordered to prepare a summary of its contents, including the index of pages where the relevant information is contained in the submitted documents. If the party fails to observe such order, the documentary evidence is deemed to be withdrawn (Article 226/4, CPA). The fore-mentioned provision was introduced in CPA with the amendment in 2008 in order to assure greater diligence of parties and their attorneys in producing documentary evidence.[344]

362. The issue whether illegally obtained evidence may be presented in court in a civil case is not regulated by the CPA and has, till recently, not been thoroughly discussed either in theory or in case law (the situation is the opposite with regard to criminal procedure). The traditional position was that all evidence, regardless of how it has been obtained, may be used in a civil case (whereas the act of illegal obtaining of evidence can result in penal sanctions). However, this issue has recently been addressed by an influential precedent of the Constitutional Court.[345] The position of the Constitutional Court is that evidence, which was obtained by unlawful means, and the taking of which would violate a constitutional right (such as the right to privacy in case of unlawful video or audio recording) may in principle not be used in court. However, a test of proportionality should be applied and the use of illegally obtained evidence may be justified by balancing the interests involved, having regard also to the plaintiff's right to effective access to court and his or her right to be heard (which the right to evidence is a part of) on the one hand and the other party's right to privacy (or some other constitutional right) on the other hand.[346]

343. Decision of the Const. Court, No. Up 266/01, 25 Apr. 2002. *See also*2 L. Ude et al.*Pravdni postopek – zakon s komentarjem* [*Civil Procedure: Act with the Commentary*]353(GV Založba in ČZ UL 2005).

344. N. Betetto, *Predvidene novosti v ZPP glede dokaznega postopka*[*The Foreseen Novelties in CPA Concerning Evidence*], 33 Podjetje in delo, 1071 (2007).

345. Decision of the Const. Court, Up 472/02, 7 Oct. 2004.

346. *Ibid.*

Chapter 4. Administration of Evidence

§1. General Observations

363. It has already been mentioned that according to Slovenian CPA, the court may not take evidence on its own motion, but only the evidence proposed by the parties (Article 7). Such system would indicate that the court retains a passive role at the gathering of evidence, but such conclusion would be wrong. First, it must be taken into account that a court should, by putting questions and hints (also regarding the distribution of the burden of proof), provoke the parties to adduce evidence (Article 285, CPA).[347] But it is foremost important, that, after the party has proposed certain evidence, it is the court, rather than the parties and their lawyers, who has the main responsibility for the achieving and taking it. It is the judge who takes the active role at, for example, the examination of witnesses and who always poses the questions to witnesses and experts first. Only afterwards, the attorneys and parties may also ask questions (Article 289, CPA). It is not obligatory for the parties to be present during the taking of evidence. Besides, there is a very narrow scope of obligation on the parties to exchange the proofs in their possession between themselves. It is the court's task to gather the proposed evidence. However, after the court takes evidence, the parties must be given the opportunity to comment orally or in writing.

364. Regarding the production and the taking of evidence, there is no distinction between pre-trial (aimed to discovering of evidence) and trial (aimed to presenting of evidence). Besides, a main hearing is not a single continuous event, and the court usually gathers and evaluates evidence over a number of (often rather short) hearings. Every party must propose evidence already in their initial submissions (i.e., a statement of claim and the answer to the claim; Articles 180 and 278, CPA). As the system of 'fact pleading' is accepted, facts must already be asserted in detail and means of proof proposed.[348] Each party must state the facts and adduce the evidence, upon which their claims are based, and by means of which they contest the facts stated and evidence adduced by the opposing party (Article 212). But, as already explained, the parties are free to propose new means of evidence till (the end of) the opening session of the main hearing and also later, if they prove that at the opening session they were prevented from presenting them by reasons beyond their control. So, in practice, the taking of evidence is often conducted in a 'piecemeal' manner. The insufficient means of production of evidence before the trial is one of deficiencies of the Slovenian CPA, for which it has already been established that it lacks an appropriate organization of the pre-trial stage in general. A partial improvement was brought by the CPA amendment in 2008, which gave the judges the power to make observations and to put questions in writing to the parties even

347. Decision of the Const. Court, No. Up 266/01, 25 Apr. 2002, Decision of the Supreme Court, II Ips 152/2003, Z. Trampuš, *Metode racionalnega vodenja postopka*[*Methods of Rational Case-management*], Pravosodni bilten, 39 et seq. (1999).

348. J. Zobec, *Nesklepčnost tožbe in zamudna sodba*[*Unconclusiveness of the Action and Judgment by Default*], 21 Pravna praksa, II (suppl.) (2002).

before the main hearing and to request from them to offer further evidence (Article 286.a, CPA). The party, who does not react, may be precluded from stating such evidence in the later stages of the procedure.

365. The court makes a formal order on the evidence (usually by dictating it for the trial records), which must include a description of the facts at dispute for which evidence is to be taken, and a description of the means by which evidence is to be taken (Article 287, CPA). If the court rejects certain proposed evidence (e.g., if facts, which the party wishes to establish, are irrelevant for the case) it must also give reasons for it. The practical importance of the order on evidence should not be undermined. For achieving a goal of acceleration and concentration of proceedings, it is essential that a judge distinguishes between relevant and irrelevant facts, as only the formed need to be, if disputed, proved. This presupposes a judge's preliminary evaluation of the legal basis of the claim as this is often necessary in order to be able to define certain evidence as irrelevant. Besides, from the order on evidence, the parties can see which facts are considered relevant for the case and may drive conclusions as to the judge's legal evaluation of the case.[349]

366. Upon a request of a party, the judge may agree to take evidence even before the claimant has filed its complaint if there is a risk that evidence could not be taken in the future (pre-action measures for the conservation of evidence; Articles 264–268, CPA).

§2. Production of Documents

367. In principle, all forms of evidence have the same weight under the principle of free evaluation of evidence (Article 8, CPA). In practice, documents are considered to be the most reliable evidence in a civil case.[350] Thereby, the CPA draws a distinction between the evidential value of public documents (*javna listina*) and of private documents. Public document is a document issued by a government body in the prescribed form and within the limits of its powers, or a document issued by a local government body or other statutory authority in the said form and manner (Article 224, CPA). The facts, referred to or confirmed in a public document, are presumed to be true. This presumption, however, is rebuttable (Article 224, CPA). In principle, a document submitted to the court, must be in the original form; a transcript (a photocopy) is sufficient only if the opponent does not request the original to be presented (Article 107, CPA).

368. In Slovenian (and former Yugoslav) civil procedure, party access to relevant information and documents, which are in possession of the opponent and

349. L. Ude, *Civilno procesno parvo* [*Civil Procedure*] (ČZ UL 2002); Z. Trampuš, *Metode racionalnega vodenja postopka(Methods of Rational Case-management*], Pravosodni bilten, 39 et seq. (1999).

350. 2 L. Ude et al.*Pravdni postopęk – zakon s komentarjem* [*Civil Procedure: Act with the Commentary*]416(GV Založba in ČZ UL 2005).

which could adversely affect the opponent's case, has traditionally been limited. The principle that no one was obliged to help his adversary win the case *(nemo tenetur edere contra se)* applied.[351] In spite of recent changes (the latest were implemented in 2017) the CPA still provides only for a very narrow scope of the duty to produce documents (Article 227). A party can request the opposing party to produce documents, which are in the possession of the latter, only in a limited number of circumstances. One of them is the case, when the opposing party has relied on or cited the documents. So, in general, a party is obliged to produce a document, which he or she has relied on – this will normally be a document which supports his or her case. But, there is no general obligation to disclose the documents, which are in a possession of a party, and which could adversely affect his or her own case or which would support the opponent party's case. There are only few exceptions, when a party might be obliged to produce a document in his or her possession and it was not that party who invoked it. A party can request the owner of a document to produce the document, where the requesting party has a statutory right (or – since the 2017 amendment of the CPA – a contractual right) to receive or see the document (e.g., a share-holder with respect to some documents of the company) or when the document is, due to its contents, regarded as mutual for both parties (e.g., a contract between these parties). If the party, in the above-mentioned cases (thus, not in cases which fall outside of that scope) refuses to adduce the documents in its possessions, the court must regard the assertion made by the other party in connection with the content of such documents, as well as the facts to be supported by the documents, as well-founded. The court's order that the opposing party must produce the documents is, however, not enforceable.[352] The court thus cannot compel the party to produce evidence; even in a case where the opposite party has a legal right (by statute or by contract) to achieve the document. There only remains a possibility for a separate action with a (main) claim for the handing over of the document in question (*actio ad exhibendum*).

369. Third parties may be ordered to submit documents. They may refuse to produce a requested document only in cases where they would also be entitled to refuse to testify on the same issue (e.g., protection of professional secrets, limited protection of business secrets, fear of criminal prosecution against the witness or its close relative, ...).[353] Unlike the order directed to the other party, the order for the production of documents directed to a third person is directly enforceable (Article 228). If a document (relied upon by a party) is in possession of a public body, the court may demand its production ex officio (Article 226/3, CPA).

370. The described system hence enables for merely a limited scope of disclosure of documents. The first key difference between this system and the common

351. S. Triva, V.Belajec &M.Dika, *Gradjansko parnično proçesno pravo*, 1986, p. 425.
352. L. Ude, *Civilno procesno parvo* [*Civil Procedure*] 267(ČZ UL 2002).
353. Before the 2017 reform, persons other than the parties may be ordered to submit documents only if such an obligation is imposed on them by substantive law or if concerning the contents of a document to be submitted it was created both for this person and the party adducing it as evidence. There was no right to production if the request is based solely on the document's relevance for the pending case, no matter whether the person possessing it had any legitimate interest to withhold it.

law concept of disclosure is that in Slovenia a party has no duty to disclose unfavourable documents in its possession on its own motion. Although the law establishes the obligation of truth for the parties (Article 9 CPA), this is merely a programmatic proclamation without any sanctions and adverse consequences for cases of non-compliance. The second major difference is that in Slovenia the party seeking disclosure must sufficiently identify the document he or she is requesting. A request for production of a document can only be successful if the party is able to describe the content of the requested document in sufficient detail so as to clearly identify it. The regulation is hence merely proper to avoid the concealing of the documents, the existence of which is already known, but not the documents, for which the seeking party does not know to a quite concrete degree what their contents are or that the other party even possesses them. This system does not facilitate any kind of discovery of new information[354] and purely exploratory evidence is not admissible.[355] The duty of the opponent to produce documents only applies if the requesting party has submitted his substantiated pleadings and explained his case in detail beforehand. It should also be noted that in line with the continental tradition (and in contrast to the US style of notice pleading) the principle of fact pleading applies in Slovenian civil procedure. This means that the party must plead detailed facts and offer exactly specified means of evidence already in the statement of claim. According to the continental procedural tradition of fact pleading the judge will only order the taking of evidence on individual facts that have been asserted by the party.

371. Parties often try to avoid this limitation by requesting 'the entire correspondence' or 'all documents relating to certain transaction' to be disclosed, but courts are usually quite restrictive in this regard.[356] In addition it should be noted that the party cannot demand the opponent to disclose evidence, only the court is (upon the party's motion) authorized to do so. Consequently, documents are handed to the court, not to the requesting party (who however will receive copies of or – in case of voluptuous documentation – is entitled to inspect the documents in the court's file). More importantly, the court's order for disclosure of documents cannot be rendered already at the preparatory stage of civil litigation, but only after the commencement of the main hearing; the disclosure mechanisms are designed to be used after the commencement of the main hearing. Consequently, they can hardly contribute to a better preparation of a trial and even less so to stimulate settlements at an early stage of proceedings. It has been already mentioned that since the CPA 2008 amendment the judge has the powers to order documents to be produced already before the main hearing. But this – at least according to the wording of the

354. Judgment of the Supreme Court No. II Ips 544/2002, 11 Sep. 2003.
355. *See,* e.g. judgment of the Supreme Court No. II Ips 560/2006
356. *See,* e.g. judgment of the Ljubljana Court of Appeals No. I Cpg 1205/2001: ' … .the law refers to specific, individualized documents, invoked by the party, and not to any documents relating to the case or even some undefined and undefinable "documentation"'.

law –merely relates to the documents in possession of the party who in his pleadings (the claim, the defence plea) adduced (but still not produced) them. Unfortunately there is no explicit provision authorizing the court in the preliminary stage of proceedings to order the party to produce documents in her possession which the other party has adduced as evidence.

372. The present situation in Slovenia, where – and even this to a very limited extent – the court's order for disclosure of evidence can only be made at the trial, is unsatisfactory. Such a system does not enable an effective preparation and a focused trial. Moreover, the goal substantive aspect of adjudication. The lack of obligation to disclose presupposes that both parties have equal opportunity to access to evidence, however there are frequent disputes in which just one party possesses important information and evidence. The number of complex litigations, which cannot be effectively pursued without broad access to information, not already in a possession of the aggrieved party, is increasing. The same goes for the number of cases where the economically stronger party (large companies, public entities) has in its possession relevant documents and information, whereas the weaker party (consumer, aggrieved individual) does not. In addition, enabling parties to realistically assess the strength or weakness of their positions at early stages of proceedings would also be a powerful device for promoting settlements. It has been acknowledged in Slovenia as well, though in a different context, that if a party cannot know before the main hearing what arguments and evidence are 'in the hands' of his opponents, he cannot realistically assess its prospects of success. In such a case, settlement negotiations during the early stages of litigation can hardly be effective.

§3. Witnesses

373. Only those persons who are able of giving data relevant as to facts to be established may be examined as witnesses (capacity to be a witness). There is no statutory limit as to the minimal age of a child who can be called as a witness, but the court should be satisfied that the child understands the duty to speak the truth.[357]

374. If, by giving a testimony, a person might violate his or her duty to keep an official or military secret, he or she may not be examined as a witness unless the competent authority releases him or her from such duty (Article 230, CPA). A witness may refuse testimony on what the party has confessed to him or her as their attorney; on what the party or other person has confessed to him or her as their confessor; on the facts of which he or she has learnt as a lawyer or a doctor or in pursuance of other activity (e.g., a mediator or a social worker), if he or she is bound to protect the secrecy of what he or she learns in the practice of such activity.[358] The stated persons must be instructed by the presiding judge on their right to refuse testimony. However, the right to refuse testimony is not absolute. The principle of

357. *Ibid.*, p. 434.
358. *Ibid.*, p. 444.

proportionality applies: a witness may not refuse to testify on the grounds of protection of a professional secret if the disclosure of certain facts is to the benefit of the public or some other person, provided that such benefit outweighs the damage caused by disclosure of the secret (Article 232, CPA). Therefore, it is the judge who ultimately decides whether the witness may refuse to give a testimony.[359]

375. Unlike in criminal procedure, there is no general relief from the obligation to testify for close family members in a civil case. As a matter of principle, they are obliged to testify. But a witness may refuse to answer a particular question for justified reasons, especially if, by answering, the witness or members of his or her close family might be exposed to a serious disgrace, considerable financial loss or criminal proceedings (Article 233, CPA). On the ground of the prevention of financial loss, a witness may not refuse to testify on legal transactions which he or she has attended as an appointed witness; on acts concerning the matter in dispute which he or she has performed as a legal predecessor or representative of any of the parties; on facts relating to property relations in respect of a family community, a matrimony other form of extramarital community; on facts relating to birth, conclusion of marriage and death.

376. Since the CPA amendment of 2008, there is (however still limited) a possibility to gather depositions and affidavits from witnesses in Slovenian civil procedure.[360] In general, attorneys are discouraged from contacting potential witnesses, and a preparation of witnesses is regarded as a breach of rules of professional conduct. However, a practice of affidavits has developed, and it is used in arbitration proceedings in Slovenia, and it has proved to be effective. It enables the arbitral tribunal to find out whether the proposed witness can testify on anything relevant at all. Besides, if the other party does not contest the statements of the witness, the examination before the tribunal becomes superfluous.[361] Since the CPA amendment of 2008, the parties may present signed statements of witnesses and also a court may request a proposed witness to give a written statement (Article 236a, CPA). Due to the principle of orality and immediacy, and also to safeguard the parties right to be heard (which a right to pose questions to witnesses is a part of),[362] a witness must nevertheless be summoned if a party requests so, even if he or she has made a written deposition beforehand.

359. *Ibid.*, p. 448.
360. N. Betetto, *Predvidene novosti v ZPP glede dokaznega postopka*[*The Foreseen Novelties in CPA Concerning Evidence*], 33 Podjetje in delo, 1073 (2007).
361. There is, however, another reason, of a rather practical nature, why there are often problems with examination of witnesses in Slovenian courts. The everyday practice in Slovenian courts clearly shows that it is one of the most important reasons for adjournments of a hearing that a certain witness, although properly served, did not appear before the court (besides also quite frequent cases, when it is established that the subpoena has not been served to the witness). This might be a question of harshness of possible sanctions for non-appearance, but it is also an expression of the general legal culture and the respect of judiciary. The latter needs time to improve. Also for this reason of frequent problems with non-appearance of witnesses, it was considered to be plausible to introduce a system of depositions and affidavits.
362. Decision of the Const. Court, No. Up 39/95, 16 Jan. 1997.

377. Whoever is summoned as a witness must comply with the summons, and must testify, unless the statute determines otherwise (Article 229/1, CPA). The CPA no longer recognizes witnesses' oaths. Perjury is a criminal offence (Article 289, Criminal Code). The witness evidence is taken at the trial before the trial judge. It is the judge who conducts the questioning, but the parties (their attorneys) may subsequently also pose questions. Leading questions must be refrained from (Article 239, CPA). New technologies e.g., video links, can be used since the CPA amendment of 2008, provided that the court is adequately equipped (Article 114a, CPA). It is still not possible (except in small claims cases) to take oral evidence (witness testimony) by telephone. In exceptional circumstances the trial judge may examine the witness at another location (e.g., in a hospital, if a witness is not able to attend a hearing). In such case, a witness may also be heard by a judge of a requested court (Article 217, CPA). In any case, the parties must be informed of the date and place of examination and have a right to be present and pose questions. If a properly summoned witness unjustifiably fails to attend, the court may order him or her to be brought by force (with the assistance of the police), at their expense, and may also impose a fine. The court may also impose such fine on a witness who attends but then, after having been warned of the consequences, declines to testify or to answer specific questions for reasons that the court deems to be unjustified. The court may, if the witness is still unwilling to testify, imprison the witness for up to one month (Article 241, CPA).

§4. Expert Evidence

378. The court must appoint an expert when special scientific knowledge, which the judge does not possess, is required for the purposes of determination or clarification of a certain fact in dispute (Article 234, CPA). Experts are designated by the judges and selected from the list of authorized experts (for different fields of technical knowledge), not by the parties. However, prior to the appointment of an expert, the court must give the parties the opportunity to be heard thereon. Except in complex situations when two or more experts may be appointed to the case, expert examination must be carried out by a single expert. Thus, the principle is that a court will appoint one expert, but such must fully comply with the demands of independence and impartiality. The expert is considered to be an assistant for the court.[363] Therefore, the grounds for disqualification of judges are applied also with regard to the experts (Article 247, CPA).

379. A private expert report commissioned by one of the parties cannot be admitted as expert evidence unless the consent of both parties is given.[364] Otherwise, such report can still be submitted to the court, but it does not have the value and significance of expert evidence. Neither does it have the force of documentary evidence; it is merely considered to form a part of a party's own allegations. A party,

---

363. 2 L. Ude et al. *Pravdni postopek – zakon s komentarjem* [*Civil Procedure: Act with the Commentary*]481(GV Založba in ČZ UL 2005).
364. Judgment of the Supreme Court, II Ips 748/2005, 15 Feb. 2007.

even if ultimately successful in the case, is as a matter of principle not entitled to costs concerning the work of a private expert. A notable exception exists if the court finds that it was absolutely necessary for the claimant to rely on the private expert before the commencement of the litigation in order to establish the damage and to be able to choose a right remedy. In such case, the courts can order the losing party to repay the costs of a private expert, commissioned by the claimant before the litigation.[365]Nevertheless, since the 2017 amendment of the CPA, a person who intends to bring proceedings, may already before filing the claim request the court to appoint a pre-action court-appointed expert and determine its terms of reference (Article 268.a CPA). This is possible in cases where expert knowledge is essential already in order to make an informed decision as to whether to bring proceedings and how to formulate a specific prayer for relief. The other party (the prospective defendant), has a right to participate in the process of selecting the expert and determining his or her terms of reference, as well as in commenting on the expert report.

380. Only a natural person can be appointed as an expert. The task may also be entrusted to a specialized institution like a scientific institute or a hospital (Article 245, CPA). But this does not mean that such an institution as a whole shall be an expert. It only means that in such case the decision, which natural person shall be designated as an expert, is left to the internal organization of the institution.[366] The court must give precise instructions as to the object of the expert's work. In any case, the object of the expert's work must be the existence of the facts, already asserted by the parties. It is not possible to appoint an expert with the goal, that the party shall on this basis obtain information, necessary for future assertions in the case or for correct formulation of the prayer for relief.[367] The task of the expert witness is to state their findings (visum repertum) and opinion (parere).[368] Expert witnesses must give their evidence in written reports unless the court orders otherwise. Parties have the right to comment on both and may pose questions.[369] The court decides whether the expert must attend the trial to give oral explanations and answer the parties' questions. If fundamental differences emerge between the information given by the expert witnesses or if the findings of one or more expert witness are unclear, incomplete or self-contradictory and such anomalies are not rectified by a fresh hearing of the expert witness, the court may order that the evidence must be taken again from the same or other expert (Article 254, CPA).

381. A party is not obliged to submit to a blood test or to a medical examination by an expert and cannot be forced to give certain body-samples. However, if the party fails to consent to such measure, the court will normally drive conclusions as

365. Judgment of the Supreme Court, Pž 1040/73, 25 Oct. 1973, Judgment of the Celje Court of Appeals, Cp 613/99, 21 Oct. 1999.
366. 2 L. Ude et al.*Pravdni postopek – zakon s komentarjem*[*Civil Procedure: Act with the Commentary*]482(GV Založba in ČZ UL 2006).
367. Judgment of the Supreme Court, III Ips 12/2004, 15 Feb. 2005.
368. 2 L. Ude et al. *Pravdni postopek – zakon s komentarjem*[*Civil Procedure: Act with the Commentary*]483(GV Založba in ČZ UL 2006).
369. Judgment of the Supreme Court, II Ips 342/2000, 7 Feb. 2001.

to the existence of the disputed facts, unfavourable to the party who failed to submit to the taking of evidence (also in a paternity suit, where the alleged father refused the DNA test[370]). This approach is logical for a regular civil case, where party autonomy should clearly prevail. However, it is doubtful whether it is acceptable with regard to paternity suits, which should, in the best interest of the child, strive to uncover the truth about an important aspect of their personal identity. It should be noted that the ECourHR has already found (in a case concerning the substantially identical regulation in Croatian law) that a lack of appropriate measures to comply with the court order for DNA tests to be carried out may (if there are also no alternative measures of proof) result in the violation of Article 8 of the ECHR.[371]

382. Quite often, technical knowledge or knowledge of general experience or knowledge of a usage or habit is necessary in order to achieve a correct interpretation of a legal norm. If for example, a legal norm defines that a doctor is liable if he or she acted in a breach of professional care, a judge must first know what the standard of 'professional care' means. In such case, a judge will often need to rely on evidence (witnesses, expert opinion), because only on that basis shall the judge be able to determine the right content of the legal norm. It is not possible to decide whether the doctor breached the standards of professional care, if it is not beforehand known what that standard means (with regard to, say, certain medical treatment). In such case, the expert does not assist the judge at the determining of how the doctor acted in the given case, but 'how the doctor should have acted'.[372]

§5. Parties' Testimony; But No Interrogatories

383. To establish the disputed facts, which are of importance for the determination of the dispute, the court may also examine (interrogate) the parties (Articles 257–264). The parties' statements can only serve as a piece of evidence, if they are given in the course of the parties' interrogation. The parties' statements in, for example, the claim and defence plea, and the preparatory written submissions or at the court hearing, but not in the course of the parties' interrogation, do not serve as evidence. However, the parties' interrogation serves only to the purpose of evidence, thus to establish the existence of the facts, previously asserted. The interrogation of parties does not serve the purpose to assert new facts.[373] If the evidence of the examination of parties is taken, the court should, in principle, examine both parties. The examination of the parties to a certain, though very limited, degree serves as a substitute for interrogatories, which are unknown in Slovenian law. A party cannot demand the opponent to answer certain questions or give explanations, but can achieve that both parties will have to stand as witnesses in litigation. Again,

370. Judgment of the Supreme Court, II Ips 127/2004, 22 Apr. 2004.

371. Judgment of the EcourHR, *Mikulićv. Croatia*, application No. 53176/99, 7 Feb. 2002.

372. 2 L. Ude et al.*Pravdni postopek – zakon s komentarjem* [*Civil Procedure: Act with the Commentary*]82(GV Založba in ČZ UL 2005).

373. Decision of the Const. Court, Up 1/96, 15 Jan. 1997.

this can only be achieved at the main hearing, and it cannot serve as a tool for the preparation for a main hearing. Besides (and this seems to be the most crucial difference with regard to interrogatories or depositions), it is aimed towards the establishing of truth from the facts, that have already been asserted, but not for the getting of information upon the facts, which the opponent has not yet asserted.

§6. Inspection (View) of Objects

384. This is direct physical inspection of the evidence by the judge. This is also understood to include touching, smelling, listening and tasting. Consequently, sound and video recordings and computer records can also be inspected (although the case law is still unsettled with regard to the question whether, for example, data saved on micro-films or computer disks should be regarded as a document or an object).[374] If the inspection concerns an object that cannot be viewed in court, the object is inspected in *locus in quo*, whereby the judge may order the tape recording of the whole course of inspection or a part thereof. The tape recording shall be enclosed to the record on view (Article 223, CPA). When specific technical knowledge is required in order to drive conclusions from the object, it is often difficult to drive distinction between the evidence of inspection and expert evidence (e.g., inspection of the blood sample).[375]

374. 2 L. Ude et al.*Pravdni po̧stopek – zakon s komentarjem*[*Civil Procedure: Act with the Commentary*]409 (GV Založba in ČZ UL 2006).
375. *Ibid*., p. 413.

Part VIII. Particular Proceedings

Chapter 1. Payment Order

385. A payment order (*plačilni nalog*) is a device for a debt collection, which is based on a practical experience that a vast number of claims remain uncontested in courts. On application of the creditor, the court orders the debtor ex parte to either dispute the claim or pay the sum of money fixed in the order.

386. A payment order may be granted only in case of pecuniary claims that are due and supported by an authentic document (the original or a certified copy); Article 431, CPA. Authentic documents include, but are not limited to, public documents; private documents on which the signature of the debtor has been authenticated by a body authorized for authentication; bills of exchange or cheques, with the protest and certificate of payment when the latter are required for the origination of the claim; certified statements of outstanding debts and invoices (faktura). Precisely the latter are practically the most important basis for granting payment orders. But, it must be taken into account that only a legal entity or a professional may issue a faktura and only with regard to a contractual obligation, and thus avail himself to the payment order procedure.[376] A physical person cannot issue a faktura concerning contractual obligations which fall outside his or her professional activity. Only if the claim does not exceed EUR 2,000, the court can issue a payment order even though the claim is not supported by an 'authentic document', however a basis and a amount of debt as well as evidence, which could prove the claimant's allegations (Article 432, CPA), are provided.

387. The court (a court's clerk) issues a payment order ex officio even if the plaintiff has brought an ordinary claim (action) and has not applied to this effect, provided that the conditions exists for the issuance thereof. There is no computerized payment order procedure and no standard forms are used. If the case does not fulfil criteria for issuing of a payment order, the case is considered as an ordinary claim and is dealt with in an ordinary litigation. No appeal is allowed against the decree dismissing the application for issuance of a payment order. If a payment

376. For example, Decision of the Ljubljana Court of Appeals, III Cpg 83/2003, 8 Jan. 2004. In the case law, it has previously been accepted that only an invoice, referring to a domestic currency can form a basis for a payment order. But the position is now reversed and the fact that the invoice refers to a foreign currency does not present an obstacle for issuing a payment order. Decision of the Supreme Court, II Ips 582/97, 4 Jun. 1998.

order is issued it contains a request that a debtor should pay the amount due within eight days or file a statement of opposition instead. The defendant shall be served the payment order together with a copy of the action. The payment order is enforceable and is a *res iudicata*, if the defendant fails to contest the claim within eight days from the day of service of the payment order (in disputes involving bills of exchange or cheques such term of payment is three days); Article 433, CPA. If a statement of opposition is filed in time, the case is automatically transferred to ordinary civil procedure (Article 435, CPA). The parties may state new facts and adduce new evidence at the first hearing session, The court shall then, after a contradictory litigation, decide whether the payment order shall remain in force or whether it shall be set aside and the claim dismissed. If the case is transferred to an ordinary civil procedure, the majority opinion is that the claimant may then amend the claim and the defendant may file a counter-claim or a set-off plea, just as if the case has been decided under general rules of civil procedure from the start.[377]

388. One legislative measure which was adopted on the level of EU and which is directly applicable in Slovenia, should be mentioned in this regard: the Regulation Number 1896/2006 of 12 December 2006 creating a European order for payment procedure. The Regulation is applicable in cross-border cases (when at least one of the parties in domiciled or habitually resident in an EU Member State other than the Member State of the court seized). The procedure established by the Regulation should serve as an additional and optional means for the claimant, who remains free to resort to a procedure provided for by national law (in Slovenia the above-described procedure for payment order as regulated by the CPA). There are certain differences between the system of the mentioned Regulation and the Slovenian CPA. For example, for a European enforcement order to be issued, the claimant does not need to possess an authentic instrument but only needs to state sufficient grounds and include a description of evidence supporting the claim and thereby establish a prima facie case. Besides, the Regulation strongly relies on the use of standard forms.

377. L. Ude, *Civilno procesno parvo* [*Civil Procedure*] 380(ČZ UL 2002).

Chapter 2. Procedure in Family Law Cases

§1. Jurisdiction and Common Characteristics of Procedure

389. The CPA contains special provisions (Chapter 27) regarding the procedure in matrimonial disputes and disputes concerning relations between parents and children. These provisions apply for family law litigation (such as the divorce procedure and the regulation of parental rights, including access rights, when these issues are decided in the framework of divorce litigation – see below). Certain family law matters that are decided in a non-contentious procedure (i.e., a withdrawal of parental right, a prolongation of parental rights over the age of maturity, a decision concerning the exercising of parental responsibilities, decision on custody and visitation rights, when parents do not live together and cannot agree on these issues) and in such cases the Non-Contentious Procedure Act (*Zakon o nepravdnem postopku*[378]) applies (in addition to rules of the CPA). A separate chapter on the enforcement of judgments concerning custody and judgments regarding rights of access is contained in the EJPMA. Important reforms of procedural aspects of family law have been implemented in 1999 and 2004 in Slovenia, foremost concerning the improvement of the procedural position of the child and the extension of the jurisdiction of the courts in family law matters (thus nearly abolishing cases where family law matters are decided in administrative procedure).[379]

390. Subject matter jurisdiction for family law cases is vested with district courts. There are no specialized family courts in Slovenia. However, there are specialized panels at district (and higher) courts, composed by judges who are being continuously educated in the field of family law. At the largest district court in Slovenia (Ljubljana District Court), there is also a special division for family law matters.

391. The principle of free disposition is restricted. A judgment by default cannot be rendered either in disputes concerning dissolution of a marriage or in disputes concerning parental responsibility or paternity and maternity suits. It is not possible to acknowledge or abandon the claim (Article 412/1, CPA). A court-settlement concerning custody and maintenance of a child is possible, but only if the court is satisfied that it is in the best interest of the child (Article 412/2, CPA). In cases concerning maintenance of under-age children, the court is not bound by the limits of the amount sought (see above). The inquisitorial principle prevails. In order to protect the best interest of the child, the court may find facts and take evidence, which neither of parents have asserted or invoked. As a principle, the court is bound by virtue of office to perform all such acts as are necessary for the protection of

378. Official Gazette RS, No. 30/86.

379. *See* K. Zupančič, *Reforma družinskega prava*[*The Reform of Family Law*], 31 Podjetje in delo, 1453–1465 (2005);V. Rijavec, *Nepravdni postopek v družinskih zadevah*[*Non-Contentious Procedure in Family Law Matters*], 31 Podjetje in delo, 1492–1512 (2005), M. Končina–Peternel, *Ukrepi za varstvo koristi otrok*[*Measures for the Protection of Children*], 31 Podjetje in delo, 1482–1491 (2005).

rights and interests of children and other persons who are not capable to protect their rights and interests by themselves (Article 408, CPA). However, in a dispute concerning maintenance between spouses, decided upon in the course of divorce proceedings, adversarial principle and principle of free disposition applies.[380] In all family law cases, rules concerning preclusion of new facts and evidence (Article 285, CPA – see above, paragraph 232) do not apply in proceedings in matrimonial actions and in actions concerning the relations between parents and children. In these proceedings, the parties may present new facts and adduce new evidence until the end of the main hearing and also in the appeal (Article 414, CPA). The prevalence of the inquisitorial principle is an expression of the safeguarding of the best interest of the child and a logical consequence of certain restrictions concerning party autonomy in substantive family law. However, it is also a consequence of the fact, as it is generally accepted, that judgments concerning personal status have an *erga omnes* effect.[381]

392. The public is excluded from the proceedings in family law matters (Article 407, CPA). The determination of costs of proceedings shall be left to the discretion of the court (Article 13, CPA).

§2. Matrimonial Disputes

393. Slovenian law does not provide for an action for the declaration of either the existence or non-existence or nullity of a marriage. Only an action for divorce and an action for the annulment of the marriage are possible. The legal impediments for marriage (e.g., bigamy, relationship, mental illness of a spouse, defective intent; Article 32 of the Marriage and Family Relations Act, *Zakon o zakonski zvezi in družinskih razmerjih*, hereinafter: MFRA) do not cause nullity of marriage but only its voidability (for which an action according to Article 36 MFRA is required). In certain cases (i.e., bigamy), an action can also be filed by the state prosecutor (against both of the spouses), and in certain exceptional cases, relatives can also file the action (i.e., marriage of an under-age child). In these cases, the action must be filed against both spouses (compulsory joinder of parties).

394. The only grounds for divorce on the basis of an action is the 'unsustainability' of the marriage; Slovenian law does not provide for grounds for divorce. A divorce can only occur on the basis of an action of one of the spouses or on the basis of a motion for the dissolution of a marriage by agreement of spouses. In both cases, a court shall decide according to the rules of contentious procedure. Before the trial, a court refers parties to the Centre for social work (*Center za socialno delo*) to conduct a marriage counselling (except in certain circumstances, for example if the spouses have no common children); Article 416 MFRA, but in practice this is just a formality.[382] In case of a divorce upon agreement, the spouses must submit to the

---

380. Judgment of the Supreme Court, II Ips 226/2006, 18 May 2006.

381. L. Ude, *Civilno procesno parvo* [Civil Procedure] 317(ČZ UL 2002).

382. Some courts, though, have started a pilot-programme of court-annexed mediation also in family law

court an agreement on the division of the community property and on the eventual maintenance of a spouse. They must also submit an agreement on the custody and maintenance of common children, whereby the court reviews whether such agreement is in the best interests of the child. For this purpose the court obtains an opinion from the Centre for social work and must also hear the child (Article 64 MFRA).

395. A final judgment whereby a marriage is dissolved or annulled may not be set aside or modified on the basis of a motion to reopen the proceedings, irrespective of whether any of the parties has made a new marriage subsequently (Article 420, CPA).

396. Besides the marriage, Slovenian law also regulates the extramarital union. The extramarital union does not commence by a formal act, and the same applies to its termination. It is not possible to bring a declaratory action of establishment of the existence, non-existence or termination of an extramarital union. Such issues can only be decided on as preliminary questions in proceedings, when the decision on the main subject depends on them; the question of (non)existence of an extramarital union can never be the main question in any procedure.[383]

397. A question of maintenance between ex-spouses may also be decided in the judgment, which the marriage is dissolved by. However, the court shall not decide upon maintenance between spouses ex officio, but only upon a claim of a spouse (Article 421, CPA). Thus, the issue of maintenance between spouses is considered to be a family law matter. However, disputes concerning joint property and other aspects of economic matrimonial regime are decided in a regular civil litigation.

398. By means of an interim injunction, issued in a course of a divorce proceedings, a court can (when children are involved) temporarily regulate the right of access and custody (as well as maintenance), issue a restraining order to a spouse as well as order the removal of a spouse from a common dwelling, if this is required to prevent violence; furthermore, the court can freeze the assets or issue a restraint order (e.g., to parents regarding certain property of the child), order a deprivation of the passport or another travel document of the child (to prevent a threatening abduction).[384]

§3. Cases Concerning Relations Between Parents and Children

399. In case a court dissolves a marriage, it must also (ex officio) rule on the custody over (under-age) children as well as on the maintenance and rights of access.

---

disputes, concerning both a divorce as well as the parental responsibility. *See,* e.g., M. Končina Peternel, *Družinska mediacija (de lege lata in) de lege ferenda*[*Family Mediation (de lege lata and) de dege ferenda*], 33 Podjetje in delo, 1303 et seq (2007).

383. *See,* e.g., D. Wedam Lukić&A. Polajnar Pavčnik, *Zakon o nepravdnem postopku s komentarjem*[*Non-Contentious Procedure Act with commentary*]47(ČZ UL 1991).

384. *See* M. Končina Peternel, Končina–Peternel, *Ukrepi za varstvo koristi otrok*[*Measures for the Protection of Children*], 31 Podjetje in delo, 1490 (2005).

The court must render such decision also in case no specific claim has been raised to this effect, while even if such claim has been raised, the court is not bound thereby. Regarding the types of custody, Slovenian law provides for custody of one parent, custody of a third person (natural person or a legal entity), and since the amendment in 2004, joint custody of both parents is not only possible but preferred.

400. The decision of the court about custody (and rights to access) can be altered upon a new action, filed by one of the parents or by a Centre for social work, if the circumstances of the case have subsequently changed (Article 421/4, CPA).

401. Besides in the divorce proceedings, custody and exercise of the right of access (visitation rights) can also be decided upon in all other cases, when the parents (regardless whether they are married or not) do not live together (Articles 105 and 106 MFRA). If they cannot reach an agreement, the court decides in non-contentious civil procedure. The parents can file a petition to the court for adjudication also in case they have agreed on the exercise of the right of access. A court also decides in a non-contentious procedure in case when the parents cannot agree on the exercise of parental right (also in case when they live together) – Article 113 of the MFRA. Apart from the case when the aforementioned issues are decided upon in divorce proceedings, it is a procedural prerequisite for the admissibility of action that the parents have beforehand attempted a mediation with the aid of the Centre for social work.

402. An action for determination of fatherhood is brought by the child, represented by her mother. An action which challenges the fatherhood may be brought either by the child or by the mother or by the presumed father (the mother's husband or the man who acknowledged to be the father of the child before a Centre for Social Work) or by a man, who claims to be a real father of the child. There is an obligatory joinder of parties on the side of the defendant (e.g., if an action is brought by the presumed father, both the child as well as the mother must be joined as co-defendants).[385]

403. In case a court establishes that the defendant is a parent of the child (the claimant), it may, depending on circumstances, also (ex officio) rule on the maintenance. The court impose the defendant the obligation of maintenance also if no specific claim has been raised to this effect, while even if such claim has been raised, the court is not bound thereby.

404. Analysis of DNA on the basis of obtained blood sample is considered to be such reliable evidence that makes other evidence superfluous.[386] The defendant, however, may not be forced to subdue himself to a blood test or to a taking of other body-samples (see also above, paragraph 375).[387]

385. 2 L. Ude et al.*Pravdni postopek – zakon s komentarjem*[*Civil Procedure – Act with the Commentary*], 259.
386. Judgment of the Supreme Court, II Ips 429/2006, 13 Jul. 2006.
387. Judgment of the Supreme Court, II Ips 127/2004, 22 Apr. 2004.

§4. PROCEDURAL POSITION OF THE CHILD

405. Recent reforms in procedural family law have emphasized on the improving of the position of a child in proceedings concerning parental responsibility. As a principle, a right of a child to be heard must be respected.[388]

406. In a matter concerning parental responsibility (including a divorce proceedings, as this obligatory results also in decision on custody and maintenance of a child, see above), a court must in an appropriate manner inform a child, who is capable of understanding the meaning of the proceedings and the consequences of the decision, of the introduction of the proceedings and of his right to state an opinion thereon. Considering the child's age and other circumstances, the child must be invited, through intermediary of the social services or a school social worker, to attend an informal interview with the judge (either in the court building or in another appropriate place). If the child has attained the age of 15, the participation of social worker in the interview of the judge with the child, may be considered to be superfluous.[389] In applying the provisions concerning the child's right to be heard, the court must act flexibly, depending on all circumstances of the case.[390] In any case, such interview may be attended by a person whom the child so designates. The judge makes a record on the discussion and, as the case may be, records the discussion on a tape. The law contains a very controversial provision, that for reasons of protection of interests of the child, the court may decide not to allow the child's parents to inspect the record or to listen to the tape recording. Since the purpose of the hearing of the child is to influence the decision of the court, but the parties to the proceedings (the parents) are not given an opportunity to acquaint themselves with these statements and reply to them, the parents' right to be heard in the proceedings is substantially encroached. It seems that this regulation (although with the purpose to ensure the best interest of the child) is going too far. Truly it is common also in other legal systems that the parents cannot be immediately present at the hearing of the child and cannot pose questions to the child; however, this is still a less severe infringement into their procedural position from the Slovenian regulation, which provides that the parents cannot gain access to the child's opinion even in writing and cannot submit their reply to this opinion to the court even later. As the European Court for Human Rights defines that a right to be heard (as guaranteed by the Article 6/1 of the ECHR) means that 'the parties to a trial must have the opportunity to have knowledge of and comment on all evidence adduced or observations filed'[391] it is highly questionable whether the presented regulation in the Slovenian law is in line with these requirements (and consequently whether a recognition and declaration of enforceability of a Slovenian judgment in another Member State could be denied on the grounds of the violation of Article 23(d) of the 2201/2003 Regulation.

---

388. *See,* e.g., Judgment of the Supreme Court, II Ips 56/2004, 22 Apr. 2004.
389. Judgment of the Supreme Court, II Ips 424/2004, 23 Jun. 2005.
390. Judgment of the Supreme Court, II Ips 943/2006, 1 Mar. 2007.
391. *See* such a definition in, for example, *Apeh v. Hungary*, Judgment from 5 Oct. 2000, No. 43465/96.

407. The child who has reached the age of 15 and has produced his opinion during the proceedings is served upon the decision, from which he or she may also take appeal.

408. The above-mentioned rules only enable a child, regardless of her age, to state her opinion. But the CPA makes one step further. A child who has attained the age of 15 and is capable of understanding the meaning and legal consequences of the acts he performs must be invited by the court to participate in a procedure as a party (Article 409, CPA).[392] In such a case, the statutory representative of the child may execute acts of procedure unless and until the child declares that he is taking over the litigation. Except in above-mentioned case, a child is represented by his statutory representative (i.e., parents). The court designates a special guardian to the child in the proceedings (*guardian ad litem*) in case the interests of the child and the parents as statutory representatives are in conflict.[393] According to the 2004 amendment of the CPA, the court designates a special *guardian ad litem* also in other cases when such is necessary to protect the best interest of the child. In principle, such regulation is appropriate. However, it can be established that in practice this provision is enforced only with difficulties. The institute of *guardian ad litem* is namely not institutionalized and the issues of expenses remain unsolved, and similarly there are no special services or a list of persons who are professionally trained to provide such service in the best interest of the child.

§5. Enforcement of Decisions Concerning Custody and Rights of Access

409. Special provisions regarding the execution of judgments regarding custody and the rights of access (visitation rights) are provided in Slovenian law only since the amendment of the EJPMA in 2002 (Article 238a–238g). The basic manner of the enforcement of judgments concerning custody is indirect coercion – the parent who is holding the child who was by the judicial decision entrusted into custody of another parent, is being coerced by manner of financial penalties to hand over the child. If such manner of execution is not successful, execution by direct coercion is possible – a bailiff physically takes the child and hands the child over to the person, who is entitled to custody on the basis of the judicial decision. The decision on execution is effective *erga omnes*– against any person, by whom the child is during the execution (e.g., the child's grandparents). If the judicial decision on custody itself contains an order that the child must be handed over to the entitled parent, such order is included into the enforcement order of the court. If the judicial decision on custody itself does not contain an order to hand the child over to the entitled parent, such order is included in the enforcement order by the court. Concerning the execution of judicial decisions regarding the rights of access, the primacy of execution by means of indirect coercion (financial penalties) is emphasized; regarding the

392. Judgment of the Supreme Court, II Ips 199/2005, 7 Jul. 2005.

393. On this issue *see*: B. Novak, *Posebni zastopnik otroka v postopku*[*A Special Representative of a Child in Proceedings*], 61 Zbornik znanstvenih razprav PF v. Ljubljani, 103–119 (2001).

issue of an execution of a decision on the right of access, direct coercion – an intervention by a bailiff who physically takes the child and ensures the exercise of the right of access in accordance with the judicial decision, is relevant only in exceptional cases.[394]

394. On this topic *see*: H. Jenull, A. Galič&M. Jan, *Zakon o izvršbi in zavarovanju s komentarjem*[*Enforcement of Judgments and Protective Measures Act with the Commentary*]417 et seq.(GV Založba 2002).

Chapter 3. Small Claims Procedure

410. A simplified civil procedure for small claims has been introduced in order to facilitate access to justice by achieving that costs and loss of time, incurred by litigation shall not be disproportionate to the value of the claim.[395] Rules of small claims procedure apply if the value of the claim does not exceed EUR 2,000 (concerning rules on the calculation of the value of the claim, see above, paragraph 142). Regardless of the value of the claim, small claim procedure does not apply for disputes relating to immovable property, disputes arising out of copyright, disputes relating to the protection and use of inventions and marks of distinctiveness or to the right to use a company title, disputes relating to the protection of competition, and disputes for disturbance of possession (Article 444, CPA). Subject matter jurisdiction for small claims procedure is vested with county courts.

411. In small claims procedure, a court may omit the oral hearing if it establishes that only law, but not the facts are in dispute. An oral hearing can also be omitted if the court opines that the disputed facts can be established on the basis of written evidence, but only if neither of the parties requested an oral hearing to take place. The court may not refuse such a request (Article 454, CPA). Nevertheless, even if an oral hearing takes place, parties are strictly prevented from asserting new facts and evidence in this phase of proceedings. Parties are allowed to state new facts and evidence only in claim and in the defence plea (Article 451, CPA). Parties may then file one further written submission each. In replica, the claimant may answer to the assertions in the defence plea, while in triplica the defendant may in answer to the assertions in the claimant's replica (Article 452, CPA).[396]

412. The court may restrict the means of evidence, and time available for taking it in order to assure compliance with objectives of simplicity and cost-effectiveness. At the taking of evidence, the judge may use her discretion in order to assure proportionality between procedural guarantees on one hand and effectiveness and acceleration of proceedings on the other hand (Article 450, CPA).

413. Sanctions for inactivity of parties are strict. If the defendant does not enter a defence plea, the court renders a judgment on the basis of acknowledgment. This is in contrast to the default judgment in a regular civil proceeding, which is rendered only if the court is satisfied that the claim is well-founded in substantive law, on the basis of facts as asserted in the claim. In regular civil proceedings, a defendant who is in default is only deemed to admit facts, asserted in the claim, but he or she is not deemed to acknowledge the claim. The sanction of losing the case with

---

395. N. Betetto, *Postopek v sporih majhne vrednosti*[*Small Claims Procedure*], 21 Pravna praksa, 15 (2002).

396. As the parties are obliged to state all facts and evidence already in their written submissions, the role of the active case management (*materielle Prozessleitung*) in the oral hearing) is practically frustrated. *See*: *Ibid.*, p. 17.

a *res iudicata* effect also applies if the party does not appear at the oral hearing, although it was him or her who explicitly requested the oral hearing to be conducted (Article 454, CPA).

414. Party must be warned in advance about procedural restrictions, which apply in the small claims procedure. Otherwise, these special rules may not apply.[397]

415. In small claims procedure, the judgment must be announced immediately after completion of the main hearing. A written judgment must subsequently also be produced, but its reasons (statement of ground) needs to consist only of a brief description of factual considerations and the indication of provisions of the substantive and procedural law which have been applied in determination of the case (Article 457, CPA).

416. An appeal is available against the judgment rendered in a small claims procedure (within the time limit of eight days); it is however restricted to violations of the substantive law and to the grave procedural errors (so-called absolute procedural violations). On the contrary, a judgment rendered in a small claims proceedings may not be appealed against on the ground of so-called relative procedural errors (those, where a possibility of a causal link between a procedural error and the substantive correctness of the judgment must be established) and erroneous and incomplete findings of facts cannot be invoked by an appeal. An independent appeal against procedural decrees of the First Instance Court is available only with regard to such decisions, which the proceedings are terminated with (i.e., the striking out of an action for a lack of procedural prerequisites) – Article 447/1, CPA. Other decrees appealable pursuant to the present Act may be challenged only by the appeal from decision by means of which the procedure is completed. Such decrees are not served upon the parties; instead, they are announced at the hearing and included in a written copy of the decision (Article 447/2, CPA). Appeals in small claims cases are decided upon by a single judge of the appellate court. He or she may however submit the case to the panel of three judges if the case concerns important legal questions, especially if there is still no settled case law concerning the legal issues in question (Article 458, CPA).

417. Under certain conditions, claimants in Slovenian court may avail themselves to the use of so-called European small claims procedure, pursuant to the Regulation No 861/2007 of the European Parliament and of the Council of 11 July 2007 establishing a European Small Claims Procedure. The objective of this Regulation is to simplify and speed up litigation concerning small claims and to reduce costs. The European Small Claims Procedure is available to litigants as an alternative to the procedures existing under the laws of the Member States (in Slovenia the above-described procedure in small claims cases as regulated by the CPA). Thus, the claimant may, in a cross-border dispute, choose whether she wants her case to be decided in 'European small claims' or in 'domestic (CPA) small claims' procedure. The Regulation can be applied only in cross-border cases (when at least one

397. *Ibid.*

of the parties in domiciled or habitually resident in a EU Member State other than the Member State of the court seized), provided that the case concerns a civil or commercial matter, where the value of a claim does not exceed EUR 2,000 (excluding all interest, expenses and disbursements). Proceedings are commenced with the use of standard form (Article 4) and are, in principle, written; oral hearing is foreseen only as an exception (Article 5). Evidence taking is simplified (Article 9) in order to reduce costs and speed up the litigation, but the adversarial principle must be respected. Concerning the costs, the principle that the losing party must reimburse the cost to the opponent, prevails; however, the court can refuse to award costs to the successful party to the extent that they were unnecessarily incurred (which is the same as in the Slovenian CPA) or are disproportionate to the claim (which is a condition that is not imposed by the Slovenian CPA).

Chapter 4. Procedure in Commercial Litigation

418. The CPA contains a separate chapter which contains norms, applicable only in commercial cases. These are however not extensive, and there are only few differences between ordinary civil procedure and procedure in commercial cases. Subject matter jurisdiction for commercial cases is vested with district courts. There are no specialized commercial courts in Slovenia, but there exist specialized divisions for commercial cases within larger district courts, as well as in the appellate courts and in the Supreme Court.

419. Commercial divisions of district courts adjudicate disputes between parties, both of whom are registered commercial companies. Furthermore, commercial litigation also exists in disputes with an institute, a cooperative, the state (the Republic of Slovenia) or a local community (Article 481, CPA). For a commercial litigation to exist, it is not necessary that the dispute between above-mentioned litigants results from pursuing commercial activity. Thus, if both parties come from above-mentioned categories, litigation between them shall be deemed commercial even if it concerns purpose which can be regarded as being outside their trade. Only with regard to physical persons, who are registered proprietors of a business (sole traders), the approach is different. Litigations between two sole traders or between a sole trader and a person from above-mentioned categories shall be commercial only if the dispute arises out from pursuing their commercial activity.

420. Certain types of disputes are always considered to be commercial cases, regardless of the status of parties. Such are disputes among partners, disputes between partners and commercial companies, disputes between commercial companies and members of their bodies of management, which must be decided on the pursuant to the Commercial Companies Act (Article 482, CPA), as well as maritime disputes (except the disputes on the transfer of passengers), disputes arising out of entries in the companies' register, disputes arising out of contracts on concession and disputes relating to patents, trade marks or the protection of competition, as well as disputes relating to bankruptcy. Commercial litigation also includes actions for annulment of an arbitration agreement, and actions for annulment of an arbitral award (provided that the arbitration concerned a dispute, which would be, if pursued in a court, be deemed a commercial litigation); Article 483, CPA. However, the rules on the proceedings in commercial litigation never apply to disputes on rights in rem in movable and immovable property and to disputes for disturbance of possession (Article 481/2, CPA).

421. Some of more important special rules, which apply in commercial litigation, are the following: an additional special territorial jurisdiction (venue) is vested with the court for the place where a contractual obligation, which the claim refers to, ought to be fulfilled (Article 484, CPA). In emergency cases, the court may fix the hearing immediately after the preliminary examination of action. In emergency cases, the court may fix the hearing by way of telephone or other means of telecommunications (Article 487, CPA). When after the receipt of the defence plea the court establishes that the state of facts is not disputed between the parties and that no other obstacles hinder the rendition of a decision, it may render the decision without having fixed a hearing (Article 488, CPA). If upon a mutual agreement the parties move for the hearing to be adjourned for an attempt of settlement, the court shall grant to such motion and inform the parties forthwith on the day and the hour of the new hearing session (Article 491, CPA). In the proceedings in small claims commercial litigation (which is the case, if the value of the claim does not exceed EUR 5,000; Article 495, CPA) the statement of ground for the judgment must contain only the indication of the claims and the facts upon which the latter are based, a legal warning on the right of appeal, and a note that, when reduced to writing, the judgment will contain the full statement of ground only if a party announces an appeal (Article 496, CPA). This is the only case in Slovenian civil procedure that the right of appeal is subject to a prior announcement of a party of her intention to file an appeal. Thereby, also a court fee for an appeal must be paid in advance. In commercial case, an extraordinary legal remedy of revision is per se admissible if the value of the claim of the contested judgment exceeds EUR 200,000.

Part IX. Seizure for Security and Enforcement of Judgments

Chapter 1. Seizure for Security

422. The provisional order (*začasna odredba*) as by far the most important protective measure in Slovenia has already been dealt with in detail in another context (see above, paragraph 289). Provisional order may aim to securing the future effective enforcement (e.g., freezing of a bank account or prohibition from disposing with immovable property) or to maintaining status quo (e.g., a prohibitory injunction). It cannot consist of an order for preliminary payment of the pecuniary debt with the only exception existing in the field of maintenance obligations. Although the creditor may request the provisional order to be given also after the termination of litigation, it is most common that provisional orders are requested and given already in the time the litigation is still pending (or even before the filing of the claim).

423. Further protective measures that serve to the purpose of seizure for security exist in Slovenian law. One is the preliminary order (*predhodna odredba*); Articles 256 et seq. of the EJPMA. This measure is available to the creditor, who has already obtained a favourable judgment of the First Instance Court, which however is still not final as an appeal against it has been filed or the time limit for the appeal has not expired yet. It must be noted that Slovenian law does not provide for provisional enforcement of first instance judgments. Only a judgment, which is already *res iudicata* is enforceable (meaning that a judgment of the First Instance Court is enforceable only if the time limit for the appeal has expired without an appeal having been lodged; otherwise only after judgment has been given on the appeal). However, a similar effect as can be achieved by provisional enforcement in legal systems that provide for this possibility can be achieved through the protective measure of preliminary order (*predhodna odredba*) in Slovenia. A creditor who is in possession of a favourable first instance judgment may request the court to, e.g., attach movable or immovable property or freeze the debtor's bank accounts (Article 260, EJPMA). The same as with regard to provisional orders, the applicant is required to specify the assets, aimed for seizure. Unlike the provisional order (see above) a preliminary order has effects in rem – it results in the creditor's obtaining a lien (a mortgage) and a priority right over other creditors. So, concerning the real estate, the creditor acquires a mortgage and such is entered into a land register, and thereby it produces effects (it can be enforced) against anyone who subsequently acquires the title to the land.

424. The motion for granting of preliminary order must be filed with the county court for the place, where also the enforcement in the same property should be sought (Article 257, EJPMA) and is decided upon in the same manner as the motion for the provisional order (see above, paragraph 289). The order is given in an ex parte proceeding, but the debtor may subsequently file an objection, which is again decided about by the county court. Then, an appeal to the Court of Appeals is possible.

425. A court can issue a preliminary order only to safeguard a pecuniary (but not non-monetary) claim and only if the creditor demonstrates, to the degree of probability, a *periculum in mora*, meaning that there is a risk that enforcement of the claim will be impossible or very difficult (Article 257, CPA). Unlike with regard to the risk as a necessary condition for granting of provisional order, the standard here is objective – it is not necessary for the risk to be caused by individual acts of the debtor.[398] For example, a critically bad financial standing of the debtor is already a sufficient grounds for a preliminary order to be issued.[399]

426. A preliminary order can also be rendered with regard to obligation for payment of future maintenance claims, which will be due within one year (Article 259, EJPMA).

427. Further possibility that enables a creditor to obtain security is to file a motion for the imposition of compulsory lien over movable (Article 246, EJPMA) or mortgage over immovable property of the debtor (Article 242, EJPMA). Only a creditor who is already in possession of *titre exécutoire* (thus: who already could move for an enforcement) can avail himself or herself to this measure. This might be plausible for a creditor, who is still negotiating with the debtor about modalities of fulfilment of the debt and who yet does not want to move for a forced execution, but nevertheless wishes to secure his or her position by obtaining priority over possible other creditors and by obtaining a lien or mortgage over the debtor's property and thus a right in rem.[400] The motion for imposition of compulsory mortgage over immovable asset is decided upon by the court that keeps the land register (Article 242, EJPMA), while the motion for imposition of compulsory lien over movable property is decided upon by the court in the place, where the property is situated (Article 246, EJPMA).

398. For example, Decision of the Koper Court of Appeals, Cpg 594/99, 2 Dec. 1999.
399. For example, Decision of the Koper Court of Appeals, VSK sklep II Cp 388/2004, 22 Feb. 2005.
400. V. Rijavec, *Civilno izvršilno parvo* [*Enforcement of Civil Judgments Law*]230 et seq.(GV Založba 2003).

Chapter 2. Enforcement of Judgments

§1. Enforcement of Domestic Judgments

I. Proceedings

428. The Slovenian EJPMA was adopted in 1998 and has already been amended several times. The adoption of the 1998 Act as well as all of its amendments pursued a declared goal to make an enforcement of civil judgments more effective and to put it in line with the principle that only with the ultimate accomplishment of enforcement, the right of access to court is effectively guaranteed.[401] In contrast, the old Yugoslav law was perceived to have emphasized too much on the protection of the debtor and that it left open too many possibilities for delaying tactics and thus frustrated the goal of an effective enforcement. However, in spite of all the reforms, the expectations were not fulfilled. The most critical situation regarding court backlogs and inefficiency of civil justice in Slovenia remains in the field of enforcement of civil judgments.[402]

429. In Slovenia, a court is involved in the enforcement proceedings from its commencement as it is necessary for the creditor to apply for a court order authorizing the enforcement. The creditor must file a motion for enforcement (Article 40, EJPMA) with the enforcement court (court, competent for enforcement proceedings), and this court shall issue an warrant of execution (*sklep o izvršbi*) by which it shall verify the title and order enforcement measures (Article 44, EJPMA). The warrant of execution is granted by a court's clerk in an ex parte proceedings, and the debtor is also not notified in advance that attachment will occur. In order to achieve a surprise-effect, the warrant of execution is served to the debtor only in the time of attachment (Article 45, EJPMA). The warrant of execution entails the creditor to proceed with physical measures of enforcement – with the methods of enforcement and to the extent, authorized in the warrant of execution. After the warrant of execution has been rendered, the enforcement proceedings remain in the domain of the enforcement court in certain types of enforcement (e.g., garnishment of debts, enforcement against real estate and enforcement of certain non-monetary claims such as injunction judgments). For certain other types of enforcement (enforcement into movable property and enforcement of certain non-monetary claims such as eviction of a tenant who does not have or no longer has a legal right of occupation), the responsibility for physical actions of enforcement is allotted to private enforcement agents (bailiffs). On bailiffs, see in detail above, paragraph 132.

430. The aforementioned warrant of execution should be distinguished from the so-called enforcement clause (*izvršilna klavzula*); the latter is obtained from the (clerk of the) court, which rendered a judgment and is a matter of purely formal

401. Decision of the Const. Court, U–I–181/99, 18 Dec. 2002.
402. *See*, e.g., H. Jenull, *Nova ravnovesja v izvršilnem postopku*[*New Balances in the Enforcement Proceedings*], 28 Podjetje in delo, 1586 (2002); I. Vovk, *Reforma izvršilnih postopkov*[*Reform of Enforcement Proceedings*], Pravna praksa, 21 (2006).

examination; it only confirms that the judgment is final and that the time limit for voluntary fulfilment has elapsed, but it does not refer to the authorization of particular enforcement measures (Article 42, EJPMA). The enforcement clause therefore does not substitute a warrant of execution.

431. Subject matter jurisdiction for enforcement proceedings is vested in county courts (Article 5, EJPMA). Concerning territorial jurisdiction (venue) different rules apply for different kinds of enforcement (and they all apply also for the determination of international jurisdiction). E.g., for enforcement in movable property, a court where this property is situated has jurisdiction. However the creditor is not obliged to define movable property, which should be attached or state where it is located; in such case, the court in the place of the debtor's domicile is competent (Article 78, EJPMA). In case of garnishment of debts or enforcement out of other intangible property, the court for the place where the debtor has his domicile, is competent. It is not necessary that the debtor's debtor (the garnishee) also has a domicile in Slovenia and in principle, if a debtor is domiciled in Slovenia, nothing prevents a Slovenian court to attach the debtor's bank accounts in a foreign bank (it will however be practically pointless in case the attachment shall not be recognized in the state of the bank). Besides, if the debtor is not domiciled in Slovenia, the court for the place of the seat or the domicile of the garnishee (e.g., a bank) is competent (Article 100, EJPMA). For enforcement into real estate, territorial jurisdiction lies with the court in whose territory the real estate is situated (Article 166, EJPMA).

432. Most important examples of enforceable titles (*izvršilni naslov, titre exécutoire*) are the following: a judgment or order rendered by a court, a court settlement, an arbitral award and a settlement, concluded in a course of arbitration proceedings and an enforceable notary deed (Article 17, EJPMA).

433. Only a final judgment (*res iudicata*) can be enforced. Slovenian law does not provide for provisional enforceability of non-final judgments (except in certain cases of non-contentious procedures). If an appeal is filed against the first instance judgment, the creditor cannot move for enforcement till the appellate court disposes of the appeal. Thus the defendant can delay the enforcement by filing an appeal and the only option for the creditor in such case is to avail her to protective measures (see above).

434. Another *titre exécutoire* in Slovenia is so-called authentic document (*verodostojna listina*). This should however not be confused with authentic instruments, referred to in certain EU regulations (e.g., Article 57 of the Regulation 44/2001 – the Brussels I Regulation). The latter are documents, which have been formally drawn up or registered as such (e.g., an enforceable notary deed) with the involvement of a public authority (with regard to the content, not just a signature) and thereby substitute a judgment.[403] However, an authentic document, as a *titre exécutoire* pursuant to the EJPMA, refers to certain types of documents, which can establish merely a probability of the existence of a claim. The notion of authentic

403. *'See Unibank' A.S. v. Fleming G Christensen*, Judgment of the ECJ, C–260/97, 17 Jul. 1999.

documents has already been described in the chapter on payment order (see above, paragraph 379) and in fact, the tool of enforcement on the basis of authentic instrument can be compared with the issuance of a payment order. Authentic instruments include, *inter alia*, also a simple invoice (*faktura*); Article 23, EJPMA. Precisely the latter is practically the most frequent ground that leads to authorizing enforcement on the basis of an authentic document. Therefore not only can the creditor, who is in a possession of an invoice, obtain a payment order (on the basis of which, an enforcement proceedings can then be initiated) but also he or she may directly move for an enforcement.[404] In such a case, a court shall issue an order, by which it will:

(1) order the debtor to pay the due amount; and
(2) authorize an enforcement in case neither the due amount is paid nor does the debtor file an objection (Article 44, EJPMA).

If the debtor files an objection, the case is transferred to ordinary civil procedure (the same as in case of an objection against a payment order); Article 61, EJPMA. If however the debtor does not file an objection, the enforcement proceedings may continue. The practical significance of the above-described system is big – experience shows that warrant of executions on the basis of authentic documents remain uncontested in the vast majority of cases. Practical significance even increased with the introduction of fully computerized system for filing of requests and issuing of warrant of executions on the basis of authentic instruments in January 2008. For this purpose, a special department within the Ljubljana County Court has been established, and it has jurisdiction to decide upon all requests for enforcement on the basis of authentic instruments (till the actions of physical enforcement commence).

435. Effectiveness of the enforcement proceedings depends, to a great extent, on the creditor's accessibility to information as to the debtor's assets.[405] Pursuant to Article 40 of the EJPMA a creditor, who is already in a possession of a final judgment or other equivalent *titre exécutoire* (but not merely an authentic document) can obtain access to official records concerning the identity of the debtor's employer (obtained through the social security authority), information about debtor's real estate (obtained through the court that keeps the land register), information about public limited companies, which the debtor is a partner in (obtained through the court who keeps companies' register), information about shares in corporations (obtained, through the authority (*klirinško depotna družba*) that keeps register of shares, listed at the Ljubljana Stock Exchange and (through an administrative authority) information about vehicles, registered to the name of the debtor (which however is not a conclusive proof of his ownership). In any case, the aforementioned information can be gathered without the debtor being aware of the attempt of enforcement. Furthermore, upon a presentation of aforementioned title, banks have a duty to disclose information as to the existence and number of transaction accounts of natural persons and as to whether the bank accounts have already been

404. V. Rijavec, *Civilno izvršilno parvo* [*Enforcement of Civil Judgments Law*]135(GV Založba 2003).
405. H. Jenull, *Nova ravnovesja v izvršilnem postopku*[*New Balances in the Enforcement Proceedings*], 28 Podjetje in delo, 1595 (2002).

attached by other creditors. Certain of the aforementioned information can also be obtained by a bailiff (and of course by the court; Article 4, EJPMA). However, information on account numbers of legal persons and on whether those accounts are frozen are already generally accessible to the public (thus, not only in connection with an imminent enforcement) via the register of transaction accounts on the Bank of Slovenia's website. It should however be noted that the creditor will in any case not be able to obtain information as to whether there are any assets on the bank account. Therefore, creditors usually request the garnishee orders to be served on all banks, where the debtor holds accounts, hoping that on at least some of them there will be sufficient assets to be attached.

436. Upon the creditor's request, the court can request from the debtor to deliver a list of all his assets (within jurisdiction and abroad) and dispositions with his property in the last year (inventory of the debtor's property). An interrogation at the court's hearing may also take place if it is demonstrated that attempts of enforcement have been or are likely to be unsuccessful. Pecuniary fines and imprisonment may be imposed if the debtor fails to deliver the aforementioned directory or if he gives false or incomplete statements as to his assets or if he does not appear at the aforementioned hearing although properly summoned (Article 31, EJPMA). There are no registers or publicly available information about the indebtment of certain debtors or about their previous inability or unwillingness to repay debts.

437. Creditors are satisfied strictly in accordance with the priority principle.[406] Priority is conferred through the seizure of movable or immovable property or with the garnishment of debt.

II. Judicial Review

438. As a general rule, objections and complaints do not have the effect of suspending the procedure (Article 9, EJPMA). However the attached property may not be sold until the warrant of execution has become irrevocable.

439. The debtor may file an objection against warrant of execution (Article 53, EJPMA). The same court (i.e., the county court that issued the warrant of execution) then re-examines the case, in the light of reasons, contained in the objection. If unaltered, the warrant of execution may then be appealed against (to the Court of Appeals). The latter applies also for the creditor if his motion for enforcement is dismissed. The debtor's objection to the court's authorization of enforcement must be sufficiently reasoned; otherwise, it is immediately dismissed. The enforcement court also has powers to decide on the objection although there are facts in dispute (Article 58, EJPMA). However, the enforcement court is not obliged to do so; if the case involves difficult questions of facts, it may simply dismiss the objection and the warrant of execution becomes irrevocable. The debtor may still file an action in

406. D. Wedam Lukić, *Civilno izvršilno parvo* [*Enforcement of Civil Judgments Law*] 15 et seq.(ČZ Uradni list 1992).

ordinary civil proceeding for declaration of inadmissibility of enforcement (Article 59, EJPMA). However, such an action does not automatically cause a suspension of the enforcement. This may continue and be accomplished. The attached property may be sold and the enforcement creditor repaid, unless the debtor succeeds with the motion for the suspension of the enforcement. But in order to succeed with such motion, the debtor will need to prove that imminent enforcement would cause an irreparable harm (Article 71, EJPMA).

440. Concerning grounds for the debtor's objection and for a separate action for declaration of inadmissibility of enforcement, it is clear that these may relate solely to the matter of enforcement and the main action in which a judgment (or another type of enforcement title) has already been delivered is not re-examined.[407] A ground for opposition to enforcement, frequently invoked by the debtor is that the debt is extinguished, e.g., due to the payment (Article 55/1, EJPMA). But such grounds can only be invoked, if they refer to payments, accomplished after the termination of the main hearing in civil proceedings, in which the judgment on merits of the dispute was rendered. This follows from inter-temporary boundaries of *res iudicata.*[408]

441. Among other grounds for opposition to enforcement are e.g., that the *titre executoire* no more exists (e.g., a judgment has been quashed upon an extraordinary legal remedy) or that the succession on the side of the claimant or the defendant is not proved or that the prescription period for the obligation, imposed by the judgment has already expired (pursuant to Article 356 of the Obligations Code the prescription time limit for an obligation, imposed by a final judgment is ten years).

442. As a principle, a bailiff cannot seize goods that are not the property of the debtor. However there is a presumption that goods in possession of the debtor are his or her property and they may be seized (Article 83, EJPMA). A third party who claims that he or she has such a right on the attached property that makes enforcement inadmissible may file an objection (Article 64, EJPMA). However, if the creditor does not acknowledge the claim of the third party, the latter's objection is dismissed (Article 65/2, EJPMA). The third party may then, within thirty days, bring an action at the court of general jurisdiction for a declaration that enforcement into a given property is inadmissible (Article 65/3, EJPMA). Nevertheless, such action does not have a suspensive effect with regard to enforcement proceedings. This may proceed and the attached property may be sold unless the third party succeeds with a motion for a suspension of enforcement. Under previous rule in order to succeed with such motion, the debtor had to prove that imminent enforcement might cause an irreparable harm (Article 71, EJPMA). Thus, even if the third party was in possession of firm evidence about her ownership right over property in

407. The Constitutional Court affirmed that it would constitute a violation of a right to judicial protection (right of access to court) if the correctness of the judgment could be re-examined in the course of enforcement proceedings. It is an integral part of aforementioned constitutional guarantee that a creditor can rely on a *res iudicata*. Decision of the Const. Court, Up 384/00, 18 Sep. 2001.

408. *See,* e.g., Judgment of the Supreme Court, II Ips 524/2003, 30 Sep. 2004.

question, the enforcement could still not be prevented if the claimant did not recognize the third party's claim. The constitutional court found that such system disproportionately infringes the third party's right to property, and the law was changed in 2005.[409] Now, enforcement may also be suspended upon motion of a third party who can present firm proofs of ownership over the attached property (Article 73, EJPMA).

443. Substantive grounds for third party's successful opposition to enforcement are foremost the ownership right, for example in a case, when the asset was in a possession of the debtor on the basis of a lease contract or in a case of fiduciary transfer of ownership for security. However, mere fact that the third party concluded a valid purchase contract with the debtor concerning the asset in question, but which has not been performed yet (e.g., with regard to real estate, the ownership of the buyer has not yet been entered into a land registry does not present a valid ground for a third party's opposition to enforcement). This is in line with a principle of Slovenian substantive law that right in rem is not acquired already in time of the conclusion of the contract but in the time of performance of the contract.[410] With regard to real estate, entry into land register is decisive. This however only applies when the title of ownership derives from a contractual basis. If the ownership is acquired *ex lege* (such as co-ownership of spouses over property, acquired in the time of marriage), the new owner will, according to the latest (but highly disputed) case law of the Constitutional Court, have a valid ground for objecting enforcement, although the third person's ownership right is not yet entered into a land register and it is the debtor, who is according to the data of the land register, the (only) owner of the real estate in question.[411]

III. Particular Types of Enforcement

444. One can distinguish between cases, when the *titre executoire* contains a pecuniary claim and cases when it contains a claim for specific performance. Another criterion for classification can be made with regard to assets against which enforcement is to be levied.[412]

445. The means of enforcement of pecuniary claims are the following: the attachment and sale of movable property, the attachment and sale of immovable property, the garnishment proceedings (including attachment of bank assets and assignment of earnings), enforcement of a claim in claims for delivery of goods, enforcement in respect of other pecuniary rights (such as intellectual property rights) and non materialized negotiable instruments, the attachment and sale of share in commercial company.

409. Decision of the Const. Court, U–I–110/03, 14 Apr. 2005.
410. For example, Judgment of the Koper Court of Appeals, II Cpg 119/2005, 22 Sep. 2005.
411. Decision of the Const. Court, Up 128/03, 27 Jan. 2005.
412. V. Rijavec, *Civilno izvršilno parvo* [*Enforcement of Civil Judgments Law*]45(GV Založba 2003).

446. The method of enforcement of a judgment is a matter for the initiative of the creditor, whereby the creditor can undertake any of the measures of enforcement provided for by the law. The principle of *gradus executionis* (in the sense that creditor is obliged first to try certain means of enforcement, which can be deemed to be a lesser burden for the debtor (e.g., garnishment of bank accounts or earnings) and only if such prove to be ineffective, further and more drastic means of enforcement, e.g., attachment and sale of real estate, could be invoked) does not apply in Slovenian law.[413] From the beginning, the creditor is free to choose any of the means of enforcement, available under EJPMA. Thus, even if the debt is relatively low and even if the debtor possesses other property, the creditor may move for enforcement into a real estate. The court can, upon the debtor's motion, substitute the enforcement into real estate with another type of enforcement, if it is probable that the latter shall be successful. If the debtor proposes, enforcement to be accomplished by garnishment of salary or another kind of income, the enforcement into real estate shall be stayed if satisfaction of the creditor's claim out of the debtor's income can be expected within the time limit of one year (Article 169, CPA). Of course, the debtor can also prevent any kind of enforcement by voluntarily performing the obligation in question; this can be done till the seized property is sold.

447. Enforcement upon movable property consists of attachment of the property and thereby a creation of a compulsory lien, determination of the value of property, its sale and by repayment of the creditor from the proceeds (Article 81, EJPMA), and in his motion for enforcement, the creditor can identify the property to be attached, but he is not obliged to do so. In that case, the bailiff is by law authorized to search a house or business premises in order to find attachable assets, if the debtor is present. Otherwise, a bailiff may force his way into a house or business premises only upon a court's warrant. In case of debtor's resistance, assistance from the police may be requested. If the bailiff finds that the debtor has property available to attach, he shall decide which property to attach and shall list, evaluate and secure it. As a rule, the property is taken into safe keeping by the bailiff, but it can also be allowed to remain in the possession of the debtor, whereby it is clearly marked and sealed (Article 85, EJPMA). If the attempt of attachment remains futile, further attempts may be undertaken on the grounds of the original warrant of execution within the time limit of one year (Article 88, EJPMA). If the claimant does not again file a motion of attachment within the aforementioned time limit, the enforcement is dismissed.

448. The value of the movable property is determined by the bailiff. The parties can, however, demand the assignment of a court expert, but on their own expenses (Article 89, EJPMA). The mode of sale of the property is determined by the bailiff; sale by auction is preferred but a directly negotiated contract or a sale through a broker (Article 93, EJPMA). On the first auction, the property may not be sold for a

413. H. Jenull, A. Galič&M. Jan, *Zakon o izvršbi in zavarovanju s komentarjem*[*Enforcement of Judgments and Protective Measures Act with the Commentary*]34(GV Založba 2002).

price, lower than the determined value, but if the first auction is not successful, on the next auction, the purchase price may be as low as a third of the determined value of the property (Article 94, EJPMA).

449. Various assets of the debtor are immune from execution, such as clothes and other items for the debtor's personal use, household equipment to the extent it is necessary for living, working tools and other equipment, necessary for the debtor's professional activity, cash in the amount of a monthly income, exempt from enforcement, means to make good a disability and therapeutic treatments, family pictures, letters, etc. (Article 79, EJPMA). Certain items are also exempt from enforcement against commercial company, such as machinery, necessary for the commercial activity, fuel and raw materials, necessary for one week's production (Article 80, EJPMA).

450. Enforcement upon real estate consists of the compulsory creation of a mortgage by notification of the warrant of execution in a land registry, determination of the value of real estate, its compulsory sale by auction and distribution of proceeds among creditors in accordance with principle of priority. It should be noted that house or apartment where the debtor lives permanently is not exempt from enforcement. The only protection of the debtor is that after the sale of the house or apartment he or she has a right to live there as a tenant for up to three years on condition of paying the market-value rent (Article 210/1, EJPMA). However, even this modest protective norm does not apply if the enforcement into real property was based on the contractually acquired mortgage (Article 210/4, EJPMA).

451. The value of the real estate is determined by the court by the court-appointed expert (Articles 178 and 179, EJPMA). In the first attempt of sale on auction, the property may not be sold for the price lower than the determined value and on the following attempt not for the price less than half of the determined value (Article 188, EJPMA). The Constitutional Court rejected the claim that the possibility for a sale for only a half of the determined value violates the debtor's constitutional right to private property as well as it rejected the claim that a possibility to have a real estate sold also for the satisfaction of disproportionately low debts violates the constitutional principle of proportionality.[414] However the Constitutional Court determined (and the law was accordingly changed afterwards) that in case when the buyer of the property is a creditor himself or a person, affiliated with the creditor, for a price lower than the determined value of the property and under the condition that the price of the property is lower than this creditor's claim, the creditor is deemed to have been repaid up to the determined value of the immovable property (now amended Article 200a, EJPMA).[415]

414. Decision of the Const. Court, U–I–93/03, 18 Nov. 2004.

415. For example, if the creditor's claim is EUR 100,000 and the value of the debtor's real estate is officially determined to be EUR 150,000, but the price reached on the auction is only EUR 75,000, the creditor will be deemed to be repayed for the whole claim (EUR 100,000) if the creditor or a person, affiliated with him bought the property on auction.

452. Distribution of the proceeds, once the value of an asset has been realized, is accomplished in accordance with the principle of priority (Article 198, EJPMA). If there are any other mortgages registered (either contractual or those, obtained by way of protective measure) prior to the mortgage of the creditor, who initiated the enforcement proceedings, those will be paid first. Besides, other creditors may join the pending enforcement proceedings. Certain claims enjoy priority *ex lege*: expenses, incurred during the enforcement proceedings, taxes related to the real estate and its sale as well as maintenance claims (Article 197, EJPMA). The distribution of the proceeds will be determined by a court order, and a hearing will need to take place for that purpose (Articles 207 and 208, EJPMA).

453. The object of garnishment proceedings can be any debt, owed to the judgment debtor by a third party. Practically most important are however garnishments of debtor's earnings and garnishment of bank accounts (whereby slightly different rules apply with regard to bank accounts, serving for payment transactions of legal entities and professionals). Enforcement is effected by attachment and transfer. The attachment is effected when the warrant of execution is served upon a garnishee (Article 107, EJPMA). The seizure of a debt secures a right of priority for the judgment creditor in relation to other creditors (Article 110, EJPMA). The seizure refers to all present and future debts' (thus, new payments into the debtor's account will immediately become subject to a seizure). If the earnings are seized and the debtor finds another employment, the garnishment order shall bind also the second employer, after it is served on him (Article 133, EJPMA). Failure to comply with the order result in the garnishee (e.g., bank or employer) being directly liable to the judgment creditor for the amount for which the seizure has been made.[416]

454. The enforcement of judgment may not result in an infringement of fundamental rights and social welfare rules. The debtor must retain a minimum income and therefore enforcement out of the debtor's earnings is subject to limitations. Up to two-thirds of the debtor's earnings may be attached on condition that the debtor still receives the income equal to the minimum salary guaranteed by law (currently cca. EUR 520) or two-thirds of minimum salary in case of enforcement of certain privileged claims, such as maintenance claims must remain to the debtor's disposal (Article 102, EJPMA). The Constitutional Court already reaffirmed that the latter is a constitutional guarantee, following from the principle of social state and respect for human dignity. In the same decision, the Constitutional Court also affirmed that it should also be taken into account whether the debtor has maintenance obligations as the minimum living standard for his or her family must also not be jeopardized. Following this decision, a law was amended so that it now provides for the additional amounts becoming exempt from seizure if the debtor has maintenance obligations. Furthermore, certain categories of income are always exempt from enforcement (e.g., maintenance, scholarship, social welfare or nursing care benefits; Article 101, EJPMA).

416. V. Rijavec, *Civilno izvršilno parvo* [*Enforcement of Civil Judgments Law*]287(GV Založba 2003).

455. Concerning the repayment of the creditor out of the attached debt, the law provides for two options. The first option is *cessio ad causam*: the claim itself is transferred to the judgment creditor (Article 127, EJPMA). In this case, the creditor takes the risk of whether the third party will be able to perform her obligations. The other option is *cessio ad processum*: the judgment creditor only obtains a transfer of standing to sue for the performance of obligation in court or to take other steps necessary to effect payment (Article 120, EJPMA). The claim against the third party remains a property of the debtor. If the third party fails to pay, the creditor can still invoke alternative methods of enforcement.[417] However, with regard to attachment of bank accounts and salaries, the first option is used as funds are automatically transferred to the judgment creditor in satisfaction of the debt once the seizure has been made and after the warrant for execution became irrevocable.

456. If the debtor is required to undertake a particular action, but this is such that it could be performed by another person, the creditor may, upon the court's authorization, have the work accomplished by a third party at the defendant's expense. Upon the creditor's request, the debtor may also be ordered to advance the money, needed to pay the third party. Depending on circumstances, assistance of a bailiff may also be authorized (Article 225, EJPMA).

457. If the debtor is required to perform a particular undertaking which cannot adequately be performed by anyone else; the enforcement is reached through use of indirect pressure; a pecuniary fine may be threatened and ultimately imposed as a means of persuading the debtor to fulfil his or her obligation. The amount of fine should depend on circumstances of the case but it may not exceed cca. EUR 4,000 for physical person or cca. EUR 20,000 for a legal person or a sole trader. If the debtor still fails to accomplish the required undertaking, the fine is enforced ex officio and another fine can be imposed till the whole amount of imposed fines has reached ten times of the aforementioned amounts (Article 226, EJPMA). If an injunction to refrain from acting is rendered against the debtor, the course of enforcement is practically the same as described in the preceding paragraph, except that there is no upper limit for the level of overall amount of fines that may be imposed (Article 227/1, EJPMA). Besides, upon a creditor's motion, the debtor may be required to advance a payment of a security for the damages incurred by the breach of obligation (Article 227/2, EJPMA).

458. Slovenian law does not permit imprisonment to be used as a sanction for non-compliance with the judgment. The fine is paid to the state. It has however already been mentioned that Slovenian law also contains a procedural device of *astreinte* (a civil fine). This periodic penalty can be invoked by a creditor for enforcement of any kind of non-monetary claim (see above, paragraph 288). The collection of fine does not extinguish the defendant's original obligation to comply with the judgment.

---

417. *Ibid.*, 288.

459. Eviction of a tenant who does not have or no longer has a legal right of occupation is enforced (after the court has given a warrant of execution) by the bailiff, if necessary with assistance of the police (Article 405, EJPMA). If the debtor is obliged to hand over specific movable property, the accomplishment of enforcement is a task of the bailiff as well (Article 214, EJPMA). If the item is not found in the debtor's possession, the creditor may instead request the enforcement court to award damages and have them enforced as a pecuniary claim (Article 215, EJPMA). If the obligation of delivery refers to generic goods and if they are not found in the possession of the debtor, the claimant may have the same kind of goods purchased at the expense of the debtor (Article 216, EJPMA).

§2. Recognition and Enforcement of Foreign Judgments

I. Rules Applicable in the Absence of a Treaty

460. A creditor who is in possession of a foreign judgment, has two options, how to have it enforced in Slovenia. The first option is to seek a recognition (exequatur) of the judgment in a separate proceeding and after the recognition is granted, enforcement proceedings may be initiated in the same manner as if it was conducted on the basis of a Slovenian judgment. Pursuant to the PILPA, district courts have jurisdiction to decide in separate proceedings of recognition of a foreign judgment. The district court first decides in ex parte proceedings. If the *exequatur* is granted, the opponent may file an objection against the decision of the district court, on which it is decided in adversarial procedure at the same court (the district court). Against the decision on this legal remedy (as well as for the claimant if the recognition is refused), an appeal is admissible to the Supreme Court. Procedure on recognition of a foreign judgment is decided upon in accordance in rules, applicable to non-contentious procedures (Article 111, PILPA). A public hearing (in the proceedings of recognition or declaration of enforceability) is not obligatory, but the court may call for a public hearing if the court considers such appropriate. (Article 7 NCPA). This applies to the issue of the 'first' decision according of the district court as well as the decision on the objection. It seems that the requirement of contradictory procedure can be sufficed also in written proceedings (therefore, a possibility that the party can respond to the statements, made in the application for recognition or in the court decision, in writing). On the appeal according to Article 34 the Supreme Court normally decides in camera). A 'claim' does not have to be specifically stated in non-contentious proceedings (Article 21 NCPA). If the applicant in the proceedings of recognition or declaration of enforceability does not state otherwise, it is considered that he or she is applying for a recognition (or declaration of enforceability) of the foreign judgment as a whole and against the person, against whom the application was filed (the opposite party must be stated in the application). According to the general rules, every party of the non-contentious procedure bears their own costs (Article 35 NCPA). However, the situation is different in case of proceedings for the recognition of foreign judicial decisions. Although also these proceedings are non-contentious, due to an explicit provision of Article 110 of the PILPA it applies the successful party has the right to reimbursement of costs from the opposite party. It may be also worth mentioning, that pursuant to the PILPA it is only possible to initiate proceedings for recognition of a foreign judgment, but not for a declaration that the foreign judgment should not be recognized.

461. The creditor, however, does not need first to obtain an *exequatur* in order to have a foreign judgment enforced in Slovenia. According to the regulation in the PILPA, in case the recognition of a judgment is raised as an incidental question in any court proceedings, that court may determine that issue. Thus, it is not necessary for the creditor first to engage in a separate proceeding for recognition of a foreign judicial decision. Thus, the creditor can directly move to enforcement proceedings in Slovenia on the basis of a foreign judgment. In the course of enforcement proceedings, the court will examine as a preliminary question (incidenter), whether the foreign judgment fulfils criteria for recognition.[418] This system seems to be creditor-friendly as it does not oblige him first to go through a separate procedure to obtain exequatur. However, it can contribute to a complication of enforcement proceedings, as it imposes on the court, that responsible for enforcement, a burden, to deal with questions concerning conditions for recognitions. These questions are often complex and demand a knowledge of specific field of international private law and as such they are clearly not suitable for adjudication by the court, which deals with enforcement proceedings.

462. Concerning substantive conditions for (denial of) recognition, the Slovenian law is rather liberal. It is clearly based on the principle of *controle limite* and a foreign judgment may not be reviewed as to its substance (no *controle au fond*).[419] Grounds of non-recognition are limited to the examination, whether the subject matter of the foreign judgment does not concern a dispute, for which exclusive jurisdiction of a Slovenian court is reserved, furthermore, the violation of public policy, the violation of the right to be heard (right to present a case and to obstacles of *res iudicata* and lis pendens (whereby the latter results only in a suspension of the proceedings on recognition). A condition is also the existence of reciprocity; however, a factual reciprocity is sufficient and its existence is presumed (thus, the respondent has a burden of proof to prove the non-existence of reciprocity). Concerning the international jurisdiction, upon motion of the defendant, recognition shall also be denied if the foreign court disrespected a prorogation agreement in favour of Slovenian court (although duly invoked by the defendant) and furthermore, if a foreign court based its jurisdiction on the grounds, which count as excessive (exorbitant) jurisdictions (such as: the nationality of the plaintiff or the presence of defendant's assets within jurisdiction (Article 98, PILPA).[420]Only judgments, which are *res iudicata* in the country of origin, could be recognized and enforced in Slovenia. Therefore, even if a judgment, although not yet final, can be

418. Decision of the Supreme Court, III Ips 64/2001, 22 Nov. 2001.

419. Judgment of the Supreme Court, Cp 2/2006, 29 Jun. 2006.

420. About the notion of excessive jurisdiction *see* Galič, *International jurisdiction based on the presence of assets*, in*Dvadeset godina zakona o međunarodnom privatnom pravu: collection of papers* 277–282(M. Zivkovic ed., Centar za publikacije Pravnog fakulteta 2004).

a subject to a preliminary enforcement in a country of origin, it cannot be recognized and enforced in Slovenia. It is an obligation of the creditor to attach to the request for recognition (also when this is sought incidenter within enforcement proceedings) not only the proof that the judgment is enforceable in the country of origin, but also that it is a *res iudicata* (Article 95, PILPA).

463. In the doctrine, public policy (*ordre public*) is construed in a restrictive manner.[421] The same applies (at least on a principled level) also in the case law.[422] Foremost constitutional provisions (including also human rights – both substantive as well as constitutional procedural guarantees[423]) but also certain norms, which are fundamental for the socio-economic order and vital interests of the state are considered to form *ordre public*.[424] But the notion of *ordre public* is certainly narrower as the notion of *ius cogens* (sometimes referred to as an *ordre public interne*– while the public order in the context of foreign judgments and foreign law is sometimes referred to as *ordre public* international).[425] Besides, the doctrine pleads that the notion of *ordre public* should be construed even in a more restrictive manner, when it concerns recognition of foreign judgments than when it concerns an application of foreign substantive law in a domestic court (doctrine of *Ordre public attenue*).[426]

II. EU Regulations and International Treaties

464. Judgments, given in other EU Member States, concerning civil and commercial matters are recognized and enforced in Slovenia pursuant to the Regulation 44/2001 (Brussels I Regulation), while judgments concerning parental responsibility and matrimonial disputes are recognized and enforced pursuant to the Regulation Number 2201/2003 (Brussels II Regulation). Both systems are based on the principle of mutual trust and recognition and provide for almost automatic recognition and enforcement. Nevertheless, a creditor, whose judgment is subject to the regime of the aforementioned EU Regulations, unlike the creditor, who is subject to the regime of the PILPA, may not directly move for an enforcement procedure in Slovenia. Prior to that, she must obtain a declaration of enforceability (*exequatur*) in a separate proceeding. This should however be issued virtually automatically after purely formal checks of the documents and forms supplied. The court has no possibility to invoke on its own motion any of the grounds for non-recognition (see

421. For example, J. Kramberger, *Javni red pri priznanju in izvršitvi tujih sodnih odločb,[Public Policy at the Recognition and Enforcement of Foreign Judgments]*, 65 Zbornik znanstvenih razprav PF v Ljubljani, 257 (2005); M. Ilešič, A. Polajnar–Pavčnik&D. Wedam-Lukić*Mednarodno zasebno pravo – komentar zakona[International Private Law – Commentary of the Act]* 24(ČZ Uradni list 1992).

422. Decision of the Supreme Court, Cpg 3/2003, 11 Sep. 2003.

423. Decisions of the Supreme Court, Cp 11/2001, 8 Nov. 2001 and Cp 6/2001, 28 Jun. 2001.

424. Decision of the Supreme Court, IIps 14/92, 3 Jul. 1992.

425. M. Ilešič, A. Polajnar–Pavčnik&D. Wedam-Lukić*Mednarodno zasebno pravo – komentar zakona[International Private Law – Commentary of the Act]* 25(ČZ Uradni list 1992).

426. J. Kramberger, *Javni red pri priznanju in izvršitvi tujih sodnih odločb,[Public Policy at the Recognition and Enforcement of Foreign Judgments]*,65 Zbornik znanstvenih razprav PF v. Ljubljani, 257 (2005).

point 17 of the preamble and Article 41 of the Brussels I Regulation, whereas the ex officio control is partially still retained in the Brussels II Regulation (Article 31).

465. The system of both EU Regulations need not be presented in this context, except certain issues, which the Regulations leave to the national law. Slovenia did not adopt any implementing legislation concerning neither the Regulation Number 44/2001 nor the Regulation Number 2201/2003, and the existing legal regulation does not provide reliable answers to many specific issues regarding the procedure for recognition and for declaration of enforceability. Regarding the questions which are according to the Regulation Number 2201/2003 left to domestic law, in Slovenia the provisions of the Non-Contentious Procedure Act, and subsidiary the provisions of the CPA. Concerning the jurisdiction, the district courts decide both upon a separate motion for recognition as well as on a motion for issuing a certificate on the enforceability. A legal remedy is admissible against the decision of the district court, on which it is decided in adversarial procedure at the same court (the district court). Against the decision on this legal remedy an appeal is admissible to the Supreme Court. At the determination of these legal remedies Slovenia evidently followed the goal that the system of jurisdictions and legal remedies in the Regulation Number 2201/2003 (same as the Regulation Number 44/2001) would be as similar as possible to the system of jurisdictions and legal remedies regarding the proceedings of recognition of foreign judgments in Slovenian domestic law (PILPA) as described above.

466. While the aforementioned EU Regulations still retain the prerequisite for an *exequatur*, in some sectorial EU legislation this has already been abolished. This applies to decisions on visitation rights and decisions on the return of the abducted child, pursuant to the Regulation Number 2201/2003; to the European enforcement order for uncontested claims (Regulation Number 805/2004); decisions, given in an European small claims procedure (Regulation Number 861/2007) and to European payment order (Regulation Number 1896/2006) as well as for the future Maintenance Regulation.

467. Slovenia shall be a party to the new Lugano Convention on Jurisdiction and Recognition and enforcement in civil and Commercial Matters. Several to numerous Hague Conventions in the field of international private law apply in Slovenia (either by ratification or by succession from Yugoslavia), such as:

- Convention of 1 March 1954 on civil procedure.
- Convention of 19 October 1996 on Jurisdiction, Applicable Law, Recognition, Enforcement and Co-operation in Respect of Parental Responsibility and Measures for the Protection of Children.
- Convention of 5 October 1961 Abolishing the Requirement of Legalisation for Foreign Public Documents (The *Apostille* Convention).
- Convention of 25 October 1980 on the Civil Aspects of International Child Abduction.
- Convention of 25 October 1980 on International Access to Justice.

- Convention of 29 May 1993 on Protection of Children and Co-operation in respect of Intercountry Adoption.
- Convention of 19 October 1996 on Jurisdiction, Applicable Law, Recognition, Enforcement and Co-operation in respect of Parental Responsibility and Measures for the Protection of Children.
- Besides, the UN (New York) Convention on the Recovery Abroad of Maintenance of 20 June 1956 is also significant from the viewpoint of enforcement of foreign judgments.

468. Certain bilateral treaties in the field of mutual legal assistance in civil matters (such as Between Slovenia and Macedonia, dated 6 February 1996, and between Slovenia and Croatia, dated 7 February 1994) also contain norms on recognition and enforcement, but they do not fundamentally depart from the above-described system of the PILPA.

Part X. Arbitration

Chapter 1. Limits of Arbitrability

469. A comprehensive reform of arbitration law in Slovenia was implemented in 2008, when the Arbitration Act (AA) was adopted. The new law is based on United Nations Commission on International Trade Law (UNCITRAL) Model Law on International Arbitration. Although there are some divergences between the AA and the UNCITRAL Model law, it can be expected that Slovenia will be put on the list of 'model law jurisdictions'. The new law already took into account latest amendments of the UNCITRAL Model law, adopted in 2006. These concern mostly the loosening of form requirements of an arbitration agreement and establishing of a more comprehensive regime dealing with interim measures in support of arbitration. Until 2008, arbitration procedure has been regulated by the CPA, except the recognition and enforcement of foreign arbitral awards, which was regulated in the Private International Law Act (PILPA). The necessity of an overall revision of arbitration law in Slovenia was recognized already in early nineties, as the old law appeared outdated, in certain aspects even 'arbitration unfriendly'.[427] The acceptance of the UNCITRAL Model law was perceived to be a proper way to make Slovenia a regionally attractive venue for international arbitration, while a reform should in general contribute to promotion of arbitration in domestic cases as well.

470. The AA does not distinguish between international and domestic arbitration, and neither does it distinguish between commercial and non-commercial arbitration. Thus, the AA applies also to purely domestic and non-commercial arbitrations and in this regard, its scope is broader than that of the Model law. There are however, certain special rules for consumer and labour disputes.

471. The provisions of the Act apply if the place of arbitration is situated in Slovenia (Article 1/1). Certain provisions (e.g., interim measures, granted by court, assistance of the court in taking of evidence) however apply even if the place of arbitration is situated outside Slovenia or has not yet been determined (Article 1/2). The law also provides for jurisdiction of Slovenian courts to decide matters of nomination, challenge (disqualification) and termination of mandate of arbitrators in

427. *See* M. Damjan, *Reforma arbitražnega prava: prevzem Uncitralovega vzorčnega zakona*[*Reform of Arbitration Law: Adoption of UNCITRAL Model Law*], 33 Podjetje in delo, 1313 et seq. (2007); Galič, A., *Arbitration in Transformation: The Experience of a Country in Transition* in*Schiedsgerichtsbarkeit in Zentraleuropa*107–130 (Oberhammer ed., Neuer Wissenschaftlicher Verlag 2005).

cases when the seat of arbitration is not yet determined. In such cases, the Slovenian court shall, upon a motion of a party, offer assistance to arbitration proceedings under condition that any of the parties has seat, domicile or temporary residence in Slovenia (Article 1/3). The Model law does not include such provision, it is however useful as there are cases that the seat of arbitration is not determined before the constitution of arbitral tribunal. In most cases, the court decides pursuant to rules, governing non-contentious procedure (Article 9/2, AA); just in case of action for setting aside arbitral award, action for declaration of (non)validity of arbitration agreement and in case of request for court's revision of the tribunal's decision on jurisdiction shall the court decide pursuant to rules governing contentious procedure (CPA).

472. Unlike the UNCITRAL Model law, the AA defines limits of arbitrability (*arbitrabilnost*). These are broad: any claim involving an economic interest (patrimonial claims; *premoženjskopravni zahtevek*) can be the subject of an arbitration agreement. An arbitration agreement concerning claims not involving an economic interest has legal effect to the extent that the parties are entitled to conclude a settlement on the issue in dispute. The doctrine, developed in the time, when a criteria of arbitrability was, whether the case concerned rights, which parties can freely dispose of opined that besides (most of) family law matters, also certain commercial disputes are not arbitrable, for example disputes regarding the validity of patents, trademarks and other registered intellectual property rights, intra-corporate disputes, insolvency and antitrust. However, claims for damages, whereby questions of violation of antitrust law is only a preliminary question, were considered to be arbitrable, just as any other tort claims.[428] At least disputes, which are solved by decisions with effect not only *inter partes* but *erga omnes*, cannot be considered arbitrable also pursuant to the new law. But pursuant to the new, larger definition of arbitrability, certain restrictions on the arbitrability of cartel disputes might be considered to be abolished. There is no condition that only contractual claims are arbitrable and therefore non-contractual tort claims are also arbitrable.[429]

473. The law imposes one further condition concerning conclusion of an arbitration agreement, conferring jurisdiction to a foreign arbitration. Such agreement is not admissible if it refers to a dispute, for which Slovenia reserves an exclusive international jurisdiction (Article 5, AA). Otherwise, also physical persons, who are nationals or residents in Slovenia, and legal entities, registered and domiciled in Slovenia (including the Slovenian State and legal entities of public-law character), can confer jurisdiction to foreign arbitration without any other restrictions.[430]

428. L. Ude, *Arbitražno parvo* [*Arbitration Law*]68(GV Založba 2004).
429. *See ibid.*, p. 67 et seq.
430. According to the old law, two Slovenian companies (even if foreign owned) were not entitled to avail themselves to an arbitration outside Slovenia. It was however highly questionable whether the violation of this restriction could result in any sanctions. *See ibid.*, p. 30 and p. 262, T. Keresteš, *Pridržek javnega reda pri priznavanju tujih arbitražnih odločb po newyorški konvenciji*[*Ordre Public Clause at the Recognition of Foreign Arbitral Awards Pursuant to the New York Convention*], 25 Podjetje in delo, 1631 et seq. (1999).

474. In Slovenia there are no strict legal conditions for and obstacles to establishing permanent arbitral institutions (*stalna arbitraža*). Nevertheless, the Permanent Court of Arbitration attached to the Chamber of Commerce and Industry of Slovenia is the only general institutional arbitration body in Slovenia, which is also active in international arbitration. There are also no obstacles for ad hoc arbitration (as distinguished from institutional arbitration) in Slovenia.

Chapter 2. Arbitration Agreement

475. By way of an arbitration agreement (*arbitražni sporazum*), the parties can agree to refer future disputes to arbitration or to refer a case to arbitration once a dispute has arisen. The arbitration agreement must be concluded with regard to certain disputes which have arisen or which may arise between them in respect of a defined legal relationship, whether contractual or not (Article 10, AA). For disputes regarding consumer contracts there is a restriction that an arbitration agreement could be entered into only after the dispute has arisen (Article 45, AA). However, there is no such restriction for labour disputes.

476. An arbitration agreement may be in the form of a separate agreement or in the form of a clause in a contract ('arbitration clause', Article 10/1, AA), whereby principle of separability of arbitration clause from the main contract is recognized (Article 19/1, AA). The arbitration agreement must be contained either in a document signed by the parties or in an exchange of letters, telefaxes, telegrams or other means of communication or data recording which provide a record of the agreement, if the information contained therein is accessible so as to be usable for subsequent usage (Article 10/2, AA). The definition is broad enough to include also modern electronic means of communication (such as e-mail). The form requirement is furthermore deemed to have been complied with if the arbitration agreement is contained in a document transmitted from one party to the other party or by a third party to both parties and – if no objection was raised in good time – the contents of such document are considered to be part of the contract in accordance with common usage (Article 10/3, AA). The reference in a contract (to general contract terms, to another contract or similar) complying with the aforementioned form requirements to a document containing an arbitration clause constitutes an arbitration agreement provided that the reference is such as to make that clause part of the contract (Article 10/4, AA). An arbitration agreement is also concluded by the issuance of a bill of lading, if the latter contains an express reference to an arbitration clause in a charter party (Article 10/5, AA; there is no such provision in the Model law).

477. Form requirements are stricter in consumer and labour disputes. The arbitration agreement must be concluded in a separate document (thus, a reference to general contract terms or even an explicit arbitration clause, included in the main contract is not sufficient; personally signed by the consumer or the labourer. A reference to a 'separate document' means that no agreements other than those referring to the arbitral proceedings may be contained in such a document.

478. A valid arbitration agreement is deemed to have been concluded also in case when the claimant brings an action in arbitration proceedings and the defendant fails to object lack of jurisdiction at the latest in the defence plea (Article 10/6, AA). The wording is a bit less restrictive than Article 7/5 (Option 1) of the revised UNCITRAL Model law, which requests the claimant to allege existence of arbitration agreement (whereas the defendant does not object this allegation). It is not clear whether the Slovenian rule applies also in case that the defendant does not file a defence plea at all. It is also an open question whether the arbitral tribunal may examine the question of existence of arbitration agreement ex officio in case of total default of the defendant, who absolutely refrains from participating in proceedings, or can also such an omission be regarded as a waiver of the right to object existence or validity of arbitration agreement.

479. The principle of competence-competence is recognized in Slovenian law, so arbitrators have the power to rule on their own jurisdiction.[431] A plea that the arbitral tribunal does not have jurisdiction must be raised not later than the submission of the defence plea. A party is not precluded from raising such a plea by the fact that he has appointed, or participated in the appointment of, an arbitrator. The arbitral tribunal may admit a later plea if it considers that the party has justified the delay (Article 19/2, AA). If the defendant raises the plea of lack of jurisdiction, the arbitral tribunal shall in principle rule on the issue of jurisdiction in a separate order (Article 19/1, AA). If in such case the arbitral tribunal rules that it has jurisdiction, any party may request, within thirty days, the court to decide the matter (Article 19/3, AA); while such a request is pending, the arbitral tribunal may continue the arbitral proceedings and make an award (Article 19/3, AA). However, the decision of the arbitral tribunal to deny jurisdiction, cannot be challenged in court at all. It is a position of a Slovenian doctrine that an arbitral tribunal cannot be forced to accept jurisdiction if it does not wish to accept it, and that a negative decision of the arbitral tribunal about jurisdiction in any case makes an arbitration agreement inoperative.[432]

480. Unlike the UNCITRAL Model law and unlike the Regulation in old Slovenian law, which left this issue unsolved, the new AA allows for a separate action for declaration whether or not arbitration is admissible, whereby such an action is allowed only if it is filed prior to the constitution of the arbitral tribunal (Article 11/3, AA). In spite of filing of the aforementioned action, arbitral proceedings may nevertheless be commenced or continued, and an arbitral award may be made, while the issue is pending before the court (Article 11/4, AA). As the action for declaration whether arbitration is admissible must be filed before the arbitration is commenced, it cannot be considered as another possibility of court's intervention in pending arbitral proceedings. It is disputable whether arbitral tribunal is bound by the findings of the court that arbitration is inadmissible or whether it can in spite of such ruling proceed with arbitration.

481. In Article 11, the AA determines how the court should react in court proceedings, which have been brought in breach of an arbitration agreement. The court must, upon the timely objection of a defendant who invokes an arbitration agreement in the defence plea at the latest, strike out on the action unless it finds that the

---

431. *See,* e.g., L. Ude, *Arbitražno parvo* [*Arbitration Law*]90(GV Založba 2004).
432. L. Ude&D. Wedam-Lukić, *Schiedsgerichtsbarkeit in der Republik Slowenien*58(Verlag Recht und Wirtschaft 1998). Also in case if a party brings an action on merits in a court and the court strikes out the claim on the grounds that it has no jurisdiction as there is a, in the opinion of the court, valid arbitration agreement, and the party then brings an action in arbitration, the arbitral tribunal is not bound by the position of the court that the arbitration agreement is valid (*seeibid.*, p. 63).

agreement is null and void, inoperative or incapable of being performed. It is, however, not clear whether in the event that there is a dispute between the plaintiff and the defendant as to the validity of the arbitration agreement the court should decide on this issue with full assessment of facts and law or just prima facie (and thus enable the arbitral tribunal to have the 'first word' in the disputed case). It is also not regulated whether it makes a difference if a parallel arbitration procedure is already pending and whether at least in such a case a court should wait until the arbitrators have first decided whether they have jurisdiction.[433] In the context of the issue of jurisdiction, it might also be mentioned that it is unclear to what extent the court may control the validity of the arbitration agreement in the event its intervention is invoked for the support of an arbitral proceedings (such as with the constitution of an arbitral tribunal).

482. Except in cases explicitly provided by law, the court may not interfere with arbitration (Article 8, AA).

433. Compare Art. 6/3 of the European Convention on International Commercial Arbitration and L. Ude, *Arbitražno pravo* [*Arbitration Law*]92–93(GV Založba 2004).

Chapter 3. Appointment and Challenge of Arbitrators

483. The parties are free to determine the number of arbitrators (thus, also an even number is possible). Failing such determination, the number of arbitrators shall be three (Article 13, AA). The parties are free to agree on a procedure of appointing the arbitrator or arbitrators (Article 14/2, AA). Failing an agreement, a sole arbitrator shall, if the parties are unable to agree on his appointment, be appointed, upon request of a party, by the court. In an arbitration with three arbitrators, each party shall appoint one arbitrator, and the two arbitrators thus appointed shall appoint the third arbitrator who shall act as chairman of the arbitral tribunal. If this fails, the appointment shall be made, upon request of a party, by the court. An intervention of the court is also possible if parties agree on an appointment procedure, however a party fails to act as required under such procedure, or if the parties, or two arbitrators, are unable to reach an agreement expected of them under such procedure, or a third party or institution fails to perform any function entrusted to it, any party may request the court to take the necessary measure, unless the agreement on the appointment procedure provides other means for securing the appointment (Article 14/4, AA).

484. A proposed arbitrator must disclose any circumstances likely to give rise to justifiable doubts as to his impartiality or independence. An arbitrator, from the time of his appointment and throughout the arbitral proceedings, must without delay disclose any such circumstances to the parties unless they have already been informed of them by him (Article 15/1, AA). An arbitrator may be challenged only if circumstances exist that give rise to justifiable doubts as to his impartiality or independence, or if he does not possess qualifications agreed to by the parties (Article 15/2, AA). A party may challenge an arbitrator appointed by him, or in whose appointment he has participated, only for reasons of which he becomes aware after the appointment has been made. The parties are free to agree on a procedure for challenging an arbitrator. Failing such agreement, a party who intends to challenge an arbitrator must, within two weeks after becoming aware of the constitution of the arbitral tribunal or after becoming aware of any circumstance justifying a disqualification send a written statement of the reasons for the challenge to the arbitral tribunal. Unless the challenged arbitrator withdraws from his office or the other party agrees to the challenge, the arbitral tribunal shall decide on the challenge (Article 16/2, AA).

485. If a challenge is not successful, the challenging party may request, within one month after having received notice of the decision rejecting the challenge, the court to decide on the challenge. While such a request is pending, the arbitral tribunal, including the challenged arbitrator, may continue the arbitral proceedings and make an award (Article 16/3, AA).

486. If an arbitrator becomes de jure or de facto unable to perform his functions or for other reasons fails to act without undue delay, his mandate terminates if he withdraws from his office or if the parties agree on the termination. If the arbitrator does not withdraw from his office or if the parties cannot agree on the termination, any party may request the court to decide on the termination of the mandate (Article 17, AA).

Chapter 4. Arbitration Proceedings

487. The parties must be treated with equality, and each party shall be given a full opportunity of presenting his case (Article 21, AA). Counsel (foreign or domestic) may not be excluded from acting as authorized representatives (Article 22, AA). Otherwise, subject to the mandatory provisions, the parties are free to determine the procedure themselves or by reference to a set of arbitration rules. Failing an agreement by the parties, the arbitral tribunal conducts the arbitration in such manner, as it considers appropriate subject to the mandatory rules (Article 23, AA). The aforementioned refers *inter alia*, to taking of evidence (Article 23/2, AA), to determination of seat (Article 24, AA) and language (Article 26, AA) of arbitration, oral or written proceedings (Article 28, AA).

488. The arbitration commences with a request for the dispute to be referred to arbitration is received by the respondent (Article 25, AA). Within the period of time agreed by the parties or determined by the arbitral tribunal, the claimant must then state the facts supporting his claim, the points at issue and the relief or remedy sought, and the respondent shall state his defence in respect of these particulars (Article 27, AA). Default of the claimant results in termination of proceedings, whereas in spite of the default of the defendant the arbitration proceedings continue without treating such failure in itself as an admission of the claimant's allegations. The arbitral tribunal may therefore request from the claimant to prove its allegations. If any party fails to appear at an oral hearing or to produce documentary evidence within a set time limit, the arbitral tribunal may continue the proceedings and make the award on the evidence before it (Article 29, AA).

489. The law provides that arbitral tribunal may seek support from the court, for example, concerning taking of evidence (Article 31, AA). It has already been mentioned that in certain cases this activities may take place also in support of a foreign arbitration or arbitration which seat has not been determined yet (see above). Parties may also request the court to grant protective and interim measures (Article 12, AA). This applies also in case of a foreign arbitration.[434]

490. The new law, in contrast to the prior regulation, empowers an arbitral tribunal to order such interim measures of protection at the request of the party, as the

434. There is no case law that specifically answers this question; however, there is already a case law supporting the view that a statutory provision that a court can grant provisional measures already before or during a proceedings on the merits apply also to the case, when there is an arbitration proceedings on merits (Court of Appeals in Ljubljana, decision II Cpg 261/99, 16 Mar. 1999). This decision was issued with regard to domestic arbitration; if it is however taken into account that there is already settled case law that a Slovenian court would grant provisional measures in a support of a foreign court proceedings (e.g., Court of Appeals in Ljubljana, decision II Cpg 318/98, 28 Jul. 1998), the combination of both statements (that a domestic arbitration equals a domestic court proceedings and that a foreign court proceedings equal domestic court proceedings) leaves no doubt, that a Slovenian court would grant provisional measures in support of a foreign arbitration proceedings.

arbitral tribunal may consider necessary (Article 20, AA).[435] As the arbitral tribunal is only empowered to regulate relations between parties to the arbitration agreement, such measures may not be directed against the third party, who is not bound by the arbitration agreement. Measures, through which an arbitral tribunal would require, e.g., a bank to freeze assets of a defendant in the bank accounts, would not be admissible. The arbitral tribunal may require any party to provide appropriate security in connection with such measure (Article 20/1, AA). Except in urgent cases, the defendant must be given opportunity to be heard before the interim measure is issued (Article 20/2, AA). The arbitral tribunal may repeal or amend the measure. It may act so upon a motion of one of the parties and in exceptional circumstances and subject to a prior notice to parties also on its own motion (Article 20/3, AA). The court may, at the request of a party, permit enforcement of an interim measure, unless application for a corresponding interim measure has already been made to a court (Article 20/4, AA).

435. Under the old law, there was no possibility for an arbitration to grant provisional measures. The rules of the Permanent Court of Arbitration attached to the Slovenian Chamber of Commerce tried to be more advanced in this regard and included the provision that 'arbitrators may grant such provisional measures as they deem appropriate'. This attempt was blocked by the Constitutional Court, which stated that only a law can authorize arbitrators to grant provisional measures, an agreement by the parties (which their submission to the rules of an arbitral institution equals; thus, those rules are merely of a contractual nature as well) that the arbitral tribunal will have such powers is not sufficient. Constitutional Court decisions U–I–37/99, 5 Mar. 1999 and Up 20/99, 25 May 1999.

Chapter 5. Arbitral Award and Its Setting Aside

491. Concerning the applicable law, the arbitral tribunal shall decide the dispute in accordance with such rules of law as are chosen by the parties. Any designation of the law or legal system of a given state is construed, unless otherwise expressed, as directly referring to the substantive law of that state and not to its conflict of laws rules (Article 32/1, AA). Failing any designation by the parties, the arbitral tribunal shall apply the legal rules, which it considers applicable (Article 32/2, AA).[436] Thus, unlike in Article 28 of the UNCITRAL Model law, a reference is made directly to the substantive law and not merely to the conflict of law norms of the appropriate legal system. Besides, a reference to 'legal rules' allows for the applicability of e.g., *lex mercatoria* and not only of the legal system of a certain state. The arbitral tribunal may decide *ex aequo et bono* or as *amiable compositeur* only if the parties have expressly authorized it to do so. The parties may so authorize the arbitral tribunal up to the time of its decision (Article 32/3, AA). In all cases, the arbitral tribunal must decide in accordance with the terms of the contract and shall take into account the usages of the trade applicable to the transaction (Article 32/4, AA).

492. If, during arbitral proceedings, the parties settle the dispute, the arbitral tribunal shall terminate the proceedings. If requested by the parties, it shall record the settlement in the form of an arbitral award on agreed terms, unless the contents are in violation of public policy (Article 34, AA).

493. In arbitral proceedings with more than one arbitrator, any decision of the arbitral tribunal must be made, unless otherwise agreed by the parties, by a majority of all its members (Article 33, AA). The arbitral award (*arbitražna odločba*) must be made in writing, and it must contain the reasons upon which it is based, unless the parties have agreed that no reasons are to be given or the award is an award based on settlement (Article 35, AA). The award must state its date and the place of arbitration. The award shall be deemed to have been made on that date and at that place. The law provides for the possibility of correction and interpretation of award and of an additional award (Article 37, AA).

494. The arbitral award has the same effect between the parties as a final (*res iudicata*) court judgment (Article 38, AA).

495. Recourse to a court against an arbitral award may be made only by an action for setting aside (*tožba za izpodbijanje arbitražne odločbe*, Article 40/1, AA). The time limit for filing of this action is three months (Article 40/3, AA). The grounds for setting aside an arbitral award are the following:

---

436. Neither the CPA nor the PILPA contained conflict of law rules concerning the determination of applicable substantive law in disputes with a cross-border elements and there was no settled case law concerning this issue either S. Mežnar, *Uporaba materialnega prava v postopkih pred mednarodnimi trgovinskimi arbitražami*[*Applicable Substantive Law in International Arbitration*], 64 *Zbornik znanstvenih razprav Pravne fakultete v. Ljubljani*, 281 et seq. (2004).

- the lack of procedural prerequisites concerning capacities of a party and proper representation;
- a lack of a valid arbitration agreement;
- a violation of a right to be heard;
- the fact that the arbitral tribunal transgressed the scope of the submission of the dispute to arbitration; and
- the fact that the composition of the arbitral tribunal or the arbitral procedure was not in accordance with the agreement of the parties (unless such agreement was in conflict with mandatory provisions of the law).

The aforementioned grounds may be considered only if invoked by the party. Nevertheless, there are two further grounds for setting aside an arbitral award, which the court may examine ex officio: the lack of arbitrability and the violation of ordre (Article 40/2, AA).

496. In contrast to the old law, the new AA provides for the possibility that the court, when asked to set aside an award, may where appropriate and so requested by a party, suspend the setting aside proceedings for a period of time determined by it in order to give the arbitral tribunal an opportunity to resume the arbitral proceedings or to take such other action as in the arbitral tribunal's opinion will eliminate the grounds for setting aside (Article 40/5, AA).[437]

497. Possibility and grounds for setting aside of arbitral award are not left to the parties' free disposition.[438] Through an agreement, parties can neither exclude the right to have an arbitral award set aside nor can they agree for more extensive grounds for setting aside the arbitral award or even determine that the arbitral award shall not be binding (in the sense that an arbitral award shall become binding only if neither of parties shall, within a certain time limit, demand *trial de novo*. Non-binding arbitration is unknown in Slovenian law. It is settled case law of the Supreme Court that if the parties conclude an arbitration agreement, which includes a provision that any party may, after the arbitral award is rendered, pursue the same claim in the court, the whole arbitration agreement (and not just this stipulation) is null and void.[439]

437. In the old law, the only possibility remaining after a successful setting aside was that a new action could be brought (where there was an ongoing controversy whether the arbitration agreement is still 'alive'). *See,* e.g., L. Ude, *Arbitražno parvo*[*Arbitration Law*], 255–257(GV Založba 2004).

438. *See,* e.g., Š. Mežnar&A. Galič, *Slovenia – Country Report: Landesbericht,* in*Arbitration in Central Europe; Schiedsgerichtsbarkeit in Zentraleuropa,* 557(Oberhammer ed., Center of Legal Competence 2005).

439. Judgment of the Supreme Court, III Ips 68/2002, 11 Dec. 2002. On the binding nature of provisions concerning setting aside arbitral awards *see also* Judgment of the Supreme Court, II Ips 308/2000, 1 Feb. 2001.

498. The Slovenian doctrine agrees (at least on an abstract level) that courts, which exercise control over arbitral awards, should apply the public policy reservation with great restraint, whereas, the concept of public policy should be construed in a very reserved manner.[440] The Slovenian Supreme Court confirmed that the public policy reservation should be applied only as 'the last resort' with extreme caution in a restrictive and reserved manner and only in cases, where this is absolutely necessary to prevent results, which would be unbearable for domestic legal order and incompatible with the system of values on which it is based.[441] It is accepted both in theory[442] as well as in case law[443] that the standard of *international* public policy should apply when it comes to control over foreign arbitral awards (and foreign judgments). However, it is also accepted that international public policy is not a concept of international or supranational legal order but a concept of *national* law (hence: international public policy of the Republic of Slovenia[444]). Pursuant to the definition, offered by the Supreme Court, public policy relates to fundamental legal principles of domestic law, i.e., those on which the domestic legal order is founded. It consists of constitutional principles, basic principles arising from laws, basic principles of the legal order of the Council of Europe, European Communities and international agreements adopted to guarantee the minimum standard of legal protection, all subject to the overriding restriction that not every mandatory norm constitutes a part of public policy but only those, the violation of which, would threaten the legal and moral integrity of the domestic legal system.[445] In addition, the notion of public policy also includes principles of international customary law: basic moral principles, and vital economic, political … interests of the state.[446] It is acknowledged that public policy contains both a substantive and procedural part. It has also already been confirmed that, for example, the respect for *res iudicata* forms a part of procedural public policy[447] as well as of fundamental procedural guarantees.[448]

499. The reference to *international* public policy in regard to control over *foreign* arbitral awards might imply that the interpretation of public policy is different,

440. Keresteš, Keresteš, Tomaž: *Pridržek javnega reda pri priznavanju tujih arbitražnih odločb po Newyorški konvenciji* [*Public Policy Reservation Relating to Recognition of Foreign Arbitral Awards Under the NYC*], 25 Podjetje in delo, 1631(1999); Ilešič, Polajnar Pavčnik&Wedam Lukić, *Mednarodno zasebno pravo* [*International Private Law*] … 25(1992).

441. Decision of the Slovenian Supreme Court No. II Ips 462/2009 dated 28 Jan. 2010.

442. Kramberger Škerl, *Javni red pri priznanju in izvršitvi tujih sodnih odločb (s poudarkom na procesnih vprašanjih)* [*Public Policy and recognition and enforcement of foreign judgments (focusing on procedural aspects)*], 65 ZZR PFL 255 do 257(2005); Ude, Wedam Lukić, *Schiedsgerichtsbarkeit in der Republik Slowenien*85(1998).

443. Decision of the Slovenian Supreme Court No. Cpg 4/2004 dated 28 Jun. 2006.

444. Decision of the Slovenian Supreme Court No. II Ips 462/2009 dated 28 Jan. 2010.

445. *Ibid.*

446. Decision of the Slovenian Supreme Court No. II Ips 462/2009 dated 28 Jan. 2010, Decision of the Slovenian Supreme Court No. Cp 16/2006 dated 7 Feb. 2007 (both cases related to recognition of foreign court judgments, not arbitral awards. The Supreme Court implicitly confirmed, though, that the standard of review of compatibility with public policy is the same in regard to foreign judgments and arbitral awards).

447. Decision of the Slovenian Supreme Court No. II Ips 82/2007 dated 10 Dec. 2009.

448. Decision of the Slovenian Supreme Court No. Cpg 4/2004 dated 28 Feb. 2006.

when it applies to the control over domestic arbitral awards (in challenge or *exequatur* proceedings). Such a conclusion would, however, be incorrect. Both the legal writing as well as the case law (at least implicitly) confirm that criteria of compliance with public policy are essentially the same, regardless of whether a foreign or a domestic award is concerned.[449] 'Domestic public policy' (*ordre public interne*) in regard to domestic awards is, again, not construed as the entirety of all mandatory (cogent) rules in Slovenian law. It already follows from the wording of the AA that the lawmaker did not see the concept of public policy as a synonym for all mandatory (cogent) rules, when it comes to control over domestic awards. Such a conclusion can, nevertheless (?), be made, if one compares general grounds for setting aside the arbitral awards on the one hand and the special regime of setting aside awards in consumer and labour disputes on the other. Concerning the latter, the grounds for challenging awards are broader (with the purpose of ensuring a more comprehensive protection of weaker parties). In labour and consumer disputes, the court shall, beyond the reasons stipulated in Article 40 (hence, public policy including), set the arbitral award aside also 'if *mandatory provisions* of the law have been violated, the application of which may not be waived ... ' (Articles 47 and 49 AA). Clearly, since the law stipulates that the violation of 'mandatory provisions' is an additional ground for challenging awards in labour and consumer disputes, the violation of public policy as a ground for challenge under general rules must have a narrower meaning.

449. Compare Ude, *Arbitražno pravo*252 and 262(2004), Ude&Wedam Lukić, *Schiedsgerichtsbarkeit in der Republik Slowenien*95 (1998)and the judgment of the Slovenian Supreme Court No. No. II Ips 14/92 dated 3 Jul. 1992.

Chapter 6. Enforcement of Domestic Arbitral Awards

500. Different rules apply to domestic and foreign arbitral awards. Domestic arbitral award is an award rendered by an arbitration with a seat in Slovenia (Article 1/1, AA), and foreign arbitral award is an award rendered by an arbitration with a seat outside Slovenia.[450] The differences between scope of control over domestic and foreign arbitral awards is however not really big. Arbitration is a private mechanism for dispute resolution, and there is no reason to differentiate sharply between the scope of judicial control over domestic and foreign arbitral awards.[451]

501. A domestic arbitral award may be enforced only if it has been declared enforceable by the competent court (The Ljubljana District Court).[452] An application for a declaration of enforceability is refused and the award set aside if one of the grounds for setting aside, which are examined ex officio (violation of ordre public or violation of limits of arbitrability) exists. Grounds for setting cannot be taken into account, if at the time when the application for a declaration of enforceability is served, an application for setting aside based on such grounds has been finally rejected (Article 41, AA). Other grounds for setting aside an arbitral award may not be invoked during the proceedings for declaration of enforceability. Thus, the party who wishes to invoke them must avail herself to an action for setting aside the award.

502. Similar rules apply as to enforcement of interim measures, rendered by arbitration. Besides, enforcement of an interim measure may be refused also in case

450. The territorial principle regarding the determination of a nationality of arbitral award did not apply in old Slovenian law. It was not the seat of arbitration, but rather the applied procedural law that was decisive for determination, whether arbitral award is domestic or foreign. Unlike in most other jurisdictions, it is possible for the parties to the arbitration, which seat is in Slovenia, to agree that arbitration will be conducted in accordance with a procedural law (*lex arbitri*) of a foreign state (under a condition that it is not contrary to Slovenian *ordre public*). So, the approach of Slovenian legislator in this regard, was liberal, as it allows the possibility that arbitration proceedings in its territory will be conducted according to foreign *lex arbitri*. The consequence thereof is that such arbitration although its seat was in Slovenia and although arbitral award was rendered in Slovenia, will not be regarded a domestic arbitration and domestic arbitral award (Art. 104/3 PILPA). The practically important consequence thereof is that a Slovenian court does not have a jurisdiction to hear an action for setting aside such an arbitral award.

451. M. Giunio, *Courts of Law and Arbitration Under the Croatian Law on Arbitration*, 9 Croatian Arb. Y.B. 209 (2002).

452. A peculiarity of the old Slovenian law was that there was no limited and ex officio judicial control of domestic arbitral awards in (or prior to) an enforcement procedure with regard to issues of arbitrability and *ordre public*). At first sight, this even seemed like an arbitration-friendly concept, but is in fact a consequence of a certain misconception of the nature of arbitration, deriving from the former political and legal order. Arbitral tribunals in Yugoslavia were (although arbitration retained its voluntary character and the party's autonomy prevailed with regard to determining procedural rules) regarded as a kind of 'self–management court'. Such treatment guaranteed their awards a priori recognition, whereby it was considered inappropriate that another court (i.e., the court competent for the enforcement of the arbitral award) would be able to control the content of their decision in any different manner than the judgment of a state court. S. Triva, *Croatian Law on Arbitration*, 9 Croatian Arb. Y.B. 134 (2002).

if the court determines that such measure, as stipulated by the arbitral tribunal cannot be enforced. In such case the court may, upon a motion of a party reformulate or adjust the contents of the interim measure, provided that thereby the original content of the measure is not substantially infringed (Article 43, AA).

Chapter 7. Recognition and Enforcement of Foreign Arbitral Awards

503. Slovenia is a contracting state of the New York Convention on the Recognition and Enforcement of Foreign Arbitral Awards. It invoked a 'commercial case reservation' as well as reciprocity clause reservation, but both reservations were withdrawn in April 2008. However, until the coming into force of the AA, Slovenian courts did not rely directly on the Convention but on the provisions on recognition and enforcement of arbitral awards, contained in the PILPA (Articles 104–111). Nevertheless, there were no substantial differences between the New York Convention and PILPA. The aforementioned provisions of the PILPA were abolished by the new AA. Now, the Act simply stipulates that for recognition and enforcement of foreign arbitral awards the New York Convention shall apply (Article 42, AA). Due to the aforementioned withdrawal of both reservations, this applies also to awards, rendered in non-commercial cases and awards, rendered in non-contracting states.

504. A foreign arbitral award may not be enforced in Slovenia unless it is recognized by the competent Slovenian court (Article 42, AA). A subject matter and territorial jurisdiction for deciding on recognition of foreign arbitral awards is concentrated in one single court: the Ljubljana District Court (Article 42/1, AA). Pursuant to the Article 9 of the Act, the court decides in a contradictory procedure (thus, the other party's right to be heard must be safeguarded before the decision is rendered). For issues of procedure, rules of the Non-contentious Procedure Act apply. Against the decision, a direct appeal to the Supreme Court is admissible. There are no further extraordinary remedies.

505. The party applying for recognition must supply the original award or a copy thereof. The arbitration agreement (or its authenticated copy) must be supply only upon a request of the court (Article 42/4, AA). Thus, the regulation is in this regard more liberal than the New York Convention, which insists on the supplying of the arbitration agreement in every case (Article 4/1). If the arbitral award or the arbitral agreement (if the court requests the presentation thereof) is not in Slovenian language, an official translation must be provided, pursuant to Article 4/2 of the New York Convention.

506. Grounds for refusal of recognition of foreign arbitral awards are enumerated in the Article 5 of the New York Convention and these rules are directly applicable in Slovenia. Before the adoption of the AA, it has been unclear which grounds for a denial of a recognition of a foreign arbitral award the court should invoke ex officio and which on the motion of a party and in the latter case, which party bears the burden of proof.[453] The wording of the PILPA implied that the court invoked all grounds ex officio. With the direct application of the New York Convention, now it

453. Š. Mežnar&A. Galič, *Slovenia – Country Report; Landesbericht*, in*Arbitration in Central Europe; Schiedsgerichtsbarkeit in Zentraleuropa* 557(Oberhammer ed., Center of Legal Competence 2005).

should be clear that only a limited the number of grounds for non-recognition can be invoked ex officio (non-arbitrability and violation of public policy) and that in all cases, the burden of proof rests with the party who opposes the recognition). Before, it was also a common position that a Slovenian court had to (as was the wording of Article 106 of the PILPA) refuse a recognition if a arbitral award has been set aside by a court in the country in which, or under the law of which, that award was made. The position now cannot be so firm any more as the wording of the New York Convention allows for a certain degree of a discretion and may recognize a foreign arbitral award even if it was set aside in its home country (as follows from the wording in Article 5 '*may* be refused ... ').

507. It has already been mentioned that form requirements of the Slovenian AA are loosened, in accordance with the latest amendments of the UNCITRAL Model Law (2006). The New York Convention on the other side provides for more strict rules on form. In order to avoid this discrepancy, the Slovenian AA includes a provision that the requirements of form concerning an arbitration agreement in a foreign arbitral award shall be deemed to be fulfilled if the arbitration agreement fulfils form criteria of the Slovenian law. Thus, a circumstance that an arbitral award was rendered abroad on the basis of an arbitration agreement which did not fulfil the form requirements of the New York Convention, shall not prevent its recognition in Slovenia, provided that at least the form requirements as provided for by the Slovenian law were respected (Article 42/3, AA).

508. The Slovenian doctrine does not support the view that the exhausting available legal remedies against the award already in the country of the seat of arbitration are a mandatory precondition for resisting recognition of a foreign award in Slovenia. Hence, a party may resist recognition of a foreign award in Slovenia, although it did not previously challenge the award in the country of the seat of arbitration. It is also accepted that in the proceedings concerning recognition of a foreign award a Slovenian court is not bound by factual findings and legal views of the court in the country of the seat of arbitration (e.g., concerning the question whether the requirements regarding the form of arbitration agreement were complied with, or whether the arbitration agreement in the given case binds a non-signatory third party).[454]

509. Under the NYC, the party applying for recognition shall, in order to obtain the recognition, at the time of the application, supply both the duly authenticated original award or a duly certified copy thereof as well as the original arbitration agreement or a duly certified copy thereof (Article 4 NYC). It is a well-known fact that especially the latter requirement often causes difficulties in practice. The Slovenian law on the other hand, provides for less stringent requirements (Article 42/4 AA). It is sufficient for the applicant to supply the original or a simple copy of the *award*, whereas it is left to the discretion of the court, whether it shall require the party to present the original or an authenticated copy of the *arbitration agreement.* The court should exercise this discretion in disputed cases and not in cases, where

454. Decision of the Slovenian Supreme Court No. Cpg 2/2009 dated 16 Dec. 2009.

the existence of a written and valid arbitration agreement has not been put in question (by the opponent). Under the old law, providing an original or authenticated copy of the arbitration agreement was (just like under the NYC) mandatory.[455] The attempt for recognition of one foreign arbitral award in Slovenia failed precisely due to this hurdle.[456] This decision of the Slovenian court was adopted in the time when the new law was already in force; however, the courts applied the old law in regard to the duty to supply the original of the arbitration agreement. The Supreme Court offered an interesting (however very restrictive) answer as to the petitioner's argument that it is in any case irrelevant, whether he can produce the original of the arbitration agreement. The petitioner, namely, argued that even if the original of the arbitration agreement cannot be provided, it should be acknowledged that the arbitration agreement was validly concluded in a tacit manner at least – since the claimant relied on the arbitration agreement in its statement of claim in arbitration, whereas the defendant did not contest jurisdiction in its defence plea. The petitioner argued that the arbitration agreement must therefore be deemed to have been concluded in a conclusive manner – if it had not already been expressly concluded. The Supreme Court did not accept this argument. It acknowledged that the arbitration agreement can indeed be concluded tacitly in a manner described by the petitioner. In that case, however, in the view of the Supreme Court, the requirement of Article 4 NYC (and the then applicable old Slovenian law) that the petitioner should supply the original of the arbitration agreement, is still relevant. In such a case, this requirement means that the petitioner should supply the original of the claim in arbitration (from which the court could conclude that he indeed invoked the arbitration agreement) as well as the original of the respondent's defence plea in arbitration (from which it could be concluded that he did not contest the jurisdiction of the tribunal).[457] It might be worth mentioning that in another case the Supreme Court seems to have accepted the view that in case, where the respondent objects the recognition of a foreign award for the lack of jurisdiction of the arbitral tribunal, it is decisive, whether he contested the jurisdiction of the tribunal already in arbitration proceedings. If the respondent does not contest jurisdiction already in arbitration proceedings, he loses the right to rely on this ground for refusal of recognition of the foreign award.[458]

455. Article 105/2 pf the International Private Law and Procedure Act.
456. Decision of the Slovenian Supreme Court No. Cpg 6/2010 dated 11 Oct. 2010. The case concerned an award adopted by a tribunal seated in the Republic of Srpska (Bosnia and Herzegovina), proceeding in accordance with the Rules of the Permanent Court of Arbitration attached to the Chamber of Commerce of the Republic of Srpska.
457. Decision of the Slovenian Supreme Court No Cpg 6/2010 dated 11 Oct. 2011.
458. Decision of the Slovenian Supreme Court No. 2/2009 dated 16 Dec. 2009.

Part XI. Mediation

Chapter 1. Legislation/Definitions

510. Mediation in Civil and Commercial Matters Act was enacted in 2008. It encourages the use of mediation (*mediacija*) as a voluntary procedure, without connection to any already pending court proceedings. Pre-action voluntary mediation is possible, but has not started to fully flourish yet although the level of awareness of and acceptance of ADR in legal and general community is gradually growing. The Act transposes the EU Mediation Directive 2008/52/EC. However, its scope is broader as it is not restricted to cross-border mediation. It applies both to purely domestic cases as well as cross border cases. The Act however does not apply to cases where a court or a judge to whom a case has been referred, in the course of a court proceeding referring to the dispute in question, attempts to facilitate the amicable settlement of a dispute, or where an arbitrator attempts to do so in an arbitral proceeding referring to this dispute.

511. In addition, in 2009, Slovenia introduced the Alternative Legal Dispute Resolution Act (or: Court-annexed ADR Act), which concerns court-annexed mediation (*sodišču pridružena mediacija*). This law imposes an obligation on all Slovenian Courts of First Instance as well as appellate courts that they must offer mediation (or another ADR method – but in practice only mediation is used) to parties. It is thus obligatory for courts to set up court-annexed ADR mechanisms, but it is not obligatory for the parties to use them (see infra). In this regard, the Act builds on the experience of court-annexed mediation programmes which existed in many Slovenian courts before enactment of this obligation.

512. Developments concerning alternative resolution of consumer disputes should also be briefly mentioned. The Alternative Consumer Dispute Resolution Act was enacted in 2012. Therewith Slovenia implemented the Directive 2013/11/EU of the European Parliament and of the Council of 21 May 2013 on ADR for consumer disputes. Nevertheless, schemes for alternative resolution of consumer disputes remain underdeveloped in Slovenia. There are no publicly funded Consumer ADR bodies. The initiative to set up and run consumer ADR mechanisms is left to the private sector (in cooperation with consumer organizations). The traders are not (except in certain specific sectors subject to special regulation, such as telecommunications, banking and insurance sector) obliged to adhere to Consumer ADR schemes, they are merely obliged to inform consumers whether they adhere to any

ADR scheme and if case they do, to provide relevant information thereof. It is however possible that all traders, who are members of a certain voluntary trade organization in a specific sector, undertake as their membership obligation, that they will adhere to an ADR scheme, set up by the association. It should also be mentioned that consumer ADR is not only mediation. Voluntary arbitration is also possible as well as ADR schemes that provide for non-binding recommendations (neutral evaluation).

513. The CPA itself, to a limited extent, acknowledges the importance of mediation, irrespective of whether it is performed independently from the court or in the form of a court-annexed mediation. A court may stay the proceedings for three months at most if the parties agree to make use of mediation or some other ADR procedure.

514. Mediation can be defined as a structured and voluntary proceeding by which the parties attempt to reach through a neutral third person (mediator), who applies special mediation techniques and skills, the amicable settlement of a dispute arising out of or relating to a contractual or other legal relationship, irrespective of whether for this proceeding the term mediation, conciliation, reconciliation, mediation of disputes or other similar term is used (cf Article 3 of the Mediation Act). Mediator is any third person who is approached to conduct mediation, irrespective of his or her title or profession and irrespective of the manner in which he or she has been appointed or approached to conduct mediation, and who accepts the request. In the proceeding a sole mediator or several mediators may participate.

Chapter 2. Rights That Can Be Subject to Mediation

515. Mediation may be used in civil, family, commercial, labour and all other disputes involving an economic interest (pecuniary matters) if they concern claims over which the Parties may reach settlement. Mediation is also admissible in non-pecuniary disputes, so far as this complies with the nature of the legal relationship out of which the dispute has arisen and if this is not excluded by a special law (Article 2 of the Mediation Act). In practice, mediation is most often used in civil and commercial matters and in family law disputes. It is also being increasingly used in labour law disputes.

Chapter 3. Mediation Agreement

516. Mediation agreement can be concluded prior to materialization of a dispute in a form of a 'mediation clause' or 'escalation clause' (mediation agreement and in case mediation fails, an arbitration agreement or international jurisdiction agreement). Where the parties have agreed upon mediation and have expressly undertaken not to initiate, until the expiry of a certain period of time or until a specified event has occurred, arbitral or judicial proceedings with respect to an existing or future dispute, the arbitral tribunal or the court must, upon a jurisdictional plea by the defendant, dismiss such an action, unless the plaintiff demonstrates that otherwise harmful and irreparable consequences would occur. The defendant must submit this plea in the defence plea at the latest (Article 16 of the Mediation Act). It should be noted that in order to produce the above effects the mediation agreement must be explicit and specific, a mere reference that 'the parties shall attempt to resolve disputes amicably' does not suffice to produce any binding legal effects.

517. Most often in practice a mediation agreement is reached only after the dispute has arisen or, in fact, after proceedings in court have already been brought. Namely, in case of court-annexed mediation parties are (unless at least one of them objects) referred to mediation following the court's referral.

Chapter 4. Persons/Institutions That Can Act As Mediator

518. There are no special requirements as to who can act as mediator. The profession is not regulated and there is no licensing or accreditation of mediators or service providers of mediation. However, there is quite substantial self-regulation by autonomous mediators' associations (accomplished training and periodical continued training as a requirement for membership) and by organizations which offer mediation. These associations and organizations also adopt codes of ethics for mediators. Certain requirements, exceeding a level of a mere self-regulation, apply only for a court annexed mediation, which aim at ensuring the quality of mediation and integrity of the process. There, the court provides a roster of mediators and establishes criteria for inclusion on the roster (such as an accomplished initial training, organized by an authorized provider).

Chapter 5. Mediation Procedure

519. Where the parties have concluded an arbitration agreement prior to the materialization of the dispute or where mediation is prescribed by law, mediation shall commence on the day on which a party receives a proposal for the commencement of mediation from the opposing party. In other cases, mediation referring to a dispute which has already arisen shall commence on the day the parties to the dispute agree to pursue mediation. If one party proposes mediation to the other party, but does not receive an acceptance of the proposal from the other party within thirty days from the day on which the proposal was sent, it may treat this as a rejection of the proposal for mediation.

520. The Mediation Act sets out only the basic rules for mediation procedure, leaving other aspects to autonomous rules and the mediator's discretion, thus maintaining the necessary flexibility of the process. The parties may agree on the manner in which the mediation is to be conducted. Failing an agreement on the manner in which the mediation is to be conducted, the mediator shall conduct the proceedings as he or she sees fit. In so doing, he or she shall consider all the circumstances of the case, any wishes the parties may express, and the need for a speedy and permanent settlement of the dispute. In any case, in conducting the proceedings, the mediator must act independently and impartially and make every effort to treat the parties equally, taking into account all circumstances of the case (Article 8 of the Mediation Act). The mediator may meet or communicate with each party separately or with all of them together (Article 9 of the Mediation Act). When the mediator receives information concerning the dispute from a party, the mediator may disclose the substance of the information to any other party to mediation, unless a party has disclosed the information to the mediator subject to a specific condition that it be kept confidential (Article 10 of the Mediation Act).

521. All information originating from mediation or relating to it is confidential unless otherwise agreed by the parties, or if its disclosure is required under law or for the purposes of implementation or enforcement of a dispute settlement agreement (Article 11 of the Mediation Act). Information obtained in mediation, views expressed by the Parties in mediation, such as admissions and other statements, the fact that a party was willing to participate or that it had indicated its willingness to accept the mediator's proposal for amicable dispute settlement; as well as documents drawn up solely for purposes of the mediation proceedings. are not admissible as evidence in (subsequent) court or arbitration proceedings. Exceptions apply to the extent required by law, in particular where reasons of public policy so require (e.g., protection of the interests of children or prevention of interference with a person's physical or mental integrity) or insofar as necessary for the implementation or enforcement of the settlement reached in mediation.

522. As to the impact of mediation on the statute of limitation: The limitation period for a claim subject to mediation is suspended during mediation (it is therefore important that the Mediation Act determines the precise moment when mediation proceedings commence -Article 6 –and when they terminate – Article 13). If a mediation proceeding is terminated without a settlement, the limitation period continues to run from the moment the mediation proceeding is terminated. The time that expired prior to the initiation of mediation is included in the limitation period laid down by law. Nevertheless, the deadline for bringing the claim cannot expire earlier than fifteen days after the termination of mediation (Article 17 of the Mediation Act).

Chapter 6. Settlement Agreement

523. The settlement agreement reached in mediation is binding as a contract, however it is not, in itself, an enforceable title and does not have an effect of *res iudicata*, unless the Parties agree that they shall request the court to endorse such agreement as an in-court settlement. The parties may also agree that the dispute settlement agreement shall take the form of a directly enforceable notarial act (hence, a participation of a public notary will be required in such case) or an arbitral award on agreed terms (hence the parties will need to appoint an arbitrator for that purpose).

Chapter 7. Setting Aside a Settlement Agreement

524. If the settlement agreement reached in mediation is concluded in the form of a contract, it can be challenged in court on the same ground as any other settlement contract. Similar method of challenging the settlement applies if the settlement takes the form of a directly enforceable notarial deed. If the settlement is endorsed as an in-court settlement, an action for setting aside the in-court settlement may be filed on strictly limited grounds (fraud, duress, gross violation of procedure, such as a lack of capacity). If the settlement agreement is subsequently taken in the form of an arbitral award on agreed terms, an action for setting aside the arbitral award can be filed.

Chapter 8. Court-Annexed Mediation

525. Slovenia may well claim to be the pioneer among the former communist countries when it comes to implementation of court-annexed ADR programmes. A pilot-programme on voluntary court-annexed mediation was initiated by the Ljubljana District Court as long ago as the late-1990s, and proved to be quite successful. These pilot programmes were 'institutionalized' in 2009 when Slovenia adopted the Court-annexed ADR Act (*Zakon o alternativnem reševanju sodnih sporov*). The Act promotes a genuine 'multi-door courthouse' approach by imposing on all courts of first instance as well as appellate courts to offer mediation or another ADR method. In this regard the Act relied closely on the positive experience of court-annexed mediation programmes which existed in many Slovenian courts before enactment of this obligation. In an overwhelming majority of cases, the courts of first instance (appellate courts to much a lesser extent) indeed offer the parties the possibility to try mediation. Any party can object, but such rejection can have adverse consequences when it comes to determination of the costs of litigation. If the court considers that a party has unreasonably declined the use of mediation it can, when making the final determination of costs of civil proceedings, order it to pay all or part of the other party's costs, regardless of the final outcome of the case (Article 19 of the Court-annexed ADR Act).

The programmes are administered by the court; in larger courts, separate ADR offices were established for that purpose. The court provides a roster of mediators and establishes criteria for inclusion on the roster, adopts rules regarding assigning neutrals to the case and guidelines for conducting the ADR sessions. Mediation sessions are held in the court. When the programmes were first introduced, most mediators were judges (who of course cannot mediate cases that are assigned to them for adjudication), but over time attorneys and retired judges were included on the roster. In practice, mediation is offered to parties automatically very early in the proceedings and the invitation letter is a general one, not tailored for a particular case. In addition, the judge may order an informational session and after such a session has been held, the court may decide whether it shall refer the parties to mediation. Parties have the right to oppose to such decision and in that case mediation proceedings do not commence. However, parties who unreasonably decline the use of mediation might, as explained above, bear costs of the judicial proceedings, irrespective of the outcome of the proceedings. Statistics show that consent of both parties for the mediation procedure is reached in about 25% of cases and about 40% of mediations are successful, thus resulting in a settlement. Equally importantly, it is observed that even in cases, where no settlement was reached in court-annexed mediation, there are positive effects for the further course of litigation; namely the parties' arguments are clearer and more focused and not rarely, the parties settle the case once it is referred back to litigation. Whereas court-annexed mediation schemes in Slovenia are undisputedly successful, a downside is that precisely the success of mediation in courts, which is almost free of charge for the parties, makes it more difficult for private ADR providers to establish their activities on a market oriented basis.

Selected Bibliography

Monographs in Slovenian Language

Galič, A. *Ustavno civilno procesno pravo – ustavna procesna jamstva in ustavna pritožba*, [Constitutional Civil Procedure – Constitutional Procedural Guarantees and a Constitutional Complaint]. Ljubljana: GV Založba, 2004.

Galič, A. & N. Betetto. *Evropsko civilno procesno pravo,*[European Civil Procedure]. Ljubljana: GV založba, 2011.

Juhart, J. *Civilno procesno pravo,*[Civil Procedure]. Ljubljana: Univerzitetna založba, 1961.

Rijavec, V. *Civilno izvršilno pravo*, [Enforcement of Judgments Law]. Ljubljana: GV Založba, 2003.

Ude, L. *Arbitražno pravo*, [Arbitration Law]. Ljubljana: GV Založba, 2004.

Ude, L. *Civilno procesno pravo*, [Civil Procedure]. Ljubljana: Uradni list RS, 2002.

Ude, L. et al. *Pravdni postopek – Zakon s komentarjem; Vol. I*–IV, [Civil Procedure – Act with a Commentary], Ljubljana: GV založba and Uradni list, 2005–2009.

Bibliography in English and German Languages

Betetto, N. 'Court-Based Mediation and Its Place in Slovenia'. In *Public and Private Justice*, edited by Van Rhee & Uzelac. Antwerpen: Intersentia, 2007.

Betetto, N. 'Implementation of European Civil Procedural Regulations in the Case Law of Slovenian Courts'. In *Enforcement and Enforceability*, Ius Commune: European and Comparative Law Series, Volume 84, edited by Van Rhee & Uzelac. Antwerpen: Intersentia, 2010, 103–110.

Galič, A., Disclosure of Documents in Private Antitrust Enforcement Litigation. *Yearbook of Antitrust and Regulatory Studies*, 2015, vol. 8, 99.

Galič, A., Establishing an Out-of-court Mechanism for the Resolution of Consumer Disputes. *Croatian Arbitration Yearbook*, 2017, vol. 24, 95.

Galič, A., New Ljubljana Arbitration Rules of 1 January 2014. *Croatian Arbitration Yearbook*, 2014/2015, vol. 21/22, 201.

Galič, A., 'Enforcement by Means of Periodic Penalties (Astreinte) in Slovenia: a Transplant Gone Wild'. InTransfor*mation of Civil Justice: Unity and Diversity*, edited by Uzelac A.& van Rhee, C.H.Kluwer, 2018, 25.

Galič, A., 'The Inconsistency of Case Law and the Right to Fair Trial'. In*Revisiting Procedural Human Rights: Fundamentals of Civil Procedure and the Changing Face of Civil Justice*, (Ius Commune Europaeum, 157), edited by Uzelac A.&van

Rhee, C.H. Cambridge: Intersentia. cop. 2017, str. 17-51. [COBISS.SI-ID 15793745].

Galič, A., 'Interpretation and Application of the New York Convention in Slovenia'. InBermann G., *Recognition and Eenforcement of Fforeign Aarbitral Aawards: Tthe Iinterpretation and Aapplication of the New York Convention by Nnational Ccourts*, edited by Bermann G.Springer, 2017, 835.

Galič, A., 'The Preparatory Stage of Civil Proceedings in Slovenia, the Czech Republic and Slovakia: Halfway There Yet?' InErvo L., Nylund A., *Current Trends in Preparatory Proceedings: a Comparative Study of Nordic and Former Communist Countries*, edited by Ervo L.& Nylund A. Springer,2016, 111.

Galič, A., 'Slovenian Civil Procedure and the Transformative Power of the EU'. InNylund A., Krans, B., *The European Union and national civil procedure*, edited by Nylund A.&Krans, B.Intersentia, 2016, 131.

Galič, A., 'The Aversion to Judicial Discretion in Civil Procedure in Post-Communist Countries: Can the Influence of EU Law Change It?' InBobek, M.l (ed:). *Central European judges under the European influence: the transformative power of the EU revisited*, edited by Bobek, M.l, Hart, 2015, 99.

Galič, A., 'Does a Decision of the Supreme Court Denying Leave to Appeal Need to Contain Reasons?' InAdolphsen, J. (ed:). *Festschrift für Peter Gottwald zum 70. Geburtstag*, edited by Adolphsen, J. München: C. H. Beck, 2014, 159.

Galič, A., '(In)compatibility of Procedural Preclusions With the Goals of Civil Justice: An Ongoing Debate in Slovenia.' InUzelac, A., *Goals of Civil Justice and Civil Procedure in Contemporary Judicial Systems*, edited by Uzelac, A.Springer, 2014, 221.

Galič, A., 'Reshaping the Role of Supreme Courts in the Countries of the Former Yugoslavia.' InUzelac, A., van Rhee, C.H. (ed:). *Nobody's Perfect: Comparative Essays on Appeals and Other Means of Recourse Against Judicial Decisions in Civil Matters*, edited by Uzelac, A.& van Rhee, C.H.Intersentia, 2014,291.

Galič, A. 'Die Anerkennung und Vollstreckung von gerichtlichen Entscheidungen in Slowenien nach dem Beitritt zur EU'. In *Zivilverfahrensrecht – Bestandsaufnahme und Zukunftsperspektiven nach der EU-Erweiterung*, edited by Kengyel & Rechberger. Europaeisches, Wien, Graz: NWV, 2007.

Galič, A. 'Sanktionen wegen Inaktivität der Parteien im slowenischen Zivilprozess'. In *Festschrift für Walter H. Rechberger zum 60. Geburtstag*, edited by Bittner, Klicka, Kodek & Oberhammer. 1. Aufl., Wien: Springer, 2005, 139.

Galič, A. 'Die Richtermacht im slowenischen Zivilprozess'. In *Richterbild und Rechtsreform in Mitteleuropa*, edited by Oberhammer et al. Wien: Manz Schriftenreihe des Center of Legal Competence, 2001.

Galič, A. 'Die Berührungspunkte zwischen Europäischem Zivilverfahrensrechts und dem nationalen Recht in Slowenien am Beispiel des Europäischen Vollstreckungstitels für unbestrittene Forderungen'. In *Der Einfluss des Europäischen Zivilverfahrensrechts auf die nationalen Rechtsordnungen*, edited by M. Kengyel& V. Harsagi. Heidelberger Schriften zum Wirtschaftsrecht und Europarecht, Bd. 54). 1. Aufl. Baden-Baden: Nomos, 2009, 135.

Galič, A. 'Party Autonomy, Court Control and the Mutual Responsibility for the Management of Civil Litigation in Slovenia'. *Party Autonomy – Civil Procedural*

Views on Party Autonomy, Franz Klein, EU Law and More, edited by M.Dahlberg. Uppsala: Iustus Förlag, 2011, 11.

Galič, A. 'From Kudla to Lukenda: Legal Remedies against Undue Delay in Civil Proceedings in Slovenia'. In *Aurea praxis aurea theoria: księga pamiątkowa ku czci profesora Tadeusza Erecińskiego. Tom 1*, edited by J. Gudowski & K. Weitz. Warszawa: LexisNexis, 2011, 1453.

Galič, A. 'Probleme der grenzüberschreitenden Vollstreckung in Slowenien: Transparenz des Schuldnervermögens und Kontenpfändung'. In *Grenzüberschreitende Vollstreckung in der Europäischen Union*, edited by M. Kengyel& V. Harsagi. München: Sellier European Law Publishers, 2011, 209.

Galič, A. 'Language Issues in Cross-Border Service of Judicial Documents'. In *Cross-Border Civil Proceedings in the EU*, edited by V. Rijavec et al. Maribor: Pravna fakulteta, 2012, 111.

Galič, A. 'Payment Order Procedure and Arbitration'. *Croatian Arbitration Yearbook 19* (2012): 41.

Galič, A. 'Die Entwicklung des Zivilprozessrechts in Slowenien'. In *Die Entwicklung des Zivilprozessrechts in Mitteleuropa um die Jahrtausendwende: Reform und Kodifikation – Tradition und Erneuerung*, edited by T. Sutter-Somm & V. Harsagi. Zürich: Schulthess, 2012, 87.

Galič, A. & C. Hodges. 'Slovenia'. In *Consumer ADR in Europe*, (Civil Justice Systems), edited by C. Hodges, I. Benöhr & N. Creutzfeldt-Banda. Oxford; Portland (Oregon): Hart Publishing, 2012, 197.

Galič, A. 'Recognition and Enforcement of Domestic and Foreign Arbitral Awards in Slovenia'. *Croatian Arbitration Yearbook* 20 (2013): 51.

Galič, A. 'A Judge's Power to Disregard Late Facts and Evidence and the Goals of Civil Justice'. In: *Recent Trends in Economy and Efficiency of Civil Procedure.* Vilnius: Vilnius University, 2013, 72.

Kramberger Škerl, J. 'The Service of Court Documents on Persons with Unknown Residence: A Comparative Analysis with an Emphasis on Slovenia'. In *Party Autonomy – Civil Procedural Views on Party Autonomy, Franz Klein, EU Law and More*, edited by M.Dahlberg. Uppsala: Iustus Förlag, cop. 2011, 121.

Mežnar, Š. & A. Galič. 'Arbitration Law in Slowenia'. In *Schiedsgerichtsbarkeit in Zentraleuropa*, edited by Oberhammer. Wien, Graz: Neuer Wissenschaftlicher Verlag, 2005, 529.

Ristin, G. 'New Legislation on Alternative Dispute Resolution in the Republic of Slovenia'. *Croatian Arbitration Yearbook* 18 (2011): 143.

Rijavec, V.&Keresteš, T.'Restrictions on the Admissibility of Evidence.'In *Evidence in Contemporary Civil Procedure: Fundamental Issues in a Comparative Perspective*, edited by C.H.van Rhee&A.Uzelac. Intersentia, 2015, 87.

Rijavec, V. 'Neue Aspekte des Gläubigerschutzes nach dem slowenischen Vollstreckungs- und Sicherungsgesetz'. *Wirtsch. Recht Osteur* 11 (1999) 411.

Rijavec, V. 'Das Institut der Vorfrage im slowenischen Zivilprozess'. In *Festschrift für Walter H. Rechberger zum 60. Geburtstag*, edited by Bittner, Klicka, Kodek & Oberhammer. 1. Aufl., Wien: Springer, 2005, 439.

Rijavec, V. 'The Recovery of Debts Secured by Mortgage or Pledge in Slovenia'. In *Access to Justice and the Judiciary: Towards New European Standards of*

Affordability, Quality and Efficiency of Civil Adjudication, edited by C.H. Van Rhee& A. Uzelac. Cambridge; Antwerp; Portland: Intersentia, 2009, 219.
Rijavec, V. 'Einstweilige Verfügungen mit Internationalem Bezug'. In *Private Law Reform in South East Europe: Liber Amicorum Christa Jessel Holst,* edited by M. Vasiljević et al. Beograd: Pravni fakultet Univerziteta, 2010, 317.
Rijavec, V. 'Efficiency versus Fairness in Civil Procedure in Slovenia'. In *Truth and Efficiency in Civil Litigation: Fundamental Aspects of Fact-Finding and Evidence-Taking in a Comparative Context,* edited by C.H. Van Rhee& A. Uzelac, Cambridge; Antwerp; Portland: Intersentia, 2012, 283.
Rijavec, V. et al. '*Die Erleichterung der Zwangsvollstreckung in Europa*'. Baden-Baden: Nomos, 2012.
Ude, L. & D. Wedam Lukić. '*Schiedsgerichtsbarkeit in der Republik Slowenien*'. Heidelberg: Verlag Recht und Wirtschaft, 1998.
Wedam Lukić, D. 'Arbitration and Article 6 of The European Convention on Human Rights'. *Arbitration (Lond.)* 64 (1998): 16.
Wedam Lukić.'The Principle of Proportionality in the Case Law of the Constitutional Court of the Republic of Slovenia'. In *Human Rights, Democracy and Rule of Law: Liber amicorum Luzius Wildhaber,* edited by S.Breitenmoser, Zürich; St. Gallen: Dike; Baden-Baden: Nomos, 2007, 1599.

Index

The numbers here refer to paragraph numbers.

Index

Index